D1482178

Blood, Guns, and Testosterone

Action Films, Audiences, and a Thirst for Violence

Barna William Donovan

THE SCARECROW PRESS, INC.
Lanham • Toronto • Plymouth, UK
2010

Published by Scarecrow Press, Inc.
A wholly owned subsidiary of The Rowman & Littlefield Publishing Group, Inc.
4501 Forbes Boulevard, Suite 200, Lanham, Maryland 20706
http://www.scarecrowpress.com

Estover Road, Plymouth PL6 7PY, United Kingdom

British Library Cataloguing in Publication Information Available

Library of Congress Cataloging-in-Publication Data

Donovan, Barna William, 1970–
  Blood, guns, and testosterone : action films, audiences, and a thirst for violence / Barna
William Donovan.
      p. cm.
  Includes bibliographical references and index.
  ISBN 978-0-8108-7262-2 (pbk. : alk. paper) — ISBN 978-0-8108-7263-9 (ebook)
  1. Action and adventure films--History and criticism. 2. Violence in motion pictures.
3. Masculinity in motion pictures. I. Title.
  PN1995.9.A3D68 2010
  791.43'655—dc22

                                2009027871

Printed in the United States of America

For my father, Dr. Lee Erik Donovan,
who also loved and valued action films

Contents

Acknowledgments

I owe heartfelt thanks to Robert Kubey, Laurie Ouellette, Lionel Tiger, and Silvio Waisbord for their advice and support of this project from its earliest conception. I am also grateful to all the interview subjects for sharing so much of their lives and experiences to help expand our knowledge about a complex and contentious topic.

Introduction

Violence and Much More

Bless me father, for I have just killed quite a few men.

—Antonio Banderas, *Desperado*

Not so long ago, while discussing a crop of films marked by critics as that year's major Oscar contenders, I realized I had no choice but to confront the fact that I have been living with a dirty little secret. I had to admit that as a responsible adult holding various advanced degrees in the social sciences, including a doctorate in film and media studies, as an educator and head of the communication department of Saint Peter's College, the only Jesuit college in New Jersey, my first choice when it comes to watching movies has always been the anarchic art of the Hollywood action film. No, I had to explain, I don't just study action/adventure, I really love these movies, too. While a graduate student in the University of Miami's film program, I had been told that a serious scholar of the cinema should not even know who Arnold Schwarzenegger is, but none of that seemed to make any difference. Gritty, bone-fracturing, cartilage-crushing, lip-splitting fights, car chases, gunplay, trash-talking put-down humor from foul-mouthed tough guys brimming with anti-authoritarian "attitude" and, most of all, city-scale, searing, pyrotechnic destruction, for a true fan, offer stimulation and delight unmatched by any other class of film.

But the visceral, blood and guts thrills of the action genre have long been on the black list of socially responsible media critics. Such films are supposed to be an entertainment form only for—in the words of critic Michael Medved—"hormone-addled, drooling, semi-literate adolescent males."[1] Professors of Catholic colleges should not belong to that same fan base. (Bless me father, for I have just enjoyed seeing the killing of quite a few men.)

Action adventure films have fascinated me since the summer of 1985 when Sylvester Stallone ruled the box office in *Rambo: First Blood, Part II*. Although I was a teenager then, the R rating of the film was hardly enforced by theaters, and my friends and I could enjoy the large-screen mayhem without interference. Life was good.

The previous year, during the Donovan family's admittedly peculiar Christmas Eve video rental tradition of seeing an action film or two before opening presents, I had seen *First Blood*—the original *Rambo* film—and been captivated by the intense story of a wrongly persecuted man fighting for his life and honor.

The summer of 1985 and *Rambo II* were an entirely different phenomenon, however. The box office success of the film was met by a good deal of controversy and an unusual number of angry people who all wanted to "have a word with Stallone." I found this immensely intriguing, not to mention amusing.

But the 1980s were a renaissance for the Hollywood action film and most of the controversy plaguing the movies dealt with violence. Sly Stallone's critical nemeses were horrified by the film's massive body count and its hyperbolic treatment of the Vietnam War. Naturally, as an avid fan, I scoffed at the criticism. I ignored the warnings that *Rambo*, *The Terminator*, *Die Hard*, *Lethal Weapon*, or any of the big-budget, ultraviolent action epics were turning me into a dangerous young man—and they didn't. Instead, I couldn't help feeling that there was something about these films, something unspoken, an afterthought, what I would later learn to call "subtext," that the violence critics were missing.

The vast majority of the action films were about men who were larger than life, who could do things ordinary men could not. Yet these action heroes were neither a happy lot nor much respected for their fantastic deeds of heroism.

Fandom eventually turned me into a historian of the action/adventure film. Looking at the origins of the action film and tracing its evolution from the earliest, shakiest silent westerns through the haunted, hard-boiled film noir thrillers, all and the way to the genre's present incarnation as digital special-effects–enhanced spectacles, I came to see something much more complex than the history of a single category of film. The history of action/adventure is the history of something much more than the evolution of cinematic technology for rendering scenes of carnage and violence. The enjoyment of action films, in turn, is much more than just the enjoyment of violence. In fact, for quite a number of people who identify themselves as action/adventure fans, violence is not even *one* of the primary reasons for seeing their beloved genre. One can see much more violence in other venues, as a matter of fact, and one can see a much higher quality of mayhem in any number of other media. If one just wanted to see violence, one could watch the news. If, as a teenager, I would have wanted to see pure bloodletting, I could have rented the *Faces of Death* "films"—perhaps to be left feeling jipped upon realizing that much of the stuff on the videotapes was really fake. Today, the Internet can easily slake one's thirst for blood. A large part of the history of the violent action film is really the history of modern masculinity. It is a history of how art reflects society's definitions of manhood, society's ideals of the perfect man, and how this genre reflects men's self-image.

Once I started talking to other action fans, the people whose thoughts and ideas make up so much of this book, I saw this interpretation confirmed over and over again. There is more to a violent film genre than violence, and it is very important to hear this coming out of the mouths of the average filmgoers. Violent films often ruminate on issues of morality, for example, the definitions and social constructions of good and evil. At their very best—or most interesting, at least—these films may even reflect on the nature of violence, on human nature, on aggression, and how a self-reflexive, moral society can deal with violence. But since men have always perpetrated so much of the violence of the world, action films, more often than not, are contemplations of the meaning of manhood. Most often, the manhood of this high-adrenaline genre turns out to be very complicated.

The history of modern masculinity projected through celluloid is also a history of pain, trauma, and contention. Looking at the action film's representation of American masculinity, one begins to see decades of film where men change from larger than life, infallible heroes to cynical, washed up, unwanted outsiders. In the beginning, men were heroes in westerns and they instinctively knew right from wrong. They rode to the rescue and saved the day in the nick of time and to the admiration and gratitude of society. Eventually, they were soldiers who won World War II, like John Wayne and Gary Cooper who still stood tall and represented incorruptible integrity and confidence. Action heroes like these personified a victorious, postwar America, as strong and self-assured, as American audiences wanted to see themselves. But in the decades to follow, the heroic men on film would begin to change strikingly and profoundly.

The explanation for the evolution of action heroes from a self-assured John Wayne to an outcast, persecuted Sylvester Stallone in the *Rambo* films is complex. One can find a number of different reasons for why heroes needed to change the way they did what they did and *when* they did it. For one, infallible heroes are basically unrealistic. We can't really relate to characters who are always right or who always win. There are only so many times a hero can overcome an entire army single-handedly or save the girl from the train tracks before an audience tires of him.

But there was a historical time and place for such a hero, when audiences wanted to see those heroes and when filmmakers were allowed to show nothing more than infallibility in heroes. In 1930, the film industry adopted the Production Code that strictly controlled and censored films dealing with violence, crime, or sex. Audiences had to be clearly shown right from wrong, that crime could never pay, villains had to be punished, and heroes had to do the right thing and be appreciated for it.

During World War II, the film industry rallied for the war effort, and heroes in the movies were fighting Nazis and the Japanese. While stars like Jimmy Stewart and Clark Gable enlisted and fought in the real battles, directors like John Ford, Frank Capra, and Howard Hawks made propaganda films for the War Department. Tough guy actors like John Wayne did their part to boost the country's morale with rousing war epics. World War II made an action hero out of Audie Murphy, a farm kid who earned a record number of decorations in combat, wound up on the cover of *Life* magazine, then came to Hollywood to star in the film version of his best-selling autobiography, *To Hell and Back* (1955).

After the war was won, the time had come again for new directions in popular culture. While Hollywood still turned out patriotic adventures about the glories of combat, like John Wayne's most famous war film *The Sands of Iwo Jima* (1949), a new cultural landscape inspired a changing vision of men and heroes on film. In the late 1940s and 1950s, the hard-boiled, private eyes of film noir became the counterpoint to the larger-than-life Wayne image. The cynical loners of film noir spoke to the culture's fears and unease of a country too much in love with itself. Was the dark side of the super patriotism embodied by a John Wayne hero the paranoia and intolerance of McCarthyism? Was the strong masculinity that won the war now a rigid, repressive patriarchy reshaping society into robotic, male-dominated conformity contained within the uniform, barrack-like rows of suburban tract housing? Many of the crinkled heroes of noir, often based on the dark, ironic fiction of James M. Cain and Raymond Chandler, were war veterans who came home disillusioned, alienated from mainstream, happy, and self-righteous America.[2]

In the following two decades, anti-trust laws that cut into the studios' box office profits, television, and the demise of the Production Code all gave Hollywood films a harder, more complex edge in a frantic need to attract a dwindling movie-watching audience. But it was the country's sinking into the ever-darkening Vietnam quagmire, coupled with the women's movement in the 1960s, that altered action film masculinity in a way that still resonates today.

It was in the 1960s that anti-heroes took over the action genre. While the 1950s made megastars of a small handful of troubled rebel males like Marlon Brando, Montgomery Clift, and James Dean, crafting a more complicated, sensitive version of masculinity that angst-ridden teenage baby boomers could identify with, these men were not action stars. But in the 1960s, particularly as the Vietnam involvement seemed to be spinning hopelessly out of control, audiences began to see action heroes embodied by anti-establishment loners. Heroes like Clint Eastwood, Charles Bronson, Lee Marvin, and Steve McQueen became a new breed of heroes who would be at odds with authority figures, who were suspicious of the establishment and the status quo and who would fight only when cornered or out of cynical self-interest. The young people who made up the rank and file of action audiences, especially the young men resisting the draft and protesting the war, no longer saw cops and soldiers as heroes. For an action hero to be attractive, he needed to be a rebel. Steve McQueen was the first rebel cop in *Bullitt* (1968), setting the stage for Clint Eastwood's *Dirty Harry* (1971), where the disobedient cop was a thorn in the side of the bureaucracy, the politicians, "the man," and "the system."

The evolution of the male hero into a marginalized outsider, however, owes an even greater debt to the women's movement. Whereas decades ago a male-dominated, patriarchal order whipped a generation of boys into fighting men to save the world from the Nazi threat, feminists now began laying a great deal of the blame for the sorry state of the world upon men. This theme of being unwanted, undervalued, persecuted, and disrespected became the standard formula for creating the typical male action hero. These heroes were not just outsiders because they were angry at "the man," they were cast aside by society for their brutish, grungy, violent ways, in effect for *being* a man. In every *Dirty Harry* film, the story starts out with a scene of Clint Eastwood being told by a superior that his "methods are out of date." The traditional tough guy method of getting things done is always frowned upon in the beginning of an action film, and even when it works, we are told that our hero will hardly be rewarded for it. Reminiscent of Gary Cooper on the end of *High Noon* (1952), Clint Eastwood takes his badge on the end of *Dirty Harry* and throws it away in disgust with a system that does not respect him.

Film scholar Neal King has brought an interesting interpretation to the phenomenon of the postfeminist action hero, giving two reasons that the modern male action hero is a tormented soul. On the one hand, he must rise to one epic challenge after another, he must risk life and limb, endure torture and bloody punishment to save his world while being unappreciated. On the other hand, this same action hero is almost a modern-day Christ figure, enduring these torments while battling other men: corrupt, rich gangsters, racketeers, crooked politicians, traitors, sellouts, and exploiters of every shade and stripe. Although the heroes might be male, their opponents are also male, the corrupt beneficiaries of unfair white male privileges. The action hero, thus, exists to redeem men of those past sins feminists so correctly hold against them.[3]

These same themes still resonate today in entertainment that addresses masculinity: in films, literature, or television shows dealing with the question of what it means to be a man. The heroes of action films are still most often mavericks, they usually have a hard time with authority figures, their love lives are in disarray, and if they have children, the heroes are often at risk of losing them. The continuity between two generations of men is still an important theme of action films to this day, although the continuity of an older generation's values onto a generation of sons is still most often strained.

As of the late 1990s, the state of American masculinity has been a point of analysis by various sociologists, anthropologists, media critics, feminists, and social commentators across the ideological and political spectrum. In her book on modern male discontent, *Stiffed: The Betrayal of the American Man*, feminist writer Susan Faludi talks with scores of men about the state of modern masculinity and listens to them reflect on a phenomenon of fathers and father figures missing from the lives of at least two generations of men over the past half century.[4] The echoes of this crisis in the action film are remarkable.

On a similar note, famed anthropologist Lionel Tiger's book *The Decline of Males* ruminates about the changing shape of the family not only in America, but also in ever more societies around the world. The ongoing cultural debates about the family and "family values," center on these changes, he argues, and this change includes the growing number of women raising children without men in their lives. The growing divorce rate is not the only contributing factor. More and more women are now *choosing* to be single mothers, and they are providing remarkably well for their children. "Our species seems to be leaping back in time to the more basic mammalian system that was the core of our evolutionary history," Tiger writes, "one founded on the primacy of the mother and child."[5] Through the development of reliable and effective birth control and reproductive technology, one gender can now control reproduction. In effect, not only can women alone control when and if they reproduce, but they can remove copulation, or contact of any sort, with a man entirely from the process. The forming debates of bioethics, trying to come to terms with the looming technology of genetic engineering and cloning, can, perhaps, now add gender relations and the gender gap to its issues when dealing with such technology.

Many action films of the twenty-first century have prominent thematic elements and plot lines concerning men who have lost families. One of the films of the past decade that made masculinity a surprisingly explicit theme is 2001's *Swordfish*, dramatizing the male hero's removal from the family after his economic status has been wrecked. The film stars Hugh Jackman in one of his early action roles, playing a whistle-blowing idealist punished for doing the right thing. As a computer expert who goes public with the National Security Agency's illegal computer-hacking activities, Jackman gets prosecuted, does prison time, and winds up being barred from working with computers in any capacity, leaving him barely able to scratch out a living on a ramshackle oil-drilling operation. As a result, his wife leaves him, taking their small daughter. The ex-wife is promptly remarried, however, to "the porn king of Southern California." Since her pornographer husband can provide her with an oceanside mansion, even the legal system sides with the ex-wife, not only denying Jackman joint custody of his daughter, but visitation rights as well. Because he is so desperate to make enough money to impress the court, the film's plot begins as Jackman agrees to help a gang of criminals break a bank's computer codes.

The issue of the job of a strong man and its impact on family and offspring comes up in an uncanny number of Arnold Schwarzenegger's films. This is of importance because well before leaving filmmaking, Schwarzenegger had already been recognized as one of the most iconic action stars in film history. He is one of the heirs to the title representative of American masculinity, a direct cinematic descendant of John Wayne. But the sort of American male Schwarzenegger seemed to have specialized in was the type with a very tenuous hold on his family. For example, as his tough cop character laments to a would-be love interest in *Kindergarten Cop* (1990): "I didn't mean to hurt you. I wish I was a kindergarten teacher. But I'm not. I'm a cop. That's all I know how to be. I have a son I've hardly seen in the last seven years. I don't mean anything to him. My ex-wife got remarried; she doesn't want me to be part of his life. I lost my family."

But broken and lost families turn up in more Schwarzenegger films, even in his most famous films. A major factor in the character development of a key protagonist in *Terminator 2* (1991) is the lack of a strong father figure. Raised by a mother (Linda Hamilton) who is eventually institutionalized in a mental asylum, the leader of the future (Edward Furlong) begins his teenage years as a delinquent and petty thief. He begins his journey to responsibility and leadership only when placed in the care of the Terminator. In a key scene, the future leader's mother realizes that in all the madness of the world heading toward nuclear destruction, the most logical father figure for her son becomes the Terminator who "would never leave him, and it would never hurt him and never shout at him or get drunk and hit him or say it was too busy to spend time with him, and it would always be there and it would die to protect him. Of all the would-be fathers who came and went over the years, this thing, this machine, was the only one that measured up. In an insane world, it was the sanest choice."

In *Terminator 3* (2003), a twenty-something John Connor (Nick Stahl), the future leader of humanity, again reflects on how the massive cyborg is the only real father he ever had.

In *Last Action Hero* (1993), a very broad parody of the action genre, the plot revolves around a young boy (Austin O'Brien) whose lack of a father leads him to find a surrogate father figure in the on-screen Schwarzenegger hero, Jack Slater. When the boy is magically transported inside the film world, it is revealed that Jack Slater's own son was killed in a previous installment of the film series. Once Slater begins realizing that his world is not real, that he is an outdated cartoon of masculinity, his greatest pain is over the fact that he was given a son, only to have him taken away on the whim of some remote, godlike power.

In *True Lies* (1994), Schwarzenegger's super-spy character's loss of influence in his family is mocked by his sidekick (Tom Arnold) (his daughter [Eliza Dushku] easily manipulates him and steals from him and his wife [Jamie Lee Curtis] is about to have an affair with a smarmy car dealer [Bill Paxton]); in *The 6th Day* (2000), he stumbles onto a clone of himself replacing him in his own house and in the arms of his own family; while in both *End of Days* (1999) and *Collateral Damage* (2002), his wife and children are murdered.

A remarkably accurate and complete synthesis of all these themes, however, shows up in one of the most popular trendsetters of the 1980s action renaissance: Bruce Willis's *Die Hard* series (1988, 1990, 1995, 2007).

In the first film, Bruce Willis's blue-collar street cop tries to reconcile with his white-collar professional wife (Bonnie Bedelia) who left him for a high-powered career. Here, the traditional, physical, strong male becomes completely disposable to his upwardly mobile wife who can provide a better paying, more secure, more respectable and fulfilling life for herself and her children when she is alone than she ever could have staying with the hero. In a very thorough commentary track on the DVD release of the film, director John McTiernan explains that the key to the Willis character is that he is a man contending with an immense sense of self-loathing and feelings of failure. As his wife has been able to take over the traditional masculine role of family provider, he has become obsolete. When the action begins with a terrorist takeover of the building, however, only the physical, violent methods of the traditionally masculine man are successful against the villains.

In one sense, the *Die Hard* films—because all four deal with basically the same themes and issues—appeal to male audiences because their hero is just an everyday guy. In the midst of the 1980s' showdown of cartoonish musculatures between Arnold Schwarzenegger and Sylvester Stallone, Bruce Willis's *Die Hard* character was a welcome return to reality. Willis does not look like a super man and he is not a former bodybuilder, champion athlete, or unbeaten martial artist. He is not even as smooth, well-dressed, or good looking as James Bond. His unimposing body and receding hairline make him look refreshingly flawed and realistic. Even the character is just an average street cop, neither a super spy nor a special forces operative.

But in another sense, *Die Hard* pressed very sensitive psychological buttons in its male audiences. The average guy in the center of this story is one who is fast losing control and relevance in the world around him. He has become useless to his family, if not altogether a burden, and he must now throw himself in the middle of the most outrageous and overwhelming peril to prove he is still worth keeping around.

Although criticism and scholarship has long identified the action film as a theater of gender concerns and conflicts, an art where late twentieth-century manhood tries to find its place in a quickly changing, feminizing society, the impact of these films cannot be clearly ascertained by a study of the text alone. Indeed, the impact, the social and psychological effects of these films, has long been a source of heated controversy. Because action films are founded on the displays of often excessive, hyperbolic violence, they have long been looked at with suspicion, even censorious hostility by educators and social and moral crusaders of various ideological and political agendas. What must the effects of all this machismo and violence be? Unfortunately, not many have bothered to go to the viewers and ask.

Until now, the focus has always been on the text. But such a focus has become inadequate if one wants to answer any of the questions raised by all the controversy. One needs to go past the films and study the viewers.

GENRE AND AUDIENCE

Studying the interaction between text and audience when it comes to the action film is a challenge, in part, because the genre itself is so chameleon-like. The action film often colonizes several genres, incorporating archetypes and iconography from films ranging the spectrum from science fiction to horror to comedy. For example, despite the fact that they portray vampires and the archetypal plot concerns of the horror genre—methods of disposing of a vampire, avoiding sunlight, living with vampirism—the *Blade* films (1998, 2002, 2004) are of the action genre, rather than horror. Chapter 3, therefore, gives an operational definition of the action/adventure film and its nuances, explaining what is considered "action" in this study. Chapter 3 also limits the definitions and focus to the traditional male action films. Although the female action story has really begun to come into its own as a new wing of the genre within the past several years (with traditions in films like the *Alien* series and a very strong female presence in Asian martial arts films), its archetypal and thematic concerns are shaping up to be so specific as to be deserving a more in-depth analysis than a mere addition to a male cultural-identity study.

The subjects of this study, each of whom is briefly identified in Chapter 2, are a varied lot. Both men and women are probed for an understanding of their use of the action film, and in Chapter 4 a fascinating picture emerges about the needs the fast-paced action films fulfill in their lives. Before talking to individuals about their interest in the thematics of the action film, about their gender concerns and readings of the text, we must deal with why they so often turn to a genre as controversial as this. As detailed in Chapter 3, the action film is set apart from numerous other genres it may closely resemble by its violence. All drama functions on tension and conflict on one level, although the action film is the only one foregrounding the aesthetics of destruction. Chapter 4 asks those interviewed for this study what it is that attracts them to the particular aesthetics of this genre. The responses prove to be multifaceted. The answers men and women give begin painting a picture of a type of individual for whom entertainment gives the greatest pleasure when delivered in a rapid-fire pace of constant tension and excitement-arousing displays of danger and confrontation. Drawing on research conducted on the psychology of suspense, this chapter helps paint a picture of arousal-craving personality types gravitating toward the action genre.

Chapter 4 also paints a picture of the socialization process that draws people to the action film, most importantly the socialization processes introducing women to the genre. The fact that all but one of the female subjects explains that they started watching action/adventure as a result of having grown up in an environment where men influenced and guided (often forced) their film-selection activities presents implications and raises questions about women's media habits.

As cultural studies scholarship argues that media use involves the active negotiation of personal value systems and life experiences with the symbolic world within the artwork's text, Chapter 5 puts the focus on both men and women as they explain their personal values and those of the action film. As the subjects begin talking about what the films mean to them, a clearer picture emerges of the argument that media violence has to be analyzed within a moral context.

The gendered talk about values, action heroes, and action stars also lets a picture emerge as to why it could be that men do not organize in order to advance their own interests. As subjects talk about their favorite characters and stars, we begin to see the extent to which men and women feel comfortable disclosing about emotions, emotional issues, and how much the narratives and values of certain action films may help reinforce a silence in some men.

In Chapters 6 and 7, men talk about the crisis of masculinity in the world and in the action film. Most of the men agree that the narratives of the genre speak to a growing alienation men feel in the culture. Some believe this is a real crisis in the culture, others do not. It once again becomes striking how unwilling people are to admit they personally feel like they are under attack.

If action films are narratives about power and powerlessness and the disenfranchisement of men, what do women see in these narratives? Besides the speed of the stories, the excitatory pleasures offered by the pacing of the films, what do women say about the meaning of the stories? As Chapter 8 reveals, female action fans look at their favorite films as a means of negotiating their ideals of manhood and their expectations of how modern masculinity needs to relate to society, women, feminism, and families. A major difference between men and women proves to be the sociability of action heroes. Women, the chapter shows, are not interested in the action hero as loner, but do enjoy watching him, no matter how powerful he may be, in the male bonding buddy action films and team-of-men-on-a-mission films. Action heroes who fight for and protect their families are also attractive to the female audiences.

Chapter 9 asks the participants in this study what the pleasures of violence are. This section of the project moves beyond the excitatory pleasure of a fast-paced narrative and asks them to comment about the controversies surrounding violence. Once more, what they reveal is complex and surprising. All but three people of the entire subject pool say there are depictions of violence they do not like to see. All but these three people explain that they find explicit scenes of blood, bodily damage, mutilation, and dismemberment disturbing and unpleasant to watch. The three people who do not mind explicit violence, who, along with action films, also love gory horror films, are women.

As for the depictions of violence, both men and women explain that violence is acceptable when it comes in a moral context. It needs to be a part of a message, a story, it needs to be a part of a statement about right and wrong. The testimonials in this chapter illustrate their definitions of morality and illustrate what the greater purpose of the violence needs to be a part of to be acceptable. Once more, unexpected gender differences present themselves.

Finally, action films, just like society, just like men and women and gender relations, change all the time. Chapter 10 looks at the most recent changes and attempts to predict the future course of this genre. Action films changed in a big way in the 1990s and then again in the 2000s. The advent of digital technology in special effects took the action even further over the top than ever before. Computer effects could create the truly impossible on screen. Basically—and unintentionally perhaps—the action films of that decade put the accent on just how much of a construct masculinity can be. A decade of digital special effects trickery had created a line of films where manly heroics looked more obviously fake, contrived, and absurd than ever. Moreover, a freshman class of action heroes, from the likes of Keanu Reeves to Matt

Damon, Ben Affleck to Orlando Bloom, younger, more callow heartthrobs, have replaced the rough-around-the-edges *men* like Sylvester Stallone, Clint Eastwood, Mel Gibson, or Bruce Willis. But only up to a certain point! The final chapter examines these turning points, from the boyish trend of the 1990s to the impact of the terrorist attacks of September 11, 2001, the cultural atmosphere under the Bush and Obama presidencies, and what the reappearance of the "old school" models of masculinity in the newly revived *Indiana Jones*, *Rocky*, *Rambo*, *Die Hard*, and *Terminator* films might mean.

NOTES

1. Michael Medved, "Hollywood's Three Big Lies about Media and Society," www.independent.org/events/transcript.asp?eventID=69 (retrieved May 28, 2009).

2. Paul Schrader, "Notes on Film Noir," in *Film Genre Reader*, ed. B. K. Grant (Austin: University of Texas Press, 1986), 229–242.

3. Neal King, *Heroes in Hard Times: Cop Action Movies in the U.S.* (Philadelphia: Temple University Press, 1999).

4. Susan Faludi, *Stiffed: The Betrayal of the American Man* (New York: William Morrow and Company, 1999).

5. Lionel Tiger, *The Decline of Males* (New York: St. Martin's Griffin, 1999), 21.

Part I

THE CONTROVERSIES, THE CRISIS, AND THE FILMS

1

The History of a Modern Crisis

It wasn't my war! You asked me! I didn't ask you.

—Sylvester Stallone, *First Blood*

I figure, for so long the U.S. has been kicking ass all over the world. Maybe this time it will get *its* ass kicked.

—Willem Dafoe, *Platoon*

The cultural history of which entertainment attracts and amuses men has long been intertwined with a fear of violent, brutal, and anti-social behavior resulting from all the rampant, unrestrained testosterone. Young men have always been a special source of concern. As Arnold Freeman wrote in 1914:

> The boy's mind is in many respects a blank sheet at fourteen, and the writing that will be engraved on it is dependent on the influences through which the boy passes. The senses of the adolescent, now open at their widest, are opened not to art, but to cheap and tawdry pantomime, his emotions are fed, not with gracious and elevating influences, but with unnatural excitements.[1]

As the very roots of mass media studies can be traced to fears of media effects in the early decades of the twentieth century, those fears were mostly founded on a fear of male misbehavior. In fact, this fear went beyond the U.S. shores. As Schwarz quotes *The Times* (London) from 1900, "[media] excitements . . . [create 'hooligans' and] our hooligans go from bad to worse . . . they hunt in packs too large for a single policeman to cope with. . . . At best they will be bad citizens. They are an ugly growth on the body politic . . . a hideous excrescence on our civilization."[2] Murdoch, quoting the *Edinburgh Review*, traces the fear even farther:

> One powerful agent for depraving the boyish classes of our population in our towns and cities is to be found in the cheap concerts, shows and theatres, which are so specially opened and arranged for the attraction and ensnaring of the young . . . when our fear of interfering with personal and public liberty allows these shows and theaters to be training schools of the coarsest and most open vice and filthiness—it is not to be wondered, that the boy who is led on to haunt them becomes rapidly corrupted and demoralized, and seeks to be the doer of the infamies which have interested him as a spectator.[3]

He also invokes a very early linear "effects" argument comparing media messages to an epidemic, written by, not surprisingly, a surgeon named G. Frank Lydston in his 1904 book *The Diseases of Society*:

> There is a moral or psychic contagium in certain books that is as definite and disastrous as that of the plague. The germs of mental ill-health are as potent in their way and, as things go nowadays, as far-reaching in evil effects as syphilis or leprosy.[4]

Such worries are the very foundation of the modern and still very powerful media "effects" school. The kindest words this area of scholarship has for the fans of violent entertainment are still best summed up by film critic Michael Medved's quip about the "drooling, sub-literate males," presented in the Introduction.

However, only recently have scholars looked to separate anti-social behavior from media content and the traditional cause and effect chain. Graham Murdoch details this as a movement from the "transportation" model, whereupon the media is the conduit for meaning from producer to viewer and the subsequent victim of an effect, to a "translational" model.[5] In the cultural studies tradition, using qualitative data-gathering techniques, the translational model "views popular representation as complex ensembles of meaning that can be interpreted and responded to in a variety of ways and, in its more critical variant, insists that people's relations with them can be properly understood only in the context of the networks of social relations and forces that envelop and shape them."[6]

The action/adventure genre is comprised of narratives of violent confrontation perpetrated by or responded to—often with more violence—by men. While the effects debate has been unfolding for well over a century, and no doubt will unfold for much longer, an approach to violent entertainment, or one specific genre of violent entertainment, will, in this book, be seen in terms of its text being responded to by both male and female audiences, being interpreted by these audiences in light of current gender relations and the concept that has been termed a *crisis of masculinity*.

As this book will bear out, those whom I discussed action films, fandom, violence, and gender issues with viewed the meanings of the films as reflections of how masculinity is altering, how relationships between men, between men and society, and between men and women are changing. The heavy viewers of these films look upon stories that may often bemoan the fate of men, criticize classical masculinity, endorse it, mock it, and negotiate their own identities and roles as men in society with the narratives.

The most fascinating aspect of the heavy viewers of action is how much they vary in their own opinions about masculinity and society. It is also interesting to see how greatly some of those whom I interviewed varied in the extent to which they were willing to speak about gender and a masculinity crisis, and how such propensities for discourse and reflection are dramatized in the films they watch, in the stars they are fans of, and how much they will admit to believing that the crisis concept is real.

One of the most important things Lionel Tiger wrote about male activism in the face of aggressively changing gender roles is how inactive many men remain in the face of their altering social status.

> Nothing males have done as a self-conscious gender group is remotely comparable, thorough, or effective. Men in groups do not appear to perceive themselves as being in a group. They do not define themselves as a member of an assembly with a collective interest. To the extent that they are conscious at all of any problems they face, men seem to assume these will be solved in the traditional public way. Their fantasy is, all they have to do is behave in reasonably civil, even gentlemanly ways. Everything will turn out peaceably and well.[7]

There is no cohesive, organized men's movement, no activism to deal with male issues, needs, and problems because men often do not like to publicly address their problems. Interestingly, on the one hand, they watch the morality plays of the action film because it gives voice and shape to their nebulous problem in the world today. Yet, on the other hand, the very language and value systems of these films reinforce the silent models of masculinity, all performed by action stars who wed their public personas to similar images of stoic, uncomplaining toughness.

Finally, this study shows the similarities and differences between male and female action viewers. Although a predominantly male audience has always patronized the action genre, it does have a number of female fans. This study inquired why the participants enjoy action, how they were socialized in entertainment use in a way that now has them turning to this genre as a first choice of entertainment, and what they think of the masculinity crisis.

THE "CRISIS"

To many, men's social relations that seek to incorporate violence as a pre-ferred entertainment form is still a troubling phenomenon. Susan Faludi details the beginnings of her research on masculinity and the feminist ac-knowledgment of a "masculinity crisis" for her book *Stiffed*. This concept is rooted in the late 1980s and early 1990s era of post–Cold War America. It is a concept born out of the question of what becomes of American masculin-ity once the United States no longer needs to define itself as a world warrior of epic threats like communism. The male capacity and willingness to wage war were essential while the United States was locked in a standoff with the Soviet Union, and it was glamorized and celebrated throughout the Reagan era. However, as the 1980s came to a close, intellectuals and gender scholars asked a question similar to one asked in the aftermath of Vietnam: what else can a man do besides fight? Faludi started with the hypothesis that the mod-ern world's curbing of man's aggression was a part of the crisis. Starting a cross-country trip to understand different sectors of male America, she began in Southern California because it was supposed to have been the "epicenter of toxic masculinity";[8] on the one hand, the site of festering resentment in the wake of the post–Cold War defense plant closings, and, on the other hand, the site of some of the most widely publicized instances of young male violence. However, as she observed in the media-image capital of Los Angeles, the fearsome images of gang members, bullet-spraying bank robbers, and rapists that one day shock and outrage in headlines, will titillate, entertain, and sell the next day in a film:

> But the bad boy was just as frequently a shipment wrapped in celluloid and airbrushed in advertising campaigns, where what had just been demonized about him could now be glamorized, his exaggerated criminality repackaged for profit, the sexual predator made sexual object. The media's nightmare visions of "wilding" boys with MAC-10s would become the commercial daydreams of Hollywood and Madison Avenue, as snarling young gangsters and rapists reformed into long-lashed Tupak Shakur matinee idols and sulky-lipped Marky Mark pinups. The Nike-shod thug with his predatory "attitude" and bare-chested Calvin Klein poster boy with his gigantic tented underwear rivaled the Marlboro cowboy's spurs for preeminence along the Sunset Strip's billboard gulch. The perfumed junior hoodlum became the prevailing male icon, lord of the unzipped flies.[9]

Faludi's conclusion of what constitutes the crisis is manifold, but it is ultimately centered on the media. She first details a number of social and economic changes that led to male alienation and resentment in American culture. The economic recession of the early 1990s dealt a major blow to the man's position of prestige as a breadwinner and provider for his family. Talking to men in Long Beach, once the home of shipyard workers in the formerly robust-defense industry, Faludi paints a picture of the crisis emerging in the early 1990s.

A second major source of male resentment she pinpoints as originating in the culture's betrayals by businesses and social institutions. Once again, the early 1990s wave of business downsizings and corporate restructuring left men feeling betrayed. What previous generations have come to believe to be an honorable compact between workers and their employers has been proven to be a lie. At the time of this writing, headlines are once again filled with cases of gross corporate fraud and mismanagement, along with the multibillion-dollar price tags of government bailouts needed to clean up the mess, and we can easily guess what action films will be doing with big business villains in the near future.

In a similar vein, Faludi argues that a sense of citizenship has been eroding in the nation. A sense of civic duty and connection to a greater social good has been evaporating. A main problem she identifies is the problem of uncommunicative, distant, or absent fathers who no longer have bonds with their sons, who are no longer willing to teach sons these civic values.

As will be the case when looking at the testimonials of my subjects, the action films' fixation on honor and values—or the subjects' interpretations of honor and values—is something that is one of the weightiest concerns for the fans. This moral betrayal appears to be well rooted in the genre.

Ultimately, however, the crux of Faludi's work is a social constructionist argument, targeting media and advertising imagery as the chief culprit in fashioning unrealistic images of masculinity. She lays a lot of the blame on what she calls the "hood ornament culture," media-created, iconic images of sports celebrities, models, music stars, and action heroes that paint a picture of the American male that—in reality—isn't true. She argues that this ornamentalization is similar to what had been oppressing women until the 1960s, the real impetus behind the "second wave" feminism launched by Betty Friedan's 1963 book *The Feminine Mystique*. Faludi states that "Ornamental culture has proved the ultimate expression of the American Century, sweeping away institutions in which men felt some sense of belonging and replacing them with visual spectacles that they can only watch and that benefit global commercial forces they cannot fathom."[10] The ornamental male image, furthermore, is also depicted in action films most of the time, slaying larger-than-life obstacles that no longer exist. It is an epic masculinity both overpowering in appearance *and* anachronistic.

This aspect of Faludi's critique is endorsed by no less an action icon than Sylvester Stallone, explaining in a 1996 *Esquire* interview with Faludi:

Everything is a display. It has a paralyzing effect on character. You take a serious gym rat, a man who lives in a gym, it's like, what do you *do* with it? You've got it, but it comes out in this vanity thing which borders on the world of exotic dancing with women. . . . The guy with the eighteen-inch-arms, the thirty-one-inch waist, the male model, chiseled Calvin Klein-ad type of person, he is, for the nineties, the woman with the triple E. He's taking the place of the blond bombshell of the fifties. The woman on the street doesn't want to be Jayne Mansfield. But if I see another guy walking through Central Park in a tank top and bicycle shorts, it's like why don't you just get a billboard that says, "Look at me! Don't take me seriously!" It's sad, because there's no sense of self-worth, and your only entrée into people's line of consciousness for a synaptic millisecond is your body, so that they go, "Oh, look at that idiot!"[11]

On the issue of slaying exaggerated obstacles to maintain the image of the male as a conqueror, Stallone continues:

Life is becoming very static for a lot of men. The options are few and far between. . . . The opportunities for men to validate themselves are diminishing. The frontiers are diminishing. So they seek these extreme outlets. The bungee cord—let's talk about that, please! Car surfing. Sixty miles per hour on the subway roof! Hanging on to the sides of buses!

Although Stallone acknowledges his hand in perpetuating the body-centered action hero, the interview does not touch on the heyday of the genre in the mid-1980s where the muscle-fetishized action hero reached its hyperbolic extreme in his competition with Arnold Schwarzenegger, practitioner of the chief sport of the hood ornament culture: bodybuilding—the true postmodern sport where the appearance of muscle surpasses its function.

Furthermore, cinematically, the hood ornament culture thesis is at the core of the anger and discontent of both the book and film versions of *Fight Club*, a forerunner of Faludi's work, its violence aimed at the advertising and consumer culture. "I was stunned when the movie was about to come out and I started reading about Susan Faludi and *Stiffed*," claims Fox 2000 Productions president of production Laura Ziskin in the published notes to the film. "I thought it was so amazing that she had been working on this for six years while (novelist) Chuck Palahniuk was under a diesel truck in Portland writing in his brilliantly hyperbolic way, about the very same things Susan was researching." "We were told we would grow up to be millionaires and movie gods. But we're not!," declares Brad Pitt to a group of disenfranchised men in the film, all of them gathered around him as he leads a revolt against society through campaigns of vandalism. Many of these followers are, in fact, financially secure, white-collar professionals, but living a life devoid of meaning other than the things they buy to be "real men." Adds producer Ross Garson Bell: "Finally a piece of material that spoke to the heart of a disenfranchised generation, my generation. Like *The Graduate* three decades before, the book spoke to the frustrations of ordinary guys trying to make sense of the sorry world previous generations were so smugly handing over to us like so much skid-marked underwear." As Bret Easton Ellis writes, whose hyperviolent 1991 novel *American Psycho* fired up controversy with its treatment of masculinity and murder, "*Fight Club* rages against the hypocrisy of a society that continually promises us the impossible: fame, beauty, wealth, immortality, life without pain . . . a relentless, dizzying take on the male fear of losing power."[12]

The hood ornament culture indictment and the idea of men as victims of unrealistic media images is lent support by psychiatrists Harrison Pope, Katherine Phillips, and Roberto Olivardia in their 2000 book *The Adonis Complex: The Secret Crisis of Male Body Obsession*. Here, men join the ranks of eating disorder and body image crisis sufferers. Whereas the body image crisis has mostly been getting press in the case of teenage girls starving themselves to death as, supposedly, prompted by the images of ultra-thin supermodels, men suffer as a result of chiseled *GQ* models, Brad Pitt's abs, Rambo, and Arnold. The male version of the body image crisis, according to Pope and his cowriters, usually manifests itself as the ironic flip side of the female affliction. Whereas women cannot get thin enough, men cannot get big and bulky enough. The media image of men is usually muscular, "ripped," and chiseled, broad-shouldered with "six pack abs" and bulgy biceps. To give a more complex picture of the situation, however, Pope adds that the crisis is likewise helped along by the disappearance of exclusively male spheres of society. As roles and jobs once reserved for men are now encroached upon by women, the only thing a man still has that he can control is his body, his muscles. As Samuel Wilson Fussell writes in his 1992 autobiography of the trip from scrawny Rhodes scholar and New York literary professional to steroid-shooting California bodybuilder, the need to feel control in an out-of-control urban world led him to the gym.[13] In a world where he felt like he was at the mercy of the whims of fate and the various brutal, violent forces of urban America, bodybuilding involved a clear cause and effect chain. He lifted weights, his muscles grew. The more he lifted, the more the muscles grew. A new phenomenon of male narcissism, seen in the rise of men having cosmetic surgery, is argued to be yet another manifestation of the ornament culture.

As Faludi seeks to present a complete picture of the masculinity crisis, she uses an interesting artichoke metaphor. There are various manifestations to the crisis and she feels compelled to go inward toward the heart of the problem, to peel away the layers and look for deeper causes to each. With this project, I likewise wanted to look at different dimensions of the concept,

considering Faludi's strictly social constructionist approach in conjunction
with all the other major current writings on the masculinity crisis.

Aside from Faludi's social constructionist, left-wing take on the masculinity crisis, right-leaning cultural critics like Christina Hoff-Sommers also
identify a crisis, but in radically different terms.[14] According to Hoff-Sommers, the real sources of the crisis are people like Faludi and the far left wing
of feminism. Leftist, social-constructionist feminism argues that all gender
behavior is but an arbitrary social construct. According to the social-constructionist point of view that Hoff-Sommers critiques, there are no typically
male or female behaviors. Instead, men and women have been conditioned by
society to act and think in certain ways. The conditioning, however, seeks to
maintain a patriarchal, male-dominated social order. Faludi and the feminist
left ultimately argue that men would all be happier and healthier if they were
raised more like women traditionally are. Men, they argue, would feel less
crippling, traumatic pressures, less of a crisis, if society was not compelling
them to be macho tough guys with a need to exert their power, suppress their
emotions, and rule everything and everyone around them. But the counter
argument to this position usually relies on sociobiological, evolutionary arguments. Biology, this position says, especially men's and women's endocrine
systems, determines gendered behavior. Hormones like testosterone and es-
trogen regulate states of mind and gendered behavior. In effect, sociobiology
states that there are natural male and female ways to act. Acting like a man
or like a woman is not merely an arbitrary social construct, but natural urges
driven by hormones that have been programmed by evolution. If gender behavior would be but a construct, this position further argues, there would be a
greater variety of male and female behavior throughout the world and across
different cultures. Therefore, the most harmful and stressful thing men and
women can be subjected to is pressure not to behave in the way evolution and
biology naturally compels them.

Supporters of this position have come from circles as predictable as Robert
Bly's late 1980s and early 1990s men's movement and as unpredictable as
the ideas of "renegade feminist" scholar Camille Paglia. Bly's movement,
discussed in his book *Iron John*, claimed that men are hurting in the postfeminist world because their natural, biologically programmed masculinity is
being suppressed and stigmatized as something aberrant.[15] Boys, Bly writes,
are not brought up with enough positive male role models in a society that
is attacking and denigrating masculinity. Boys, in turn, caught between their
budding biologically compelled masculine instinct and society's contempt for
traditional masculinity, are suffering. Camille Paglia has likewise endorsed
the biologically based explanation for gendered behavior, arguing, simply,
that the biological and genetic position can be proven. Too much of the social

constructionist and postmodern feminist schools of thought have no solid, rigorous proof to back a lot of their positions, nothing that can be accepted as scientific.[16]

Another discipline that has been interested in media representations of biologically programmed gender relations is anthropology. An anthropological perspective on literary criticism, for example, has sought to find common motifs on gender, family, and reproduction strategies in literature across cultures. As Tiger's influential work on the "decline of males" seeks to understand how female empowerment and economic autonomy has, in a matter of a few swift decades, upset historical rules governing everything from family affairs to reproduction to morality, he shows how popular culture products reflect a world where everything from male influence over reproduction to spheres of male exclusivity have disappeared.[17] He writes that the modern battles where the genders vie for power are fought over "startlingly new politics . . . about what is right, wrong, good, and bad, and about a whole new array of issues. Single motherhood, gender styles, infertility, government food for babies, sexual harassment, homosexual infantry, women in combat, abortion, clitoridectomy, human breeders under contract—these are the issues undreamed of by writers of political science textbooks five or even two generations ago."[18] The anthropological framework seeks to understand a combination of female political/economic empowerment, combined with an empowerment over reproduction through technology and how this contributes to men's sense of crisis. For the first time in history, women are able to control reproduction alone, and legal codes—from family law favoring custody to mothers to legislature protecting family leave and mandating child support—now all support society's reorganization in line with the most basic mammalian model. Modern men, Tiger argues, have been alienated from their means of reproduction. Similar to the literary criticism anthropologists have undertaken, their view of the masculinity crisis can also be applied to the film and the action/adventure genre to see how the gendered social changes are reflected in the narratives of the action film.

Anthropologist Helen Fisher's view of the "women's movement" and the "masculinity crisis" is that the concepts should be viewed as a symptom of the modern, postindustrial, bureaucratized economy.[19] The organizational, communication, and media-structured world, she argues, is better suited to tap the inherent talents of women. While controversial among feminists, she cites empirical data from genetics that the female brain is more optimally hard-wired for the media/high-tech work environment.

Although some media scholars have argued the action/adventure genre in the realm of capitalist/economic metaphorical representation,[20] another look at the post-1960s action film offers a very tempting and convenient analysis made along the lines of anthropological tenets. For example, the idea of inherent differences better equipping women to cope in the modern, bureaucratic, information society over men's physical, aggressive natures is among the tried and true thematic formulas. The heroes of action films are often at odds with women in their lives because such men lack adequate communication skills. They are not "sensitive" enough, or "in touch with their feelings." Their penchant for violence and primal, physical masculinity has no place in a woman's world. More and more women are filling the role of the exasperated bosses and politicians who get angry at the unacceptably violent methods of tough, lone wolf male cops. Starting with the Pierce Brosnan *James Bond* films and continuing even in the latest Daniel Craig films, even Bond's boss is a woman. In her very first appearance in *GoldenEye* (1995), she declares that she considers him nothing less than a "sexist, misogynist dinosaur." The bedrock formula also often involves the women leaving the gruff, monosyllabic, violent lone wolves for men better suited for the information society: lawyers, accountants, businessmen, and various white-collar types. These men, of course, are less "macho," less muscular, lacking martial arts and combat skills, but they are men who can communicate their feelings, and are stable, dependable, and well-providing organization men. Essentially, the nature-made characteristics of men that allowed them to conquer and tame rougher agrarian and industrial societies that needed ruling and taming are useless in an information society that needs to be managed. As Stallone again ruminates:

> The male is necessary in the actual — well, in technological procreation, no, he's not. It can be mechanically induced . . . we've lost what it *means* to be masculine . . . it's just the masculine endeavors — the jobs, the positions, the challenges — are diminishing. It's like some great nomadic tribe that's slowly being fenced in. And as they fail to wander, they no longer seem to exist.[21]

THE EYE OF THE BEHOLDER: A CULTURAL STUDIES APPROACH TO MEN, FILMS, AND VIOLENCE

The study of masculinity and male images in popular culture is relatively new, since men are generally seen as the guardians of the status quo, the ones in power, the ones with the leverage, the ones against whom all the "others" of social science and cultural studies research are measured. When it comes to male problems, there are few sympathetic ears. As Faludi explains quite succinctly:

> Men feel the contours of a box, too, but they are told that the box is of their own manufacture, designed to their own specifications. Who are they to complain? .

. . For men to say they feel boxed in is regarded not as laudable political protest but as childish and indecent whining. How dare the kings complain about their castles?[22]

Cultural studies' concern with women, immigrants, racial, ethnic, religious, sexually oriented, among myriad other, subcultures, subgroups, and oppositional social circles is most often placing its subjects in contrast to one larger "dominant" culture, or the status quo. Men are clearly identified as this dominant entity. They are the patriarchal "hegemony." Media images created within this society, even of the various subcultures, are "hegemonic" in the cultural studies parlance. According to Stuart Hall, "the definition of a hegemonic viewpoint is, first, that it defines within its terms the mental horizon, the universe, of possible meanings, of a whole sector of relations in a society or culture; and, second, that it carries with it the stamp of legitimacy—it appears coterminous with what is 'natural,' 'inevitable' 'taken for granted' about the social order."[23] The Marlboro Man, Rambo, the Terminator, and James Bond, or even the buff *GQ* models, upon first glance, are considered hegemonic because of their images of strength and domination. They make male strength the natural order of things, male positions of power normal. At the same time, female images can be hegemonic as well. The models on the cover of the *Sports Illustrated* swimsuit issue are hegemonic for two reasons. First, they are the male ideal and the women are the sorts of physical specimens that very rarely occur in nature. Second, the fact that the model is only in the spotlight because of her looks, because nothing else about her, other than her body image, is important or known, is again no challenge to the male hegemonic order. In contrast, the comedy routines of Jeanine Garofallo (one of Stallone's costars in *Copland* [1997]), most often railing against not being able to measure up to the dominant supermodel standard, would be resistant to the patriarchal hegemony for exposing the apparatus of cultural domination. Usually her monologues state this in very exact language.

Even if the Frankfurt school of critical cultural analysis is to be given its due—and the Marxist concepts of class struggle and domination indeed lay among the founding stones of the cultural studies school—the "culture industry,"[24] churning out a deluge of seemingly uniform and uniformly mindless entertainment, is actually creating an indoctrination and control apparatus, naturalizing the hegemonic elite's position of power.[25] But, writes Fiske, "the cultural studies tradition does not view ideology in its vulgar Marxist sense of "false consciousness," because this seems "inappropriate to the late twentieth century, which appears to have demonstrated not the inevitable self-destruction of capitalism but its unpredicted (by Marx) ability to reproduce itself and to incorporate into itself the forces of resistance and opposition."[26] But in this schema, there still lies the implication of the ruler and the dominated, the one who has the power and the one being manipulated into accepting a subordinate position. It is still haunted by the subtle specter of the hegemonic (male) dominator, inserting his will not by coercion but by the very *consent* of the dominated "subaltern." However, if men are, in fact, as powerful and dominant as this tradition of research indicates, why is their primary choice of entertainment a genre that presents disenfranchised male characters having no choice but to resort to violence—as well as belligerence, sarcasm, and all the requisite displays of rebellion and "attitude" that are important to the development of the archetypal action hero—to assert themselves? How, in fact, do men—and women even—see these movies and how do they see their positions within a world where one gender is facing a crisis of identity? To understand how cultural products intersect with the altering landscape of gender identity, the tenets and methodology of cultural studies need to be applied to the most active users of action/adventure entertainment.

Tracing the origins of cultural studies to the Birmingham Centre for Contemporary Cultural Studies (CCCS) in Britain, founded by Richard Hoggart in the 1950s, one finds a line of scholarship that treats media products as a text. Although the Birmingham school was originally interested in how class affects media interpretations, the methodology is now equally effective in exploring gender. Cultural studies position the text as a cultural battlefield of sorts, where meanings are created, contested, or rewritten based on its audience's, as well as the creator's, social position. The fact that this school of thought emerged from literary criticism is therefore important to the textual analysis aspects of the discipline. That they sought to give both high and low, or "mass culture," texts their equal time in analysis is important to the approach to a genre like the action/adventure film. Furthermore, the fact that in its infancy the CCCS was attempting to *criticize* mass cultural forms for their deleterious effects on traditional working-class communities is noteworthy. How many media scholars still don't give the action genre this respectful consideration is also significant, although it will be dealt with later. But chiefly, at the discipline's core, from its inception, was the acknowledgment that societies are "structured unequally, that individuals are not all born with the same access to education, money, health care, etc., and it [cultural studies] worked in the interests of those who have the least resources."[27] Today, in our study of gender, we find the arguments stating that men are now this group with the inordinate access to power.

As this study does put the focus on masculinity, the mechanics of how the text's language is created and how the reader deciphers and makes sense of it should briefly be reviewed.

Several landmark cultural studies works have expounded on the interaction of audience and text and the methodology for understanding this process. One of the most important ones is Stuart Hall's article "Encoding, Decoding," originally presented as a CCCS stenciled paper in 1973. This piece takes to task and critiques the traditional American linear effects model. The "encoding" and "decoding" refer to the activities on the two ends of the old-fashioned hypodermic needle model of communication. Hall, however, critiques these concepts, examining the processes of meaning creation and negotiation as they occur in complex social systems. The most crucial point of Hall's analysis, in fact, is the complexity of a social system, the heterogeneity of any audience and how the "mass" audience must not be understood as a monolithic block of similar tastes, experiences, opinions, and so forth. These various groups are all, in some way, related to the dominant forces of society. But communication between them will likely be confused by friction, signals moving from media producers to audiences, or vice versa, and often distorted. Hall is interested in the divergent readings that can be made of media texts, but he allows for a limited view of audience activity. On the one hand, he claims that many media texts may be polysemic, readily made available for various alternative readings. But he also argues that the fact that an audience resides in a particular culture will automatically place them under the control of various dominant codes, or rules of language, grammar, style, acceptable and unacceptable modes of behavior, beliefs, or worldviews. For example, there are many meanings in film or television text that audiences need not interpret because they have learned their codes early in life or in their earliest experiences of media use. For example, the grammar of visual storytelling is so constant in film or television that an audience, having watched a lifetime of television or movies, has come to understand and accept them as being natural. For example, certain musical scores, lighting, or camera movements have been established as the natural codes for inducing anything from fear to suspense, to laughter, to romance. When hearing a certain rhythm of music, a television audience has already been conditioned to recognize it as "ominous" music and will indeed expect a plot to take a turn toward suspense, shock, or violence. However, taking this concept to another level, there are various themes and messages that may be made natural in storytelling, too. Themes like good always triumphing over evil, the family being sacred, or crime not paying can also be naturalized. As such concepts all have political shadings, ideological positions can be made hegemonic, or established as "natural."

But the important part of Hall's encoding/decoding work is the paradigm he established for explaining how an audience, within the framework of a dominant culture, can actively contest meanings or create wholly unexpected, idiosyncratic alternate meanings. The paradigm presents three "hypothetical" decoding acts an audience may take to make sense of a message. They can make a "preferred" reading, a "negotiated" reading, or an "oppositional" reading. Through a preferred reading, the audience accepts the dominant position encoded in the message, in effect allowing for and endorsing the hegemonic reading. When negotiating a meaning, the audience's reading of the text "contains a mixture of adaptive and oppositional elements: it acknowledges the legitimacy of the hegemonic definitions to make the grand significations (abstract), while, at a more restricted, situational (situated) level, it makes its own ground rules—it operates with exceptions to the rule. It accords the privileged position to the dominant definitions of events while reserving the right to make a more ne-gotiated application to 'local conditions.'"[28] In an oppositional reading, the audience understands the meaning of the text, but "he or she detotalises the message in the preferred code in order to retotalise the message within some alternative framework of reference."[29] In action film criticism, this is best illustrated in one of the (very many) vitriolic attacks by Pauline Kael on the *Dirty Harry* films (among her greater body of contempt for Clint Eastwood's work). Having decoded (erroneously, or rather oppositionally) the films as extolling fascism and racism, she repeatedly issued outrage at how the films had a very large and avid following among inner-city blacks and Hispanics. In the Kael argument, blacks and Hispanics were retotalizing the message with an alternative framework.[30] An academic study of this phenomenon was presented by Vidmar and Rokeach in 1974 on a racist fan faction of *All in the Family*.[31]

The Hall paper's importance also lies in its function as inspiration for qualitative research work with audiences. One such work of importance here is David Morley's 1978 study of viewers of the *Nationwide* British news program. Through a set of interviews conducted with people from a wide cross-section of the population, the researcher sought to understand the *Nationwide* viewers' decoding "derived from the objective position of the individual reader in the class structure." Morley's findings, however, proved more complex.

> The meaning of the text will be constructed differently according to the dis-courses (knowledge, prejudices, resistances, etc.) brought to bear upon the text by the reader and the crucial factor in the encounter of audience/subject and text will be the range of discourses at the disposal of the audience.[32]

What he realized was that as he had a collection of *Nationwide* viewers ranging from schoolboys to apprentice groups, women and professionals, all across the British socioeconomic scale, their reactions to the program and interpretations of the text could not be predicted simply along class lines. As he concludes, while the reader can appropriate the text, the text cannot "determine the reader, interpretations are not arbitrary: they are subject to constraints contained within the text itself."[33]

However, even in cultural studies, the argument for the power of the text overwhelming the activities of the audience still has a certain following. The constraints of the text, especially the film text, has been analyzed by the *Screen* film journal staff of critics, a branch of cultural studies devoted to textual determinism, in opposition to the greater British cultural studies tradition. The *Screen* theorists focused on semiotic analysis and deconstruction of film, arguing the film's power to position the audience within the narrative's dominant ideologies.

Feminist film theorists like Laura Mulvey and Tania Modleski have argued the hegemonic male power over female representation along the lines of the *Screen* approach. The gaze of the camera, the composition of images, always favor the male viewer, these theorists argue, and the female in the audience needs to divest herself of subjectivity, especially when it comes to the pleasures of voyeurism. For example, only males are given the pleasure of observing, deconstructing, and fetishizing the body—the female body. As film has always been given to undressing and objectifying the human form, the target of objectification is always the attractive female. Any heterosexual female, thus, is automatically alienated from so much of the majority of mainstream cinema, as identification is almost only invited of men. In American action cinema, only the 1980s muscle trend (the male ornament culture) paved new ground in expanding the opportunities of the subjective female gaze. For the first time, the meticulous deconstruction of the male body was performed on the spectacularly muscled physiques of Sylvester Stallone, Arnold Schwarzenegger, and the bare posteriors of Mel Gibson and Jean Claude Van Damme. In fact, the industry's own audience research has shown that nearly half of the *Rambo II* viewership was comprised of women, and Jean Claude Van Damme's (short lived) stardom was due to a very large female fan base.[34] Concurrently, the gay subtext in the action film has long been of interest to some film scholars.[35] However, as Susan Bordo argues, the fetishization of the male body does not empower the female viewer quite the same way as a woman's body framed in extreme close-up because the characters on the screen are still more powerful than women.[36] As much as the camera may fetishize Rambo's body, he is still the power that controls the narrative, he is the hero of the story rather than a passive ornament on the sidelines to be looked at.

Another important strain of cultural studies methodology deals with subcultures and their appropriation of dominant culture artifacts. Of chief importance here is Hebdige's 1979 work with British youth subcultures. Looking at members of the "teddy boys," "mods," "rockers," "punks," "hipsters," "beats," "glam," and "Rastafarian" subcultures, he studied how the artifacts of the hegemonic society—mostly clothing—can be taken, altered, or worn

in ways so antithetical to their original design as to make the reconceptualization of the original a statement of protest and rebellion.[37]

Hobson, Radway, Livingstone, Bobo, Gillespie, and McKinley have looked
at such various texts as soap operas, romance novels, music, fashion, or religious programming and their consumption by subcultures of housewives,
teenage girls, or religious immigrant communities, and how such individuals'
connection to a subculture shapes their reading of mass entertainment.[38]

But, remaining constant among all these works, as is the case for the
greater field of cultural studies, is the concern for understanding the behavior
and experience of the individual user. The methodology of working with the
user, whether in one-on-one interviewing, focus groups, or the ethnographic
insertion of the researcher into the world of the audience, borrowing heavily
from anthropology and sociology, seeks to let the native speak and tell his or
her own story.

One approach that puts a great deal of power in the hands of the audience
comes from an important school of communication research that produces
large loopholes in the strong-media-effects approach. Fan culture scholarship
paints a complex interaction between media creators and active audiences.[39]
In fact, today it can be said that most details of a film or a television program,
quite literally down to the actors' haircuts, have probably gone through exten-
sive rounds of audience opinion polling. Still famous is the story of Warner
Brothers television network executives in the late 1990s watching in horror
as the ratings of their powerhouse show *Felicity* plummeted after their star
radically changed her hairstyle.

The attempt has also been made to bridge the issues of textual power and
audience activity when taking note of the polysemic nature of popular entertainment. As Turner writes:

> As something of a reaction against the dethroning of the text, many have ar-
> gued that, especially in the case of television or popular texts, this potential for
> resistant readings is in fact a property of texts themselves, and not merely the
> audience members' socially produced methods of reading them. Where once
> the endeavor was to alert us to the construction of a consensual reading, a con-
> siderable number of studies have now begun to describe strategies of resistance
> within the text; networks of ambiguity and contradiction that invite and accom-
> modate the reader's adoption of different, even ideologically contradictory,
> subject positions.[40]

When Marchetti analyzes action/adventure specifically, she points out that
as the speed and visceral, startling action is choreographed to be the very
central concern of the films, even logic or any coherent semblance of a plot,
message, or point of view may take leave of the story.[41] This is reminiscent of

McRobbie's arguments about the pleasures of the text, where the construction of anything from a film to a music video can, in itself, offer viewing pleasures and meanings that can contradict each other.[42] Adding to this issue, Fiske argues that popular entertainment as a whole is designed to create "illicit" pleasures in the viewer, letting him feel like he is standing in opposition to the forces of the ruling ideology by enjoying something he is not supposed to like.[43] As one of the characters in the *James Bond* film *Never Say Never Again* remarks "now that you're on the case, I hope we can look forward to some gratuitous sex and violence," almost as if specifically designed to rankle every censorious anti-violence crusader, watching an action film well loaded with attractive bare skin, explosions, blood, and a lot of firepower creates that pleasurable, rebellious feeling of watching something the hegemonic powers that be would sneer upon. Inspired by Hartley's perfectly titled *Encouraging Signs: Television and the Power of Dirt, Speech and Scandalous Categories*,[44] Fiske writes of the semiotic excesses of popular entertainment:

> I suggest that it is more productive to study television not in order to identify the means by which it constructs subjects within the dominant ideology (though it undoubtedly and unsurprisingly works to achieve precisely this end), but rather how its semiotic excess allows readers to construct subject positions that are theirs (at least in part), how it allows them to make meanings that embody strategies of resistance to the dominant, or negotiate locally relevant inflections of it.[45]

Then, once more emphasizing hegemonic reach, Fiske argues:

> The preferred meanings in television are generally those that serve the interests of the dominant classes: other meanings are structured in relations of dominance-subordination to those preferred ones as the social groups that activate them are structured in a power relationship within the social system. The textual attempt to contain meaning is the semiotic equivalent of the exercise of social power over the diversity of subordinate social groups, and the semiotic power of the subordinate to make their own meanings is the equivalent of their ability to evade, oppose, negotiate with this social power. Not only is the text polysemic in itself, but its multitude of intertextual relations increases its polysemic potential.[46]

At the core of this brief metaanalysis of cultural studies and the media lies both the reasons for the traditional exclusion of masculine analysis and the rationale for this book. Whether cultural studies, critical studies, or feminism has ever dealt with the issue of masculinity, the paradigm has always been the same dualistic approach. There have always been, essentially, two camps. There has been the hegemony and the subjugated, the elite and the mass, them and us. In this schema, the male has always been "them" and the feminine "us."

But within the cultural studies methodology also lies a more productive alternative. By carefully looking at the text of the action films and talking to their fans, one can examine if the modern American man truly is as powerful as his critics always claimed. Are they really kings? And if they are, why are they so drawn to a theater of suffering, disenfranchisement, and angst?

NOTES

1. Arnold Freeman, *Boy Life and Labour* (London: P. S. King and Son, 1914), 151.

2. Bill Schwarz, "Night Battles: Hooligan and Citizen," in *Modern Times: Reflections on a Century of English Modernity*, eds. Mica Nava and Alan O'Shea (London: Routledge, 1996), 101–128.

3. Graham Murdock, "Reservoirs of Dogma: An Archeology of Popular Anxieties," in *Ill Effects: The Media Violence Debate*, eds. Martin Barker and Julian Petley (New York: Routledge, 2001), 150–170.

4. G. Frank Lydston, *The Diseases of Society* (Philadelphia: J. B. Lippincott, 1904), 160.

5. Graham Murdock, "Visualizing Violence: Television and the Discourse of Disorder," in *Mass Communication Research: On Problems and Policies*, eds. Cees Hamelink and Olga Linne (Norwood, NJ: Ablex Publishing, 1994), 171–191.

6. Murdock, "Reservoirs of Dogma," 165.

7. Lionel Tiger, *The Decline of Males* (New York: St. Martin's Griffin, 1999), 256.

8. Susan Faludi, *Stiffed: The Betrayal of the American Man* (New York: William Morrow, 1999), 42.

9. Faludi, *Stiffed*, 44.

10. Faludi, *Stiffed*, 35.

11. Susan Faludi, "The Masculine Mystique," *Esquire* (December 1996): 91.

12. Ellis's notes of analysis and endorsement of *Fight Club* were published in the liner notes of the DVD release.

13. Samuel Wilson Fussell, *Muscle: Confessions of an Unlikely Bodybuilder* (New York: Avon Books, 1992).

14. Christina Hoff-Sommers, *Who Stole Feminism?: How Women Have Betrayed Men* (New York: Simon and Schuster, 1995).

15. Robert Bly, *Iron John: A Book about Men* (Reading, MA: Addison-Wesley, 1990).

16. Camille Paglia, *Vamps and Tramps: New Essays* (New York: Vintage Books, 1994).

17. Tiger, *The Decline of Males*.

18. Tiger, *The Decline of Males*, 11.

19. Helen Fisher, *The First Sex: The Natural Talent of Women and How They Are Changing the World* (New York: Random House, 1999).

20. John Fiske, "British Cultural Studies and Television," in *Channels of Discourse, Reassembled*, ed. Robert C. Allen (Chapel Hill: University of North Carolina Press, 1992), 214–246.

21. Faludi, "The Masculine Mystique," 93–94.

22. Faludi, *Stiffed*, 13.

23. Stuart Hall, "Encoding and Decoding," in *Culture, Media, Language: Working Papers in Cultural Studies, 1972–1979*, eds. Stuart Hall, Dorothy Hobson, Andrew Lowe, and Paul Willis (London: Routledge, 1980), 516.

24. Theodor Adorno and Max Horkheimer, "The Culture Industry: Enlightenment as Mass Deception," in *The Cultural Studies Reader*, ed. Simon During (New York: Routledge, 1996), 29–44.

25. The arguments for mass deception and popular entertainment subtly legitimizing a ruling elite's position of power were also forwarded by Antonio Gramsci, *Selections from the Prison Notebooks* (London: Lawrence and Wishart, 1971) and Todd Gitlin, "Sixteen Notes on Television and the Movement," in *Literature in Revolution*, eds. George Abbot White and Charles Newman (New York: Holt, Rinehart, and Winston, 1972), 335–336.

26. Fiske, "British Cultural Studies and Television," 286.

27. Simon During, ed. *The Cultural Studies Reader* (London: Routledge, 1999), 2.

28. Hall, "Encoding, Decoding," 516.

29. Hall, "Encoding, Decoding," 517.

30. Pauline Kael, *Deeper into Movies* (New York: Warner Books, 1980), 475.

31. Neil Vidmar and Milton Rokeach, "Archie Bunker's Bigotry: A Study in Selective Perceptions and Exposure," *Journal of Communication* 24 (1974): 36–47.

32. David Morley and Charlotte Brunsdon, *The Nationwide Television Studies* (London: Routledge, 1978), 18.

33. Morley and Brunsdon, *The Nationwide Television Studies*, 148–149.

34. Frank Sanello, *Stallone: A Rocky Life* (Edinburgh: Mainstream Publishing, 1998).

35. Neal King, *Heroes in Hard Times* (Philadelphia: Temple University Press, 1999).

36. Susan Bordo, *Twilight Zones: The Hidden Life of Cultural Images from Plato to O.J.* (Berkley: University of California Press, 1997).

37. Dick Hebdige, *Subculture: The Meaning of Style* (London: Methuen, 1979).

38. The studies can be found in the following works: Dorothy Hobson, *Crossroads: The Drama of Soap Opera* (London: Methuen, 1982); Janice Radway, *Reading the Romance: Women, Patriarchy, and Popular Literature* (Chapel Hill: University of North Carolina Press, 1991); Sonia Livingstone, "Audience Reception: The Role of the Viewer in Retelling Romantic Drama," in *Mass Media and Society,* eds. James Curran and Michael Gurevitch (London: Edward Arnold, 1991); Jacqueline Bobo, *Black Women as Cultural Readers* (New York: Columbia University Press, 1995); Marie Gillespie, *Television, Ethnicity, and Cultural Change* (New York: Routledge,

1995); E. Graham McKinley, *Beverly Hills 90210: Television, Gender, and Identity* (Philadelphia: University of Pennsylvania Press, 1997).

39. Notable and interesting fan studies can be found in Ien Ang, *Watching Dallas* (New York: Methuen, 1985); Ien Ang, *Desperately Seeking the Audience* (London: Routledge, 1991); Angela McRobbie, *Feminism and Youth Culture: From "Jackie" to "Just Seventeen"* (London: Macmillan, 1991); Henry Jenkins, *Textual Poachers: Television Fans and Participatory Culture* (New York: Routledge, 1992), and Cynthia W. Walker, "A Dialogic Approach to Creativity in Mass Communication," unpublished doctoral dissertation, Rutgers, the State University of New Jersey, New Brunswick, NJ, 2001.

40. Graeme Turner, *British Cultural Studies: An Introduction* (London: Routledge, 1996), 108.

41. Gina Marchetti, "Action-Adventure as Ideology," in *Cultural Politics in Contemporary America*, eds. Ian Angus and Sut Jhally (London: Routledge, 1988), 182–198.

42. Angela McRobbie, "Just Like a 'Jackie' Story," in *Feminism for Girls*, eds. Angela McRobbie and Trisha McCabe (London: Routledge, 1984), 110–124.

43. John Fiske, *Television Culture* (London: Routledge, 1987).

44. John Hartley, "Encouraging Signs: Television and the Power of Dirt, Speech, and Scandalous Categories," *Australian Journal of Cultural Studies* 1, no. 2 (1983), 62–82.

45. Fiske, *Television Culture*, 213.

46. Fiske, *Television Culture*, 127.

2

The Audience Matters

Do you understand the words that are coming out of my mouth?

—Chris Tucker, *Rush Hour*

For a greater understanding of how viewers position the text of violent entertainment in their lives, a qualitative, interview-oriented approach can open up a new avenue toward valuable data. As Annette Hill writes:

> What critics and theorists have to say about violent movies is certainly interesting, but does not notably contribute to answering the basic question: why do people choose to see violent movies? Unless researchers actually talk to consumers of violent movies they will not be able to explain the appeal of such movies.[1]

The overview of the action/adventure film in the next chapter will define the art form. It deconstructs and analyzes what an action film is, and conversations with the actual high users of the genre help provide connections between the research and theory scholars have called for in the past.[2] According to David Buckingham:

> Qualitative approaches . . . have clearly shown that research which engages respondents with the focus of study, such as television depictions of violence, are much more likely to reveal their actual feelings, concerns, interpretations and preferences . . . than simple surveys which seek to keep television separate from the other questions in respondents' minds.[3]

Similarly, Lindlof writes that "for too long in the history of communication scholarship, we have focused on what messages refer to, or the effects they

23

have, without examining what the messages are or how their articulation creates social realities for speakers and audiences."[4] The qualitative method em-
ployed in this study should help lead to a better understanding of that social
reality experienced by the action audience. The approach to media violence
research as a phenomenon where aggressive images are hypothesized to
reproduce aggressive behavior in viewers ignores the very subjective social
reality of that viewer, the meaning that viewer may bring, and individualisti-
cally shape the viewing experience. Understanding the interaction between
the violence viewer and the text has to be probed through the qualitative gathering of thick data from self-professed high-using watchers to offset a tradition of research whose quantitative methods largely ignore the individuality
of the viewers. Fowles states that "Viewers are conceived of as feckless and
vacuous,"[5] and Luke critiques the treatment of subjects in effects scholarship,
stating these studies look upon the audience as "passive and devoid of cognitive abilities . . . that viewers may bring anything other than demographic
variables to the screen was conceptually excluded."[6]

The major focus of this study is whether messages about masculinity are at
the heart of the modern action film. Through a series of directive and semidirective interview techniques,[7] the study tries to determine the reasons fans
watch and their expectation and their likes and dislikes of various aspects of
the action genre, chiefly the genre's social meanings and statements.

There are, however, critiques of qualitative interviewing and self-report
techniques in mass communication studies. Essentially, we must satisfy the
question of how reliable individuals' assertions and self-reports can be. How
can we be sure they are telling us the truth? David Gauntlet critiques the
highly quantitative traditions in media effects scholarship and argues that the
standing tradition has proven inadequate in shedding light on the cognitive
and behavioral effects of media messages. He writes that "the researchers do
not seem to have considered that instead of simply stockpiling correlational
data, they could actually ask the respondents about the possible mediation and
formation of their attitudes through television."[8] Qualitative interviewing of
people in cultural studies research about their understanding of media content
has produced valuable information concerning children and their television
use, women's use of VCRs, and women's viewing of violence.[9] Kubey and
Csikszentmihalyi found that "inferences about internal states made by outsiders are generally less reliable than reports made by research subjects."[10]

The most important part of the study participant selection process has been
the selection of people who watch the action film of their own accord because
it is their favorite form of entertainment and that they are actually watching
films that have been defined as "action/adventure." A major criticism, for example, of David Morley and Charlotte Brunsdon's famous *Nationwide* study

was the fact that they showed the news program they intended to study to a group of people who were otherwise not fans.[11]

The participants for this study were selected on an individual basis, as was the interviewing process itself. Since there is little to no organized audience activity among action fans—no conventions as in the case of *Star Trek* or *The X-Files* or various science fiction movies and television programs—finding the high-using action watcher had to be done on a person-by-person basis. While there are groups of devotees around spy literature and films, namely *James Bond* or *The Man from U.N.C.L.E.*,[12] such fans are not necessarily fans of the general action genre. While they might follow Bond or similar stylized spy heroes—such stylized fare meeting the definition of the "action" film, as will be discussed in Chapter 3—many of these people will not also enjoy films like the *Lethal Weapon* series, the *Die Hard* series, or the *Rambo* series. In turn, while such obscure fare as *The Man from U.N.C.L.E.* might still sustain organized fandom—people gathering at conventions, writing original *U.N.C.L.E.* stories, and maintaining websites—such relatively recent action films as the *Lethal Weapon* entries or *The Fast and the Furious* films do not have the same organized fan movement. Among the participants are a number of individuals who are very avid fans of Mel Gibson and his action films like the *Lethal Weapon* series, for example, while, at the same time, they are also fans of actors like Bruce Willis or Sylvester Stallone. However, they do not organize activities the same way the Bond fans do or focus their attention on single films. There is one exception among the several avid Sylvester Stallone fans in my subject pool. This is a twenty-three-year-old male participant who maintains a Web page devoted to *First Blood* (1983) and displays essays concerning only that first film in the *Rambo* series.

Interviews, therefore, were gathered using a convenience sample of undergraduates from several very large—300 to 400 student—lecture classes at a large east coast state university; a jujitsu martial arts club I used to be a member of; a snowball technique gathering action users through personal acquaintances both on the east coast and the Midwest; and fans in the Sylvester Stallone fan community with whom I have been in touch since I wrote my master's dissertation on the *Rocky* films.

This method has been successful in gathering a subject pool of both high-using men and women, totaling thirty-one men and thirteen women. The participants range between eighteen and fifty-seven years of age. This is a significant point, especially for the male participants, because there are several generations represented. This means that the oldest participants lived through important social upheavals regarding gender roles and have seen gender representation in the genre altering and modifying through the years. The age ranges can be broken down as follows: eighteen men from eighteen to twenty-five; seven men between twenty-six and thirty; six men from forty to fifty-seven; and thirteen women between nineteen and fifty-three. Mindful of the subject pool sizes of similar research projects, I tried to keep the number of participants as far toward the high end as possible. Comparable cultural studies media research by Hobson included six participants, Radway forty-two, Seiter, Borchers, Kreutzner, and Warth (twenty-six), Press (forty-five), McKinley (thirty-six), and Hill (thirty-six).[13] Furthermore, the convenience sampling and snowball techniques were also used in the above-mentioned work, yielding useful data.

The interviews were conducted individually to ensure the participants would not feel inhibited talking about such personal and controversial topics as violence, gender roles, and identities. The interviewing was either done in person or over the phone. These interviews were tape recorded and later transcribed with each participant's permission. For several interviews with participants who do not live in either the east coast area or in the Midwest, the Internet was used, exchanging e-mail questions and answers.

The following list includes the interview participants—names changed—with a brief biographical description of each person.

MALE PARTICIPANTS

Charles is an eighteen-year-old undergraduate. Although he intends to be a pharmacy major, he was one of the participants selected from a 100-level media systems course he was taking as an elective. His family, including his mother, father, and sister, lives in Washington, D.C. His parents are of a working-class background.

Vin is a twenty-one-year-old communications major. He was in his junior year when the interview was conducted, another student selected from a large communication lecture class. His family emigrated from Costa Rica, but he grew up on the east coast. Both his parents are of a working-class background.

Vipul is a twenty-year-old economics major, minoring in communication. His family lives in India, and he is only in the United States to complete his education. After his studies, he explained, he will be returning to India to work in his father's firm. He is from an upper-class family.

Tim is a twenty-one-year-old junior, majoring in communication with an interest in public relations. He is an east coast native, having been born and raised in the same general community, in a middle-class family.

Dwayne is a twenty-one-year-old undergraduate, doing a double major program in journalism and psychology. He is very interested in a career in entertainment, and he explained that he would particularly like to orient himself toward work in talent management or script writing, although he has had a recent interest developing in radio. One of his passions, however, is professional wrestling, of which he has an encyclopedic knowledge. He has a very large extended family all over his home state, he explained, and he grew up in a middle-class family.

Brett is a nineteen-year-old undergraduate, majoring in criminology. I know him through the jujitsu club where I used to train. He grew up in a middle-class family. Brett has always been active in sports and, aside from the martial arts, he is an avid soccer player. He explained that he has an uncle who works in the pit crew of a CART open-wheeled race car team and that team was used as extras in the Sylvester Stallone film *Driven* (2001).

Peter is a twenty-three-year-old civil engineering graduate student. He is engaged to his high school girlfriend, also a fan of violent films but not an action fan (she prefers horror). Peter grew up in a middle-class family.

Richard is a nineteen-year-old undergraduate, intending to complete a communication and acting double major. Ultimately, he wants to be an actor. He grew up in a middle-class family.

Brad is a twenty-three-year-old film school student in Vancouver. He is one of the acquaintances I made through an Internet Sylvester Stallone fan community. He grew up in Vancouver in a middle-class family.

Ray, a nineteen-year-old undergraduate, is another training partner from the jujitsu club. He intends to major in psychology and criminology in his junior year. He was born in Poland and raised in Greece and the United States by a single mother. His mother divorced his father when Ray was two years old and he never knew his father.

Jeff is a twenty-three-year-old undergraduate in his senior year. He is a communication major interested in organizational communication, hoping to start a career related to computer work or Web design. He grew up in a middle-class family of Chinese descent.

Sam, twenty-seven years old, became an acquaintance through relatives and friends in the Midwest. He grew up in the suburbs of a Midwestern city and was raised by a single, working-class mother. His mother and father divorced when Sam was six years old. He has a high school education, but was trained through an accounting firm's computer training program where he works as an office manager. Over the past several years, he took occasional film history and literature courses at a local college.

Anthony, twenty-eight, is a personal acquaintance from another Midwestern city. He grew up in a lower middle-class family. He has a college degree in finance and works as a mutual fund manager.

Patrick, thirty, grew up in a working-class family. He holds both undergraduate and graduate degrees in computer engineering. He is married and a member of the jujitsu club.

Kirk, twenty-seven, is a personal acquaintance from the Midwest and he grew up in a middle-class family. He has bachelor's degrees in accounting and actuarial science and a master's degree in business administration. He is working on a law degree as well.

Cliff is a twenty-three-year-old college graduate who works as a bookkeeper for a wholesale book company. He used to be a philosophy major and studied some communication courses, including one of the large lecture courses where I originally found him as a prospective study candidate. Outside of his work, he is an aspiring fiction writer. He grew up in a working-class family, and his mother and father divorced when Cliff was eleven but they shared custody. He claims both parents exerted an equal influence over him growing up. Cliff is also an avid sportsman, regularly diving, practicing aikido, in which he holds a black belt, and has joined the jujitsu club I trained in.

Rom is twenty-eight years old and from an upper-class family from India. His family immigrated to the Midwest when he was seven years old. He holds bachelor's and master's degrees in finance and information systems management. He currently works as a consultant and recently got married to a woman he met in India. His wife is not an action fan.

Darren is twenty-four years old and started his graduate studies in biochemistry in a large east coast state university. He completed his undergraduate education at the same school. He grew up in another east coast state in a middle-class family, with both parents in the health care industry. At one point he trained extensively in kung fu. He intends to earn a Ph.D. and work in academia, teaching and doing research.

Allan is twenty-seven years old, a senior who returned to college after taking several years off from school. He grew up in a middle-class family. He majored in communication, with a psychology minor and looks forward to working in some "computer-related" aspect of communication one day. At the time of the interview, he was largely undecided about his postcollege career, however.

David is a twenty-five-year-old African American graduate student in an east coast university's physics Ph.D. program. He is very active in the martial arts, holding a black belt in ninjutsu and a high rank in jujitsu in my jujitsu club. He grew up in the Midwest in a middle-class family, earning a bachelor's degree from a major state school there. He, more than likely, will work in academia after completing his degree, teaching and doing research.

Carl is a twenty-five-year-old senior, majoring in communication. He grew up in a middle-class family. He has always been very active in sports, most notably competitive weight lifting.

Steve is a twenty-two-year-old African American undergraduate, originally from Jamaica. His family lived close to the Goldeneye estate of James Bond creator Ian Fleming. Having heard so many stories of Ian Fleming growing up, he gravitated toward the *James Bond* films, becoming a very active viewer, along with his affinity for all action films. He is a communication major. He has worked for his university's police department and the library system at one point.

Jake, twenty-four, is a college graduate, living on the east coast and working as a computer programmer. He grew up in a middle-class family.

Luke is a twenty-five-year-old college graduate living on the east coast. He grew up in a middle-class family and he holds a degree in computer engineering and works in software design.

Chad, twenty-eight, is from the online Sylvester Stallone and action film fan community. He grew up in and lives in an eastern state, where he works as a computer programmer. He is a husband and father of three children.

Harry is forty-four years old and a personal acquaintance from the Midwest. He works as an accountant and lives in a suburb of a large Midwestern city. He grew up in a large working-class family. His father was a police officer.

Ken, forty-three, is an employee of a large computer-manufacturing firm, working in an east coast city where he grew up in a working-class family. He is a divorced father of three teenaged children. His girlfriend is not an action fan. I made his acquaintance through the jujitsu club.

Dirk, forty-three, is a librarian for one of the major Midwestern universities. He grew up in places from Mexico to Hong Kong, the son of a career military officer. When he was thirty-two years old, he joined the U.S. army, eventually qualifying for the special forces. He has been active in the *James Bond* fan community. On occasion, he works as a copy editor.

Louis, fifty-seven, is a family acquaintance, a physician living in a large Midwestern city. He grew up in Hungary and emigrated to the United States in the early 1970s. He is a husband and father of three grown children.

Edward is a forty-seven-year-old carpenter living in a large Midwestern city, a divorced father of two grown children. He grew up in the city he lives in today, in a working-class family, and worked for most of his life in construction. At one point, he worked as a part-time police officer.

Victor, forty-three, is a computer programmer and husband and father of two on the east coast. He very actively maintains an action film–related Web page.

FEMALE PARTICIPANTS

Kelly, nineteen, is a college freshman. She was selected from one of the introductory courses. She grew up on the east coast and was raised by her father. Her family background is working class and she talks of being drawn toward traditionally male pastimes like working on cars and racing motorcycles. She is a member of the women's rugby club in her school.

Cindy, twenty-three, is also from a working-class family. She was raised on the east coast and was a communication major at the time of this interview. She was in her senior year.

Jane is a twenty-seven-year-old graduate student, having grown up in a rural working-class family in the South. She studied psychology and law as an undergraduate and now studies information systems in her graduate program. She readily describes her childhood as being very physically active in sports and all types of outdoor pursuits. As will be detailed in Chapter 4, she also admits to an attraction to violent sports like boxing and wrestling.

Erika, twenty-one, is an undergraduate communication major. She describes herself as an avid, lifelong athlete, a "total jock." She was raised in a middle-class family. Most of her film watching, she explains, is done as a social activity, usually going out to the movies with a group of friends.

Lonni, twenty, is an undergraduate, intending to become a communication major, although unsure of what career she might pursue. Law is something she has been thinking about. She was born and raised on the east coast in a middle-class family, although her parents emigrated from Korea. She describes herself as being very active, playing a lot of sports, running track at one point, and growing up partaking in every type of rowdy "boy" activity with her two brothers.

Connie, nineteen, was born in the Philippines, but raised in the United States. She is an undergraduate with intentions to majoring in communication. She grew up in an upper middle-class family.

Ruby, twenty-seven, is the graduate of a large east coast state school, holding a master's degree in computer engineering. She still lives close to her alma mater and works as a computer programmer. She was born in Guyana and grew up in a working-class family that emigrated to the United States.

Diana, thirty-three, is married to Harry. She, too, grew up in the Midwest in a working-class family. She and Harry had been married for five years at the time of the interviews and they were expecting their first child. Diana is a college graduate and worked in a bank until the later stages of her pregnancy.

Selina, twenty, is an African America east coast native. She is a communication major and, aside from her active action watching, she is an avid horror fan. Her mother, who never married Selina's father, raised her. She does not know her father.

Amy, thirty-five, is a freelance writer living in the South and a member of several Sylvester Stallone and action film online fan communities. She is from a middle-class family.

Stephanie, twenty-four, is an east coast native, having grown up in a working-class family. She attributes her action watching to her father and brothers, the ones who controlled most of the television watching and video renting in her family. She also speaks of partaking in typically male activities growing up, like fighting and wrestling and competing with her brothers. She is a communication major and works for a mortgage company.

Helen, fifty-three, is a divorced mother of a grown daughter, living in a northwestern state. She works as a clerk for the government agency regulating permits for oil and gas exploration in that state. She avidly talks of her hobby of showing horses, and she is a big fan of Sylvester Stallone. I made her acquaintance through one of the Stallone Web pages where she indicated having written a treatment for *Rambo IV*, several years before the fourth installment in the *Rambo* series was made. She mailed it to Stallone, but had never received a reply.

I met Kathleen, twenty-five, through the Stallone community. She is an art student in a small college in the Midwest and works part-time at an art gallery. She grew up in a working-class family and was drawn to the arts at an early age due to her strong voice and singing abilities. Although undecided about a career after college, her interests lie in singing, acting, and writing.

SOCIOECONOMIC STATUS

The issue of socioeconomic class of the participants raises questions and suggests avenues for further research. The subject pool divides in a not entirely even way between those of a middle-class background and those of a working-class background. However, the notable fact is that the majority of the women identify themselves as either having been in the blue-collar working class growing up or still being in that class today. Since the women claim to have, at one point, been subjected to action films by the men in their lives, as will be discussed in Chapter 4, the information seems to reinforce the image of the genre as entertainment for middle-class males. Textual analysis of the greater body of art that comprises the genre favors working-class, blue-collar heroes. Thus, the brothers, boyfriends, and fathers of these women fit the expected demographic audience base of the action film. Nine women of the thirteen comprising the female participant pool come from blue-collar roots, with three women identifying their backgrounds as middle class and one positioning herself as upper class.

In the case of the male participants, however, more of the men identify their backgrounds as middle class than working class. Only two men put themselves in the upper class, although both are also of foreign origins. Rom and Vipul, the two men hailing from India, are of upper-class backgrounds. Eleven men are from working-class backgrounds, although these men are in college, looking forward to professional futures. There are thirteen men participants who identify their backgrounds as either middle class or working class. There are eleven men in medical, technological, finance, and managerial positions. One man is a physician, another holds a master's degree in business administration and is working on a law degree, and several work in computer fields. Two men are in graduate programs looking forward to careers in academia, and the rest are college students, all hoping for various professional futures.

This socioeconomic breakdown of the study participants is important, in light of the information they will give in the next several chapters about their enjoyment of the action genre. But perhaps the class position should be considered important in light of what they do not say. Class conflict and rivalry never enters into either the women's or the men's reasons for enjoying the action narrative. They never talk about enjoying films where the rich are punished or about films where corrupt businessmen get their just comeuppance.

Two of the participants who come closest to touching on the subject of class conflict are Steve and Selina, both from working-class roots. Steve is a *James Bond* fan and he explains that he enjoys the Bond films because they show relatively realistic—although stylized and exaggerated—villains such as corrupt government figures and corrupt businessmen who are punished for their crimes. However, he also explains that he takes these stories as morality tales about what should happen to the corrupt few, the rogues within the government and business worlds who break the rules. Such corruption, he believes, is usually the exception, not the rule. The *James Bond* stories of the few rotten apples, the megalomaniacal business tycoons who want to rule the world, Steve feels are accurate and not, in accordance with the critical theory of the media trying to whitewash the entirely corrupt capitalist system, a camouflage to let dissatisfied citizens vent their frustrations. Selina is more cynical than Steve, however, and believes that both the government and business worlds are equally corrupt. As she will be quoted in Chapter 8, she likes action films, especially conspiracy-themed action films, because they dramatize the corruption of the world as it exists. Cindy will voice similar opinions, finding the U.S. government highly suspect—"the most corrupt in the world" she will explain. She also believes the worlds of big business and finance to be thoroughly corrupt.

In Chapter 9, we hear what both men and women have to say about the morality of action heroes, the social good, and what the films are saying about government and social institutions. The class significance of this is commented upon in the Conclusion.

DATA

The data analysis involves work with the spoken and written records provided by the participants. All information provided through interviews done in person, over the phone, and through e-mail correspondence is treated as data valuable to the understanding of the participants' personal and social identities and how they negotiate the text of the action film with those identities.

The interviews themselves are structured as semidirective to directive interviews, as the participants' penchant for discussion requires. I did approach all of them with the broad statement that I need to understand their film-viewing habits and how they regarded the action film. However, as the study is concerned with masculinity and identity, several times I needed to very specifically guide them to these issues and prompt them into talk.

As will be detailed in the following chapter, the action film is an art form that has received limited critical attention or respect until very recently. Although this study is attempting to correct some of the flawed and inadequate analysis, my own positioning in relationship to the text should be noted here. As I explained in the Introduction, I have been an active viewer of the genre for as long as I have been watching films, or rather watching as much action at a young age as allowed or as I was able to get away with. Therefore, I know the genre very well, know the important films of the genre, its stars, and archetypes. However, as a communication scholar I was able to take the tools of media theory and textual analysis hand-in-hand with my own use of the genre and, I feel, I was better able to probe the participants' viewing activities. Furthermore, this familiarity with the films helped me convince the study participants that I understood, to a certain degree, why they liked a type of film that is so often loudly criticized. It convinced them that I, essentially, was one of them. This, I am certain, helped them open up and talk about the pleasures of watching violence and helped dispel any ideas any one of them might have harbored that an academic study would be run by an elitist researcher looking to pass judgment on them and their popular diversions.

NOTES

1. Annette Hill, *Shocking Entertainment* (Luton: University of Luton Press, 1997), 7.

2. The calls to better understand the subjective experience of media users have been discussed in Sean Moores, "Dishes and Domestic Cultures: Satellite TV as Household Technology," paper presented at the Fourth International Television Studies Conference, London, 1990; and David Buckingham, *Moving Images: Understanding Chil-*

dren's Emotional Responses to Television (Manchester: Manchester University Press, 1996).

3. David Buckingham, *Children Talking Television: The Making of Television Literacy* (London: Falmer, 1993), 103.

4. Thomas R. Lindlof, *Qualitative Communication Research Methods* (Thousand Oaks, CA: Sage, 1995), 22.

5. Jib Fowles, *The Case for Television Violence* (Thousand Oaks, CA: Sage, 1999), 49.

6. Carmen Luke, *Constructing the Child Viewer: A History of the American Discourse on Television and Children* (New York: Praeger, 1990), 281.

7. Charles L. Briggs, *Learning How to Ask: A Sociolinguistic Appraisal of the Role of the Interview in Social Science Research* (New York: Cambridge University Press, 1990).

8. David Gauntlet, *Moving Experiences: Understanding Television's Influences and Effects* (London: John Libbey, 1995), 101.

9. For excellent examples of qualitative research into the use and experience of popular entertainment that helps dispel simplistic media "effects" models, the following studies look at children and television, women and the use of the VCR, and how women view and experience violent entertainment: Patricia Palmer, *The Lively Audience: A Study of Children around the TV Set* (Sydney: Allen and Unwin, 1986); Buckingham, *Children Talking Television*; Ann Gray, *Video Playtime: The Gendering of a Leisure Technology* (London: Routledge, 1992); Phillip Schlesinger, Russell P. Dobash, R. Emerson Dobash, and C. Kay Weaver, *Women Viewing Violence* (London: British Film Institute Publishing, 1992).

10. Robert Kubey and Mihaly Csikszentmihalyi, *Television and the Quality of Life: How Viewing Shapes Everyday Experience* (Hillsdale, NJ: Lawrence Erlbaum, 1990), 57.

11. Graeme Turner, *British Cultural Studies: An Introduction* (London: Routledge, 1996). Turner's book highlights the criticism that had been raised over Morley and Brunsdon's selection of subjects.

12. Cynthia W. Walker, *A Dialogic Approach to Creativity in Mass Communication*, unpublished doctoral dissertation, Rutgers, the State University of New Jersey, New Brunswick, NJ, 2001.

13. For studies using similar methodologies and subject selection techniques, the following books may be a useful comparison: Dorothy Hobson, "Soap Operas at Work," in *Remote Control: Television, Audiences and Cultural Power*, eds. Ellen Seiter, Hans Borchers, Gabriele Kreutzner, and Eva-Maria Warth (London: Routledge, 1991); Janice Radway, *Reading the Romance: Women, Patriarchy and Popular Literature* (Chapel Hill: University of North Carolina Press, 1991); Ellen Seiter, Hans Borchers, Gabriele Kreutzner, and Eva-Maria Warth, "Don't Treat Us Like We're So Stupid and Naïve: Towards an Ethnography of Soap Opera Viewers," in their book *Remote Control*; Andrea L. Press, *Women Watching Television: Gender, Class, and Generation in the American Television Experience* (Philadelphia: University of Pennsylvania Press, 1991); E. Graham McKinley, *Beverly Hills 90210: Television, Gender, and Identity* (Philadelphia: University of Pennsylvania Press, 1997); Hill, *Shocking Entertainment*.

3

The Modern American Action Film

It's the action. Good old American action.

— Sylvester Stallone, *Tango and Cash*

A squalid shoot 'em up for the moron trade.

— 1967 *Newsweek* review of *Bonnie and Clyde*

Woody Allen's *Manhattan* (1979) has a particularly amusing scene illustrating the chasm between the sensibilities of the intellectual class and everyone else. The Allen character, representing the common man, is at a party where the topic of a neo-Nazi rally comes up. He quickly remarks that he would like to get some people with bricks and baseball bats together to go down to the rally and break some Nazi heads. One of the (female) intellectuals gives the issue some serious consideration, then says that she would rather write a satirical magazine piece about the affair, critiquing the Nazis. Sharp, pointed satire, she feels, is the best response. Allen thinks about this for a moment, then replies, "I still think a baseball bat to the face is a better idea."

Although cultural critics have by now embraced popular entertainment, and even the cultural studies school, which originated in critiquing "mass" entertainment, has accepted such forms of entertainment as rock music—in all its various genres—romance novels, comic books, soap operas, sports culture, and science fiction, there is still a certain unease when dealing with violence. For the well-read, well-mannered intelligentsia of all ideological and political persuasions, an entertainment form where problems are ultimately resolved through nonverbal conflict resolution techniques—fists, bullets, knives, explosives, or feet propelled by expert roundhouse kicks—might be an unpleasant vehicle to validate. Although many in popular culture studies have argued against the "ghettoization" of popular entertainment, films of the action/adventure genre are still having a difficult time moving up from the ghetto. Teen slasher horror films are particularly stuck in the back alleys of the culture ghetto.

As Neal King writes in his typological analysis of the action film, the genre is severely lacking in scholarship, and what studies exist are usually incomplete and inaccurate:

> Many of them provide little support for their arguments; the writers did not intend close study and simply pass quick judgment. A few manage mini genre studies, analyzing a handful of similar interracial-male-bonding movies. Though some analysts pay more attention to the uniquely cinematic qualities of these stories than do others, virtually all regard the movies in terms of race, class, gender, and sexuality. Many critique the genre as hiding its politics; and most find movies to be in some way racist, homophobic, individualist, pro-Reagan, capitalist, or misogynist. Some analysts seem to have fun finding loopy subtexts, homoerotic mainly; at least as many seem offended by the movies.[1]

At the core of the critical repulsion with the genre, however, is its violence—a very special sort of violence to be analyzed shortly—and the sort of feelings it might inspire in the great-unwashed masses of moviegoers. As the modern cultural analyst feels most at ease in the role of the defender of these same masses, championing the masses while worrying about whether or not they are smart enough not to be driven to antisocial, destructive frenzy after watching a good shoot 'em up film could possibly carry an unpleasant flavor of hypocrisy. Writing for the *New York Times* in 1967, Bosley Crowther, reigning among the *important* film critics of his day and an ardent critic of all violent films, hurled invective at the newly released *Dirty Dozen*, writing of its action scenes: "a raw and preposterous glorification of a group of criminal soldiers who are trained to kill and who then go about this brutal business with hot sadistic zeal . . . an astonishingly wanton war movie, morbid and disgusting beyond words."[2] Raising his ire specifically is the fact that the film's "heroes" are a collection of sociopathic criminals taken out of prison because their blood lusts and pathologies are perfect for a suicide mission behind enemy lines. Crowther adds: "to bathe these rascals in a specious heroic light—to make their hoodlum bravado and defiance of discipline, and their nasty kind of gutter solidarity, seem exhilarating and admirable—is encouraging a spirit of hooliganism that is brazenly antisocial, to say the least."[3]

Andrew Sarris's piece in the *Village Voice* further clarifies the unease of the progressive critic who would otherwise hail opposition to the "system."

He calls the film "a glorification of the dropout well suited to slum fantasizing." Then, he expands with:

> Jean Renoir has observed that people are moved more by magic than by logic. To sit in the balcony of the Capitol while Clint Walker and Jim Brown are demolishing two finky noncoms is to confirm this observation. All the well-intentioned Operation Bootstrap cinema in the world cannot provide underdog audiences with the emotional release achieved almost effortlessly with one shot to the solar plexus. It's sad, but true. Blood is thicker than progressive porridge.[4]

Jumping forward in time, Nigel Andrews's 1996 biography of Arnold Schwarzenegger quotes Carole Lieberman, psychiatrist and chairperson of the National Coalition on TV Violence, voicing her distaste for Schwarzenegger's films because of their possible power to incite the angry and the marginalized:

> Lieberman ups the "anti." Summarizing her film-by-film analysis of violent acts—*The Terminator* has eighty-four violent acts per hour, *Raw Deal* one hundred and forty four, *Commando* one hundred and sixty five—she pronounced: "Arnold Schwarzenegger has become an American icon, worshipped as the god of violent power by the disenfranchised and powerless masses."[5]

To give a taste of some of the global criticism, Andrews quotes British critics Ian Penman and Gilbert Adair, respectively: "He is American fascist art exemplified, embodied." "Repellent to the last degree . . . insidious Nazification . . . [an] appeal rooted in an unholy compound of fascism, fashion and fascination."[6] Schwarzenegger's Austrian roots and thick, teutonic accent give these criticisms an eerie zing.

Yvonne Tasker further comments on the critical and scholarly hatred of the action film in political tones in a very thorough scholarly book on the genre:

> The critical language with which a popular film such as *Rambo* or its star, Sylvester Stallone, has been discussed has tended to extend that rhetoric of the monstrous, anthologizing the film's audience. In this critical process, particular cultural products and forms come to seem dangerous, signifying anarchy or the threat of it. As concerns for the effects of a mass culture or the social body have so frequently testified, such responses are not new. The fear and loathing that muscular movies have inspired in the liberal/cultural elite as well as the popular press in the mid-1980s ("No, No to Rambo" screamed a headline in the *Daily Mirror*) seems to indicate in part a fear of the audience for such films.[7]

Harkening back to 1967, however, and the release and subsequent critical outcry over *Bonnie and Clyde*, Hoberman demonstrates the politicized nature of the controversy. The fear, as usual, was over the influence exerted upon the masses, but then the right wing was angrier than the left. Quoting English critic Charles Marowitz, he explains that the violent film was quickly co-opted by various factions of the left in both the United States and the United Kingdom:

> If you are a bonnie-and-clyder, you are pro-camp and anti-Ugly; pro-permissiveness and anti-authoritarian; an advocate of the easy, improvised approach to life rather than the Five Year planner. You pledge allegiance to the Pink Floyd and the Rolling Stones and all they stand for, and walk imperturbably toward the exit-doors while the National Anthem is playing . . . the heady ecstasy with which Bonnie and Clyde break the law is echoed in the arcane pleasure that attends pot parties in north and southwest London.[8]

Hoberman continues: "In the United States . . . the youthful outlaw culture not only encompassed taking drugs but equally included demonstrating against the government, evading the draft, and, in the most extreme case of the Black Panthers, shooting it out with the police."[9]

Although not as pervasive as the fear over action because of its potential to foment anarchy, but equally pointed and intense when applied, is the gender-oriented assault on media violence. As Jib Fowles metaanalyses the history of scholarship damning media violence, he draws attention to a trend of female opposition to media violence. Quoting statistics of how many women actually experience violent, aggressive, or coercive behavior aimed at them by the time they reach adulthood, he points out that women will more often be critical of violence in "its flattened, symbolic form. . . . The figment may draw too close to the real thing, whether experienced or imagined, to permit a degree of unimpeded pleasure that male viewers might enjoy."[10] This has been the case in both the United States and, at least, in England since surveys have been conducted querying whether or not there is too much violence in action films.[11]

Radical feminism begins with the drawing of males in demonic shades. Davis writes in *The First Sex*:

> The era of the cult of masculinity is now approaching its end. Its last days will be illuminated by the flare-up of such comprehensive violence and despair as the world has never seen. People of good will seek help on all sides of their declining society, but in vain. Any social reform imposed on our sick society has only value as bondage for a gaping and putrefying wound. Only a complete destruction of society can heal this fatal disease. Only the fall of the three-thousand-year-old beast of male materialism will save humankind.[12]

But even 1990s' conservative media violence criticism, as voiced by Michael Medved, charges the iconic strong male action hero with "retrograde," harmful masculinity when criticizing Schwarzenegger. As summed up by Andrews:

> Even on those occasions when he isn't *supposed* to be playing killer robots, the Big Guy deals death with mechanical, deadpan precision; in many instances, the only twinges of humanity allowed to creep into his characterizations are those murderous *bons mots* with which he rids the world of the human rubbish around him. The Schwarzenegger canon has just one retrograde message: Deadly and unreflecting efficiency as the ultimate standard of manliness.[13]

The attacks on the action film, obviously, are spread well across the ideological and scholarly spectrum. Its criticism is, perhaps, the most politically correct stance. It is not easy to go wrong attacking media violence. In the 2000 presidential elections, Republicans attacked Hollywood's violent products, as did the Democrats, as well as Independents. When fund-raising for Al Gore, even Hollywood celebrities attacked entertainment violence. As David Link remarked, today "no one defends violence . . . and when Americans all line up on one side of an issue, you know something is terribly wrong."[14] Whereas in 1996 presidential candidate Bob Dole's critique of entertainment could at least inspire a loud round of spirited condemnation from the Hollywood community, by the 2000 elections only screenwriter Joe Eszterhaz's (*Basic Instinct* [1992], *Showgirls* [1995]) full-page ad in *Daily Variety*, warning of censorious currents in the air, was the most vocal opposition to the anti-violence rhetoric of both major parties.

With so much concern over fans, this study must move beyond these reactions and put the focus on the audience and understand the action film from their perspective. But before we seek to make sense of what the subject pool of action aficionados says about their favorite movies, the basic archetypal structure of the action genre must first be understood.

WHAT IS ACTION? THE ARCHETYPES OF THE GENRE

Conducting a textual analysis of the action/adventure genre must begin with the slippery task of defining what exactly "action" is. A comedy can be easily defined, that genre does not pose a difficult semantic challenge. The romantic melodrama is not much of a challenge either. Many dramatic genres, however, especially since many can accommodate violence quite easily, may overlap into the "action" category. For example, films dealing with crime and investigation most often fall into the categories of "suspense," "mystery," "crime thriller," or "police drama." However, when certain cop films are made in a certain way, they must be categorized in the "action" genre. Similarly, most films dealing with soldiers and war are "war" films, or films dealing with robots, aliens, and other planets—"science fiction." But done in a certain way, the film can be classified "action." In this sense, the "action" film often colonizes a lot of other genres, borrowing archetypes and transforming them into an entirely new breed of entertainment. But to begin understanding action, one must go back to its roots in literature.

Film scholar John Cawelti started tracing the roots of the genre in heroic, adventure-oriented literature. "The central fantasy of the adventure story is that of the hero—individual or group—overcoming obstacles and dangers and accomplishing some important and moral mission," he writes, "often, though not always, the hero's trials are the result of the machinations of a villain, and, in addition, the hero frequently receives, as a kind of side benefit, the favors of one or more attractive young ladies." Although his typology of adventure is drawn from his analysis of literature, it can just as easily be applied to film. The typology, Cawelti writes, can be applied to "more recent cultural situations—crime and its pursuit, war, the West, international espionage, sports."[15]

The encompassing nature of the "action" label is also well documented by Murray and his analysis of a literary category emerging in the late 1960s and early 1970s, a type of male-oriented novel that could not be categorized under any preexisting genre.[16] Don Pendleton, in an ongoing saga of Vietnam veteran Mac Bolan who declares a one-man vigilante war on the Mafia, first applied publishing's use of the "action" label to books of *The Executioner* series. The books were published starting in 1968 by Pinnacle, an imprint of former porn publisher Bee-Line. The books numbered each entry in the series, reminiscent of the *Doc Savage* adventure books of the 1930s—classified as science fiction—and, although the books mainly dealt with crime fighting, they did not fit into either the mystery or detective category. The chief reason here was the violence, as Murray describes:

> A case could also be made that the *Executioner* books are a kind of pornography of violence in which the action scenes—brutal, violent and often gratuitously graphic—substitute for what in Pinnacle's Bee-Line titles would be the requisite sex scenes. Certainly the early *Executioners* are a series of bloody confrontations strung along a thin plotline.[17]

In terms of Pendelton's theme, plot, and style, he writes:

> Although his style might remind some of a truck driver who has read too much Mickey Spillane, it possesses a vitality and energy seldom found in more seasoned writers. His Mack Bolan is a single-minded man on a mission. There are seldom digressions from the action, even for sex. For a series written primarily

for males and published by a former porn house, there is little sex, gratuitous or otherwise, in the *Executioner* books. Bolan has had a couple of girlfriends at different points in the series, but they seldom survive for long. Ramboesque urban violence is the sum and substance of these books.[18]

However, through success, inspiring numerous imitation series with titles like *Death Merchant*, *The Penetrator*, *The Butcher*, *The Chameleon*, *The Exterminator*, *The Eliminator*, *The Liquidator*, and *The Sexecutioner*, what can be identified as a very specific genre rose to prominence through the 1970s. The books mainly consisted of the threadbare plot discussed by Murray, larger than life, stylized violence, and heroes who forsake normal lives and love for the higher calling of single-handedly wiping out evil. Most often, since these characters work as vigilantes, the very system they swear to defend hunts them as criminals.

As a side note, what has been argued as the surest sign of an established tradition in art being the parody, the highly successful *Destroyer* series by Richard Sapir and Warren Murphy has also been a cutting satire of the action novel phenomenon, as well as action films, tough guy action heroes, and the martial arts. In one installment of the series, very precise aim was taken at the Mafia-fighting theme of so many books, where the Destroyer tangles with an amateur group of crime fighters called the Rubout Squad, headed by the Eraser and his compatriots, the Exterminator, the Baker, and the Lizard. In 1985, the central concept of the series, bumbling Newark cop Remo Williams trained to become a super assassin by the Korean master of the martial art sinanju, was adapted into the film *Remo Williams: The Adventure Begins*. As neither Sapir nor Murphy (the later of whom sometimes sidelined as a screenwriter, responsible for the scripts behind Clint Eastwood's *The Eiger Sanction* [1975] and *Lethal Weapon 2* [1989]) was involved in the project, the screen adventures of Remo Williams also ended with that one film, failing to capture the books' wit and satire, or its readers.

As the action literature tradition peaked in the 1980s, many of them were influenced by the war-on-terrorism theme of major action films of the time, like the original *Die Hard* (1988), *Delta Force* (1986), and *Invasion USA* (1985), but even more heavily by the back-to-Vietnam-to-free-the-POWs tradition of *Rambo II* (1985), *Uncommon Valor* (1983), and Chuck Norris's *Missing in Action* (1984, 1985, 1988) series. Nearly all of the books had a back-to-Vietnam plot at one time. There were plans, in fact, to adapt *The Executioner* books with Sylvester Stallone in the Mac Bolan role and *French Connection* (1971) director William Friedkin helming the project. The American box office failure of *Rambo III* (1988) and Stallone's subsequent quest to change his image halted the project, however.

In film, as in Cawelti's and Murray's studies of action in literature, that all-encompassing extra element of stylized, hyperbolic speed is the "convention of connection"—in Leo Braudy's terminology of the archetypes connecting a specific genre[19]—that will qualify a film as an action film and not a police drama, even though its main characters are cops, or as an action film and not a war movie, or, once more, an action film and not a science fiction film.

To further clarify the nomenclature of "action," some very successful films and "action" films should briefly be compared. When asked what qualifies as action, could the scholar simply say that violent films made by Joel Silver are action, or the (former) team of Don Simpson and Jerry Bruckheimer (now just Bruckheimer, since Simpson's death in 1997) are action films? But would this make a film like *Dangerous Minds* (1995), produced by Simpson and Bruckheimer, an action film? Or would the Simpson/Bruckheimer films *Top Gun* (1986), *Beverly Hills Cop I* and *II* (1984, 1987), *The Rock* (1996), *Armageddon* (1998), and *Blackhawk Down* (2002) be their only action films? The story of Michelle Pfeiffer contending with a crime-ridden inner-city high school is an intense film and has its moments of violence, but is it an action film? Similarly, is the Joel Silver–produced *The Matrix* (1999), with its story of futuristic, robot-controlled societies and travel through cyberspace, science fiction? Or does its heavy dose of martial arts and machine gun mayhem make it an action film? Among the signature series in the Silver Pictures company's lineup of ultra-kinetic films are the first two *Die Hard* films (1988, 1990). The third and fourth entries in the series, 1995's *Die Hard with a Vengeance* and 2007's *Live Free or Die Hard* (not from Silver), are clearly action films, but where does that same production company's *Lethal Weapon* (1987, 1989, 1992, 1998) series fall? Could the *Weapon* films be better classified as police drama, or, at least as far as entries two through four are concerned, comedy? Standards of the action film since the 1980s, the *Rambo* series (1982, 1985, 1988, 2008), would certainly fall into the category, or would it? Wouldn't it be more accurate to call them war films, even though the first film in the series is more of a chase picture, involving a Vietnam veteran and the story taking place nowhere near a real war zone, or in a time of war for that matter. Wouldn't the trilogy be more likely categorized with films like *Saving Private Ryan* (1998), very graphic and violent, or *The Thin Red Line* (1998), a film consisting almost entirely of combat and destruction sequences, or *Blackhawk Down* (2001) or the Gulf War film *Jarhead* (2005)?

In classifying the above-mentioned films, *Dangerous Minds* should not be considered an action film. *The Matrix* should be, but an action film with science fiction elements. The *Lethal Weapon* films, like the *Die Hard* films, are action films (films two through four comedic action films, but action nevertheless), and so are all four of the *Rambo* films, but not *Blackhawk Down* or *Jarhead*.

Mark Gallagher argues that the "action" film's roots can be traced back to the late 1960s, and he calls it a true postmodern genre.[20] Richard Schickel, *Time* magazine film critic and Clint Eastwood's biographer, invokes postmodernity when writing about the *Dirty Harry* (1971, 1973, 1976, 1983, 1988) series, analyzing the films in their self-conscious use of style and their mannered execution, to discuss a trend in adventure and violence-oriented entertainment whose chief purpose seems to be its willingness to dwell on its artifice. While, in fact, action/adventure can safely be traced farther back in cinematic history than the 1960s, as shown by film historian Lawrence Alloway in his exhibit "The America Action Movie: 1946–1964" presented at the Museum of Modern Art in 1969, from the 1960s onward films dealing with heroic confrontation have taken on the sort of hyperbolic, violence-centered orientation that marks the action films as something quite separate from the war film, the police story, or science fiction, among other genres.[21]

"All action movies are finally about—yes—action," writes Schickel, "movies of this type routinely subvert their own plausibility, along with such ambitions toward fine moral distinction and high moral instruction as their makers may harbor, on behalf of sustained and exciting movement,"[22] in analyzing the *Dirty Harry* series and all its attendant controversy about hidden ideological statements. The action film is one that emphasizes and foregrounds spectacle, mainly violent spectacle, and subverts everything else in the narrative, including, as Schickel assesses, its own plausibility. As a matter of fact, "a complete understanding of dialogue or plot is not necessary; instead, the main pleasure of the text revolves around spectacular fights, gun play, torture, and battles," writes Marchetti,[23] tracing the genre's easy movement from culture to culture. The main archetype of the action film, then, is violence itself, and its rendering in the most creative, original, funny, or colorful ways possible is the genre's major ambition.

To illustrate clearly why violence becomes the central archetype that unifies certain films in the action genre, despite their individual narratives and settings, closer attention should be given to a series like the *James Bond* films, originating in the 1960s and lending credence to the argument of the 1960s being the starting point of the modern prototypical action film. While dealing with a spy and plots centered on the world of espionage, the *Bond* films' central concern was never any particular statement about espionage, but their performance of style. With their outlandish and clearly unrealistic stunts and science fiction whimsical "gadgets" that are still a staple of the series, the *Bond* films have been, from the moment of their adaptation from Ian Fleming's novels, an exercise in style, in the performance of spectacle. Adapted to film at the height of the Cold War, producers Albert Broccoli and Harry Saltzman very diligently avoided clear commentary about East-West relations, instead always pitting

Bond against the fictional villainous cabal of SPECTRE.[24] (The acronym stood for Special Executive for Terrorism Revenge and Extortion, or general bad guy mayhem and evil, rather than any particular political ideology.) The group's modus operandi, in fact, was extorting *all* the world's countries for astronomical fees in return for not unleashing some doomsday weapon. This was the plot of *Thunderball* (1965), *You Only Live Twice* (1967), *On Her Majesty's Secret Service* (1969), among many other entries in the series. Any commentary the films ever made about the East-West conflict was vaguely analogous. "Action films present graphic violence and pyrotechnic spectacle as exaggerated simulations of real violence and destruction rather than as credible, discomfiting representations of these phenomena," explains Gallagher in his reading of the postmodern action film, and his impression clearly fits the surrealistic world of Bond.[25]

James Bond's (filmic) origins in the early 1960s British cinema are an interesting precursor, however, to the late 1960s and early 1970s self-referential, postmodern poaching style of a new generation of American filmmakers educated in specialized films programs. Many of these people endeavored not only to make films, but to represent all of film history in one all-encompassing statement about film art itself,[26] often trying to make summary statements about entire genres in one all-encompassing film. The self-consciousness, artifice, and style of this time helped shape the hyperbolic world of the action film. If James Bond was the originator of the modern form of the genre, *Dirty Harry* (1971) carried on the tradition and became the yardstick for the American version. Not so much concerned with the realistic details of police work as with confrontation, gunplay, and over-the-top mayhem, *Dirty Harry* reinforced the practice of self-conscious stylistic performance. The tagline quip by Clint Eastwood became an important part of the series ("You feel lucky?" "Go ahead, make my day!"), repeated as ritual and spoken exactly twice in each film, once in the beginning, once in the end. Only in 1991 did another action film tip its hat to this artifice, *The Last Boy Scout*, where private eye Bruce Willis explains to a new sidekick, "This being the nineties, you can't just smack a guy in the face, you gotta say something cool. . . . If you hit someone with a surfboard, you gotta say, 'Surf's up, pal!'" Carrying stylized, ultra-graphic violence to a level that transcended genres like war or police films, however, were the 1980s and 1990s action Renaissance films in the *Rambo*, *Die Hard*, and *Lethal Weapon* series.

According to Yvonne Tasker's cultural studies–oriented textual analysis of the action film, the very postmodernist, pastiche format of the genre has contributed to the lack of serious attention from scholars.[27] With scholars most often looking for the meaning of narratives and whatever dominant hegemonic messages must surely be encoded within the text, they would eventually turn away from the genre once the text proves to lack sufficient narrative power. Once they interpret the genre as being one of predominantly visual display and pleasure rather than a consistent narrative, the action film is, at best, labeled as insignificant and unworthy or scholarly attention. "Dumb movies for dumb people" is Tasker's very concise summary of so much of the scholarly view of the genre to date.[28] She remarks about the 1980s controversies about the representation of the Vietnam War to various degrees of accuracy in action films in general, and the first two *Rambo* films in particular, writing: "while the success of *Rambo* has generated numerous commentaries, these have largely been framed in terms of an address to the truth, or otherwise, of the cinema's rendition of the saga of American involvement in Vietnam."[29] On this note, legion are the critiques of the *Rambo* films—as well as most action films where lone tough guys take on hordes of evil—as to how a dozen villains can spray hundreds of rounds of gunfire and never hit the hero while all of Rambo's shots are on target, the unrealistic use of weapons and vehicles, or inaccurate re-creations of battle maneuvers.

This approach to the genre, however, is futile simply because it refuses to acknowledge the spirit in which it was created. The action genre, first and foremost, as it encompasses and colonizes genres like the cop drama or the war film or science fiction, is a ritualistic, stylized representation of social concerns. Altman writes that all genres are a representation of a social concern and a symbolic solution,[30] and the action film is simply more symbolic, hyperbolic, and over-the-top than most other genres. To judge a *Rambo* film or a *Pearl Harbor* (2001) according to the hyperrealistic depictions of a *Blackhawk Down* or *Private Ryan* is a pointless exercise because it applies the standards of one tradition of art to another. Noteworthy here is the critique of James Fennimore Cooper's *Leatherstocking* novels by Mark Twain in his famous essay, "Fennimore Cooper's Literary Offenses."[31] Twain's complaints focus on the various inaccuracies in the depiction of the wilderness and action sequences. As Twain wrote, Hawkeye's adversaries always managed to step on a dry twig and make noise exactly when Hawkeye needed the bad guys to make a mistake and give themselves away. In this instance, just as in the critiques of the marksmanship displayed by the action film's villains, the conventions of realist literature are being applied to novels written in the Romantic tradition. The critique is ultimately an exercise in futility. To put the matter in very simplified terms, an action film like *Rambo* would be to a war film like *Platoon* what professional wrestling would be to Olympic Greco-Roman wrestling.

On a similar note, however, one can see how some artists can get away with certain comments balancing on the very edge of good taste if they keep their films well within the bounds of hyperbole, while others catch blistering heat for their work and behavior if they attempt to present their films as anything other than fantasy. A good case in point is the Schwarzenegger/ Stallone action rivalry in the mid-1980s and how close to reality or sensitive subjects their films strayed. The critical beating Stallone took for the *Rambo* films was perhaps in part due to a stylized fantasy genre dealing not only with war, but also with the most controversial and divisive war in American history. Aside from the academic critics, the popular critics labeled the films ultra-right wing and jingoistic and Stallone as the "Jane Fonda of the Right."[32] This stems largely from a tacit endorsement of the films by Ronald Reagan in one part and, in another, perhaps by the monologue closing *First Blood* that included the line "I come back here and I see those maggots at the airport protesting, spitting at me, calling me a baby-killer and all kinds of vile crap. Who the hell are they to protest me unless they've been there and been me and know what the hell it is they're yelling about?" In the critical outcry over the films, however, lost is the fact that none of the films ever endorse the Vietnam War. Part of the same *First Blood* monologue is the complaint that Rambo was sent to a war he did not want to fight—"It wasn't my war. You asked me, I didn't ask you"—then got cast out for doing what he was forced to do. In the sequel, another closing exchange with his commanding officer includes the line "this might be wrong, this whole war might have been wrong, but don't hate your country for it." In fact, the duality of the films, of the entire Stallone action persona, is analyzed perfectly in Nigel Andrews's comparison of the two action icons:

> If the hour brings forth the man, then Stallone was a creature of the 1970s—Carterite dove in hawk's clothing—while Schwarzenegger was the distillation of battle-glamour Reaganism. Stallone's militarism carries its own deconstruction programme. We *know* this man wants to get out of these war situations, because he wears his misery in that gaunt face with the dragged-down cheeks and in those near-feminine lips and eyelashes that seem to plead for peace even when they're clenched for battle.[33]

Schwarzenegger, however, in the same era, cavalierly stretched propriety to its limits as he talked about tasteful killings—with no critical backlash. In one interview, he was quoted as saying:

> We probably kill more people in *Commando* than Stallone did in *Rambo*, but the difference is that we don't pretend the violence is justified by patriotic pride. All that flag-waving is a lot of bull—we're all in the entertainment business. And if killing is done with good taste, it can be very entertaining indeed.[34]

Of course, Schwarzenegger never dealt with Vietnam or any controversial issues in his films. When dealing with East-West relations in *Red Heat*, it was a politically correct celebration of glasnost with Schwarzenegger cast as a heroic Russian cop. During the controversy over aid to Nicaragua and the Reagan administration's anti-communist efforts in Central America, *Predator* (1987), about a team of mercenaries on a Central American mission, slickly sidesteps politics. The film never mentions where exactly in Central America Schwarzenegger's team is going, who the "diplomats" they have to rescue are, who the "rebels" holding them hostage are, or what they are rebelling against. The main storyline does not even involve the captured diplomats, but Schwarzenegger battling an alien creature that comes to Earth and lands in war zones to hunt the most violent humans on the planet. This proper distance from real controversies and political situations has kept Schwarzenegger a sort of Teflon action hero throughout his film career, despite conservative credentials a lot stronger than Stallone's (who has only recently endorsed a candidate for public office, backing John McCain for the presidency in 2008) and campaigning efforts for George H. W. Bush in 1988.

The angry critical response to *Pearl Harbor* in 2001 was a similar instance of the uneasy mix of reality with a fantasy genre. A film, placing its emphasis on action and violence, selling itself on how exhilarating its scenes of mass slaughter are—mass slaughter that actually occurred, survivors of which are still alive—was criticized on the grounds of tasteless opportunism and the exploitation of suffering, rather than any political grounds.

Those scholars not dismissing the genre, however, almost invariably read it as a reassertion of traditional masculinity rather than a reflection of or dialogue about the various positive and negative aspects of strong masculinity and the patriarchy. Fiske's analysis of the action genre, calling it the "muscle genre," is a tight, concise representative example of this approach:

> The typical male hero can be seen as literally embodying patriarchal capitalism. . . . It is comparatively easy to see how this merges indistinguishably into the overlapping ideologies of individualism, competition, and a form of "social Darwinism" that proposes that morality is always on the side of eventual winners. These ideologies, in turn, merge into a particular construction of American and Western nationalism—a right wing version of the nation that sees it as masculine (exerting in the international sphere power over others in the service of the weak or of a higher morality), based on competitive individualism and social Darwinism.[35]

Although some of Fiske's work with the genre's foreign audiences, as in one study where he observes Australian Aborigines reacting to and interpreting *Rambo II*, add to the understanding of how an audience negotiates meaning and identity with the text, the above-quoted reading of the archetypal action text is inadequate. The fact that male heroes in the *James Bond*-to-millennium era of action films are so often outsiders, marginalized and disrespected, characters given to as much self-loathing, guilt, and self-abuse as their world heaps upon them, counters these uncomplicated liberal readings. Instead, King provides a more accurate summary:

> [C]ops (action heroes) often spell out the place of racism, misogyny, and capitalist greed in their world. The genre concerns itself directly with political struggle, in a way that anyone who listens to what these characters say can hear. *Heroes often describe themselves as spoiled louts who deserve punishment for their collective sins.* When others say as much, heroes tend not to argue. At the same time, they are these movies' heroes, and they expect a lot of attention paid to their faults and to their dreams of solving their own and their nation's problems. At the very least, I find little reason to think that cops cannot reckon their political situation, their responsibility for it, or the political impulses that drive them into male-bonding and bone-crunching battle. Rather than regard these movies as pernicious, vacuous, illogical, or contradictory, then, I assume that they can make useful sense about the political culture of "losing ground" in which people feel their world going to hell.[36]

To summarize King's typology of action, the generic action hero is fighting to regain lost ground and respect, losses that might originally have been quite *justifiable.* At the core of the justified loss, King interprets, are the historic abuses of power and privilege by white men. In a sense, King confirms the conservative critique of the hegemony arguments, that most of the villains in action films are rich, powerful white men. As a black cop (Chris Tucker) explains ever so concisely in *Rush Hour 2* (2001), "Let me tell you Carter's theory of criminal investigation: Always follow the rich white man! If there's a major crime committed, there's always a rich white man behind it." However, it is

> the bigoted and reckless bonding of criminals [that] causes the problems that have cost straight, white, working-class men so much public legitimacy in the first place. Exposure of their corruption has led sidekicks, bosses, families, and community members to blame white men as bullies and to distance from them as such. These men know that they cannot return to the status of "normal" or "human"; white manhood must bear the stain of their sins. Nevertheless, they can round up the baddest of white men, blow them away for public show, and claim the attention they want with their self-hating immolation.[37]

Aside from this more complex reading of the genre's social and political statements, it is now time to reexamine just how the action film is engendered. Going past the simplistic reading scholars usually afford these films, very succinctly summarized by Tasker as "a simple enactment of white male supremacism,"[38] a more thorough reading of the texts reveals a dialogue about the anxieties of manhood in decline. These dramatized anxieties are very much in line with current anthropological thoughts on the obsolescence of maleness.

Violent behavior as a metaphor for natural masculine traits thus can be seen as a point of examination, if not contention, in the 1960s to 2000s action era. Although the study wants to let its audiences talk about action heroes, general observations can still be made here to establish the nature of the genre's archetypes. As King argues, it is easy to see that, for the most part, the male action hero is not a happy character. In his work on Clint Eastwood, Schickel analyzes *Dirty Harry* as dealing with "the frustrations of the typical American male, in relation to his work, in relation to whatever system he served, most accurately, while at the same time portraying his impotent rage, his growing sense of isolation in a rapidly changing world."[39] In *First Blood*, the story is capped by its protagonist's rage at a changing world where his service in Vietnam is not honored but mocked, while he is so displaced that even though in the war he "was trusted with million-dollar equipment, [he] could fly a gunship, drive a tank, [he comes] back here and can't even hold down a job parking cars."[40] Gallagher states that "for men in contemporary capitalist society, a society that provides a social and economic structure that severely limits and codifies bourgeois male's ability to establish his identity through physical activity, action films provide fantasies of heroic omnipotence and of escape from, or transcendence of, cultural pressures."[41] In *The Matrix*, Keanu Reeves's dissatisfied, frustrated protagonist lives life as a drone-like rank-and-file computer programmer in a vast complex of office cubicles, instinctively feeling that no matter what he tries to do with his life, he just cannot fit in and find satisfaction. Of course, he soon realizes the world he lives in is not real, that it is all part of a false collective consciousness generated by the Matrix, a super computer into which all humans in the world are plugged through millions of pods. Eventually, realizing that he is the messianic "The One," his rebellion against the Matrix involves martial arts and high-tech weapon-outfitted hand-to-hand combat, his physique and "manly" combat skills foregrounded, with Reeves's body in its leanest, most muscular and angularly chiseled shape of his career.

Another interesting aspect of the action genre that needs to be recognized and will be discussed with the study subjects are the value systems the genre seems to carry or comment upon. Although postmodern in their stylized construction, action films also seem to be remarkably hostile to postmodernism when it comes to its pliant moral relativism. Aside from their mannered presentation, the internal universe of the action film is one of morally superior, masculine heroes fighting for what is right in a bureaucratized (and feminized) world where clear-cut right and wrong are no longer recognized. Unlike Fiske's reading, morality in the action film is *not* defined by whomever happens to be on the winning side, but morality is a universal absolute. In the world of the action film, there is a clearly identifiable universal Truth, with a capital T. In this world, what is almost as dangerous, reprehensible, and worthy of punishment is not only evil—the drug dealer, the terrorist, or the gangster—but bureaucrats and intellectuals who condone and excuse evil and destructive behvior.

In the *Dirty Harry* series, not only is Clint Eastwood outraged by crime, but also by the way an inefficient, bureaucratic white-collar/intellectual world is more concerned with public relations, talk, and analysis rather than meting out punishment. "Certain segments of the community don't believe in your ideas," a bureaucrat criticizes Eastwood in one installment of the series, soon after calling him a Neanderthal. "What ideas are those?" Eastwood retorts. "That murder is wrong and it should be punished?"

In *Rambo II*, the mission to free POWs is betrayed by a government agency that organized Rambo's effort in a gesture of political public relations, then betrays it in order to avoid an "international incident." "It wasn't my war, Colonel, I'm just here to clean up the mess," the Washington bureaucrat (Charles Napier) running the operation says indifferently. Then, after orchestrating a betrayal, his reasoning is more complex than mere "right" and "wrong." "Can you imagine a burned-out POW showing up on the six o'clock news? What do you want to do then, start the war all over again? Have everybody screaming 'armed invasion!' 'Bomb Hanoi!' Do you think someone's gonna get up on the floor of the United States Congress asking for billions of dollars for a couple of forgotten ghosts?" Colonel Trautman (Richard Crenna), Rambo's commanding officer retorts with: "Men, God damn it! Our men!" To the bureaucracy, the men are little more than cogs in the wheel and quite expendable. As Rambo explains to his female companion, "Expendable? That's when you're invited to a party, but don't show up . . . nobody cares." Similarly, in *Rambo III*, he is forced into action (initially he refuses to fight, opting to stay in the pacifist Buddhist monastery, outfitted in a hippyish flower-embroidered shirt) when Trautman is left behind enemy lines and disavowed by the government.

An interesting twist to moral absolutes in the *Rambo* films, however, comes in the 2008 installment of the series, simply titled *Rambo*. Here, blind, unyielding idealism proves to be just as dangerous as bureaucratic, moral relativism used to be in the past. The plot of the latest installment of the series (as of this writing) involves an even angrier, more disillusioned Rambo being asked to get involved in another war-torn region of the world. This time, a group of pacifist Christian missionaries asks him to help deliver supplies, Bibles, and medicine to besieged Karin tribes people in Burma. The cargo, he is told by the missionaries, "will help make a difference." "Will they be taking in weapons?" is Rambo's simple, suspicious reply. When he is told "of course not," he knows that the mission is doomed to failure. Yet in this film, the unyielding moral absolutes the missionaries live by turn out to be useless and deadly. Their code of Christian pacifism leaves the group as helpless targets in a land full of genocidal maniacs. The missionaries, especially their self-righteous leader Michael (Paul Schulze), may verbally spar with and debate the ethics of nonviolence with Rambo when they are safely removed from the combat zone, but once they are alone and their philosophy is tested, idealistic pacifism comes up far short. When the missionary group is administering to a village of the besieged Karin, patching up the wounded and sick, distributing the Bibles and singing hymns, they come under a swift and merciless attack. The faith of the Christian group does nothing to spare the majority of the villagers from being blown up, set ablaze with flame throwers, shot, bayonetted, and dismembered with machetes. There is idealism and then there is the real world, the film declares. If anything, violence guided by idealism is the only sane and realistic compromise in the view of the film. As angry and nihilistic as its hero might be, the film still does not endorse a complete dismissal of ethics. People who turn out to be just as useless in the face of genocidal violence in *Rambo*, after all, are a group of mercenaries who function on the mirror image opposite of the spectrum from the pacifists. The mercenaries hired by the missionaries' home church simply kill for pay, not beliefs and not idealism. They are specialists in fighting, but only so long as the odds are in their favor and they do not risk getting killed. But they prove to be equally inadequate in a world of depraved evil because they have absolutely *no* code of honor and idealism whatsoever. In fact, the film's tagline, "Live for nothing or die for something," comes from a scene where Rambo, feeling something of a reawakening of his own long-dormant ideals, threatens to kill the leader (Graham McTavish) of the mercenaries if he refuses to try to rescue the captured Michael and his group.

In Stallone's *Demolition Man* (1994), not only are crime and anarchy raging in a not so far off future, but materialism and greed go unchecked. In one scene, Stallone's credentials as not only a maverick but also a highly ethical hero are established as he single-handedly saves a child from kidnappers holed up in an expensive shopping mall complex. Naturally, Stallone demolishes the whole mall to save the child's life. In the aftermath, an outraged reporter asks, "How can you justify destroying a hundred million dollar shopping complex to save *one* girl's life?"

The revival of *Mission: Impossible* with Tom Cruise's films (1996, 2000, 2006) firmly focuses on this theme of personal honor in the face of organizational, institutional treachery. The original *Mission: Impossible* television series made famous the phrase "should you fail or be captured, the secretary will disavow all knowledge of your activities."

As Annette Hill argues, these standards of right and wrong, moral and immoral codes of conduct often have strong class connotations.[42] The masculine, morally superior heroes are more often than not blue-collar, working-class men. Even in *Dr. No* (1962) the villain taunts James Bond (Sean Connery) with "you're nothing but a civil servant, Mr. Bond. A glorified cop." Upper-class, professional, white-collar men are not only more effete, softer, less attractive in comparison to the rough-hewn heroes, but they are morally relativistic, easily corruptible, if not outright villainous. In *Dirty Harry*, the intellectual class raises the hero's ire when he hears a college professor argue that all the prisons should be opened and the criminals let loose.

The values of the violent action film can be compared to a line of scholarship on violent entertainment in relation to the "civilizing process."[43] Whereas conventional wisdom may state that a truly civilized, enlightened society needs no violent entertainment, this school of thought argues that the very civilizing process may feed the need for such entertainment, especially for men. The value system of the action film bears this out.

"You and I are a part of the same hypocrisy" are the famous words of Michael Corleone (Al Pacino) in *The Godfather, Part II* (1974). Although not an action film, the sequence perfectly illustrates the "civilizing process" argument for the appeal of moralized violent entertainment. The quote is in the context of a retort to a politician's claim that "decent" people and "good" people are those on the side of the law, the social order, government, and the establishment, and evil is in the organized crime of the Mafia, a subculture based on loyalty to the family above all. The broader context of the scene includes the information that a certain politician is corrupt and living off of bribes. The Mafia, on the other hand, operates according to strict, unwritten codes of personal and family honor. The civilizing process, in the terms of macrosociologist Norbert Elias, involves a concentration in the power of the state, the differentiation and compartmentalization of individuals into specific specialties, and the state alone reserving the right to arbitrate disputes and conflict through force if need be.[44] Of course, when the state, or its various organs or agents, becomes corrupt or ineffective, as often happens in societies, all are a part of the same hypocrisy. Action adventure films may be a symbolic way of dealing with the frustrations of this process, especially for men. The genre most often equates civilization with the feminine—the future world of *Demolition Man* is, on its utopian surface, the most civilized, with war and violence eradicated, but it is also the most feminized. Ethically, these civilized societies are the most prone to corruption when they are the most technologically and bureaucratically advanced, with their citizenry nonphysical, feminized, and nonviolent. The scores of action films dealing with good men pushed too far and needing to take revenge because the justice system is ineffective, unfair, or thoroughly corrupt further dramatize this concept. The comments of this study's participants on this issue in Chapter 6 bear out the civilizing process theory.

Research into the cognitive and biological reactions elicited upon viewing violence have shown some excitatory effects, with an increase in aggressive impulses in viewers.[45] But proving that such arousal is lasting, or that it will spill over into actual violence, has been elusive. In other words, young men may wander out of a movie theater after an action movie with more of a swagger and they might get the urge to drive a little faster after seeing a *Fast and Furious* film, but the real world, according to every study ever done on the immediate effects of viewing violence, soon comes intruding into the fantasy, and they will resume their normal, habitual behavior. Anthropological analysis of the enjoyment of violence, approached from an evolutionary perspective, argues that displays of violent contests can likewise stimulate short-term testosterone increases in males, articulated in the "eminence/dominance" argument.[46]

From an evolutionary approach, a penchant for competition and domination ensures a male's chances in securing a mate and creating offspring. Such a direct drive to physically vanquish competitors for food and females is the impulse of domination. Yet, it is an impulse that needs to be curbed as humankind becomes civilized. However, similar assertive behavior does exist in the civilized world. Where physical domination is no longer acceptable, such competitive behavior takes on the form of "eminence." Thus, it is the movement of the male from securing a position of prestige through combat and physical prowess to securing prestige in a more cerebral way, through economic success and intellectual accomplishment. Simply, in the civilized world, the men most competitive for the affections of women are not the ones who are simply tough, muscular, and macho, but those with the more expensive cars, houses, clothes, and stable, well-providing and socially respectable careers. These are also the types of men who make up the ranks of action film villains (corrupt businessmen, corrupt politicians, drug lords) or comic foils (the boss, the mayor, the internal affairs investigator, or the sensitive and dependable accountant or businessman for whom the hero was dumped by a wife or girlfriend) who need to be mocked and humiliated by the physically dominant hero in a morality play about the ethical purity of the physical man and the corruptibility of the upper classes and intellectual classes.

The action film critiques a society that tries to suppress the male impulse for domination. In fact, it states that a world where competition is done on the intellectual level is no less violent or dangerous. In fact, the moral relativism of such a world can be equally threatening. Very succinctly dramatizing this is the climactic exchange between an anarchistic psycho and his maverick cop pursuer in *Cobra* (1986). "You will never get rid of us," taunts the psycho,

"Your filthy society breeds us. . . . You won't shoot, will you, pig? You have to take me in. Even I have rights, don't I, pig? The courts are civilized." Replies the cop: "But I'm not. This is where the law stops and I start, sucker!"

Early exceptions to the class/intellectual dichotomy are in the *Indiana Jones* films (1981, 1984, 1989, 2008), *Tango and Cash* (1989), and the *Bad Boys* series (1993, 2003). Harrison Ford's hero of the eponymous Indiana Jones films is a college professor, "Indy" to his closest allies, but "Dr. Jones" to most supporting characters, with the films always reminding of his intellectual standing. In *Tango and Cash*, Sylvester Stallone plays an independently wealthy cop, attired in three-piece Armani suits and often seen reading the *Wall Street Journal*. When asked why he is a cop if he has so much money, he replies, "it's the action, all-American action." In a similar vein, Will Smith's Mike Lowry character in the *Bad Boys* films is a wealthy playboy who wears stylish designer clothes and drives sports cars. He is a cop, however, out of a need for excitement.

Concerning the issue of class and masculinity, in a new twist on genre conventions, many recent films seem to be looking beyond the rough-cut blue-collar men and finding heroes among the lower white-collar, middle-managerial class as well. As commentary by the study participants will illustrate, today even these men, supposedly privileged until now, have to fight for their place in the world, have to fight obsolescence in a postindustrial society. *The Matrix* finds its hero in what appears to be a white-collar, skilled computer programmer driven to frustration and impulses to rebel and break free of his stifling, dehumanizing world. "Do I have the kitchen furniture that defines me?" mulls the worn-out protagonist of *Fight Club*, similarly driven to acts of vandalism by a world where he feels the only avenue afforded to self-expression is conspicuous consumption. "We are the middle children of history," explains his hypermasculine alter ego, meaning a world that does not afford men true challenges that are, on the one hand, real and meaningful and consequential, such as a threat, a war of some type, the Cold War, the communist enemies of a true masculine hero like Rambo a decade earlier. On the other hand, this world of the middle children does not provide true masculine challenges that only real men can meet, challenges that will define them as men. Thus, while different in narrative structure from the classic action film, a film like *Fight Club* makes very explicit what the traditional, male-oriented action film has been quietly implying through subtext; the postmodern, postindustrial world is one that is both emasculating *and*, at the same time, morally and ethically bankrupt. Fighting back with the innate male instinct for and thirst for aggression, by turning the aggression against the by-products of this society like the evil of crime (*Die Hard*) and corrupt institutions (*Fight Club*, *The Matrix*), becomes true righteous violence.

An action subgenre—or some would say science fiction subgenre with very strong action/adventure elements—that has also brought a new dimension to the class structure of these narratives is the burgeoning superhero film. Superheroes, in fact, have often been more affluent than most of the traditional action heroes. Especially those superheroes who do not possess some sort of superhuman ability are more apt to be either wealthy businessmen or scientists. The former characters channel their wealth into the creation of everything from super vehicles to high-tech weapons and an array of ultra-sophisticated crime-fighting gadgets and computers. Batman is the most successful example of the wealthy, self-made crime fighter. Batman, however, is also the crime-fighting guise of a man who is forever contending with a boyhood loss of power and victimization. The later characters, the scientists, will often create either the super crime-fighting technologies, or they will use biological, chemical, or genetic experimentation to give themselves, or others, superhuman abilities.

Although the most successful Batman films have been those under the directorship of Christopher Nolan, the 2005 and 2008 *Batman Begins* and *The Dark Night* iterations, analysts of filmic masculinity have long found the 1989 and 1992 films much more fertile grounds for study and discussion. The late 1980s and early 1990s films, starring Michael Keaton, manage to put a greater emphasis on the idea that powerful, traditional versions of masculinity are very much constructs. Whereas in the new versions of the Caped Crusader story actor Christian Bale is a hulking, imposingly muscular figure—whether he is Batman or Bruce Wayne—there is a much more conspicuous duality between the two versions of the character in the Michael Keaton films. In the old films, Bruce Wayne has a rather average-looking build. Keaton's hyper-masculine Batman is but a facade constructed out of the armor plating of his costume. Much of the strength and physical prowess of this version of the superhero comes from the gadgets and machines fitted all over his bat suit.

But other than personal tragedies, male superheroes, even ones who are either wealthy or men of intellectual eminence, have tended to face a lot of angst born out of bureaucratic capitalism. In *Iron Man* (2008), Tony Stark (Robert Downey, Jr.) is a spoiled, obnoxious heir to a wealthy weapons manufacturing empire he did not build himself. He is but a womanizer and a drunk, a parasite living off the millions his late father's company lavishes on him. Stark, in fact, is kin to *Fight Club*'s sad-sack protagonist, the middle child of history living in the shadow of a distant and absent father. Stark is a man without a purpose, an obstacle, a way to prove his manhood. The entire narrative of *Iron Man* can also be seen as the logical continuation of *Fight Club*'s themes all the way into the post-September 11 world of the war on terror and the Iraq invasion. Whereas *Fight Club*'s men complain of being lost without wars to fight, the lost, irresponsible, and inebriated Tony Stark wakes up to a whole new war against Middle Eastern terrorists. In a way, he gets to fulfill the wish of all the men of *Fight Club*. He does not need to pick pointless street fights to get in touch with his masculinity. He is given a brand new chance to fight a brand new war in George W. Bush's America. At this point, however, *Iron Man* takes a sharp liberal turn, condemning weapons manufacturers as nothing more than war profiteers. Whereas the men of the *Fight Club* era are victimized by the end of one war and the stultifying consumerism of Madison Avenue and the "hood ornament culture," the men of the new millennium are turned into cannon fodder in pointless wars by greedy and incompetent bureaucrats who cannot even keep their weapons from falling into the hands of their enemies. Tony Stark's moral awakening and elevation to superhero status begins when he not only turns himself into superman by way of a robotic suit, but also decides to shut down the family's weapons manufacturing enterprises.

The crisis-suffering eminent man is also the focus of both the 2003 and the 2008 versions of the Marvel Comics superhero the Hulk (in 2003 "art house" director Ang Lee made *The Hulk*, and in 2008 action film director Louis Leterrier "rebooted" the franchise with *The Incredible Hulk*). The Hulk of the 2003 version of the film is a bit more complex, the sources of hero Bruce Banner's (Eric Bana) angst and rage being more than merely a gamma ray experiment gone awry. Here, Banner has the genetic predisposition to turn into the Hulk because of his father's experiments and repressed memories of his father attempting to kill him fuel his subconscious rage. Other sources of frustration for Banner are remarkably similar to Neal King's marginalized action hero typology. Although a scientist, technically an intellectual, Banner is victimized by the repressive corporate machinery that is the traditional enemy of the working-class action heroes. The corporate control of scientific research and funding degrades his work as a professional and threatens to turn him into a lowly service provider for the business and military establishments.

The same themes turn up in both the underperforming *Daredevil* (2003) as well as the very successful *The Fantastic Four* (2005). The hero of *Daredevil* is an upwardly mobile professional, successful lawyer Matt Murdoch (Ben Affleck). Murdoch, however, has also been a victim of an irresponsible father and corrupt big business polluters whose toxic waste blinded him in childhood. *The Fantastic Four* likewise revisits the theme of the emasculation of the idealistic American male intellectual by shifty, exploitative corporate capitalism.

But perhaps the most disrespected smart superhero *and* the ultimate figure of a powerless male's compensatory fantasy is *Spider-Man*. In director's Sam Raimi's faithful adaptations (2002, 2004, 2007) of the Marvel comic books,

Peter Parker (Tobey Maguire) is a brainy nerd who is regularly pushed around by bullies and ignored by the object of his crush, Mary Jane Watson (Kirsten Dunst). Although Peter is smart and talented, possessing both a keen mind for science and the skills to be a good news photographer, these attributes still do not get him society's respect. Scientists and photographers are but the lowly cogs in the corporate machinery that runs modern America. Moreover, once Peter becomes Spider-Man, he still does not fare much better most of the time. After he starts battling crime in New York City, he falls victim to the other major organ of power in the modern world: the media. Spider-Man quickly incurs the wrath of Peter Parker's boss, the blustery windbag editor of the *Daily Bugle*, J. Jonah Jameson (J. K. Simmons). Jameson decides to portray the superhero as a reckless vigilante menace and calls for the authorities to do everything in their power to apprehend and prosecute him. The corporate media, the film subtly hints, is the ultimate power broker in today's America, an institution with the ability to shape people's perceptions of reality. Most often this power is used in insidious ways, twisting the truth and arbitrarily casting good people as villains, all for the sake of sensational headlines. By the end of the first film, Spider-Man has become a sort of Christ figure, suffering the scorn of the people he is trying to save and mocked and tempted by the Green Goblin (whose face mask somewhat resembles a grinning devil) into forsaking all the ingrate New Yorkers who have turned on him.

What scholarly attention has been focused on the action genre has pointed out a series of archetypal plots, situations, and characters that set the genre apart from all other film forms that may contain violence. These are films peopled with male heroes who fight an often-futile battle for redemption as they try and counter forces of evil a morally relativistic society no longer wants to recognize. The action films function as morality tales of modernity and postmodernity, with men in the absolutist, modernist camp and women in the world of rising postmodernity. Male heroes of the action genre are often lonely figures, their reason for existence becoming their crusades as families and lovers cast them by the wayside. But, ultimately, the genre is about aggression and the male capacity for it. The films foreground the visual spectacle of destruction. But what relevance, impact, and effect all this may have on society must be gauged by first looking very closely at the thoughts of the most avid viewers of these films.

NOTES

1. Neal King, *Heroes in Hard Times: Cop Action Movies in the U.S.* (Philadelphia: Temple University Press, 1999), viii.

2. Bosley Crowther, "Review of *The Dirty Dozen*," *New York Times*, June 16, 1967.

3. Crowther, "Review of *The Dirty Dozen*."

4. Andrew Sarris, "Review of *The Dirty Dozen*," *Village Voice*, June 29, 1967.

5. Nigel Andrews, *True Myths: The Life and Times of Arnold Schwarzenegger* (Secaucus, NJ: Birch Lane Press, 1996).

6. Andrews, *True Myths*, 137.

7. Yvonne Tasker, *Spectacular Bodies: Gender, Genre and the Action Cinema* (New York: Routledge, 1993), 9.

8. J. Hoberman, "A Test for the Individual Viewer: *Bonnie and Clyde*'s Violent Reception," in *Why We Watch: The Attractions of Violent Entertainment*, ed. Jeffrey H. Goldstein (Oxford: Oxford University Press, 1995), 134.

9. Hoberman, "A Test for the Individual Viewer," 134.

10. Jib Fowles, *The Case for Television Violence* (Thousand Oaks, CA: Sage, 1999), 67.

11. *Violence on Television: Programme Content and Viewer Perceptions* (London: British Broadcast Corporation, 1972).

12. Elizabeth Gould Davis, *The First Sex* (New York: Dent, 1973), 351–352.

13. Andrews, *True Myths*, 137.

14. David Link, "Facts about Fiction: In Defense of TV Violence," *Reason* 25, no. 10 (March 1994): 22–26.

15. John G. Cawelti, *Adventure, Mystery and Romance: Formula Stories as Art and Popular Culture* (Chicago: University of Chicago Press, 1976), 40.

16. Will Murray, "*The Executioner* Phenomenon," in *Murder Off the Rack: Critical Studies of Ten Paperback Masters*, eds. Jon L. Breen and Martin Harry Greenberg (Metuchen, NJ: Scarecrow Press, 1989).

17. Murray, "*The Executioner* Phenomenon," 140.

18. Murray, "*The Executioner* Phenomenon," 139.

19. Leo Braudy, "Genre: Conventions of Connection," in *Film Theory and Criticism*, eds. Gerald Mast, Marshall Cohen, and Leo Braudy (Oxford: Oxford University Press, 1992), 435–453.

20. Mark Gallagher, "I Married Rambo: Spectacle and Melodrama in the Hollywood Action Film," in *Mythologies of Violence in Postmodern Media*, ed. Christopher Sharrett (Detroit: Wayne State University Press, 1999), 199–226.

21. Richard Schickel, *Clint Eastwood* (New York: Alfred A. Knopf, 1996), 275.

22. Schickel, *Clint Eastwood*, 280.

23. Gina Marchetti, "Action Adventure as Ideology," in *Cultural Politics in Contemporary America*, eds. Ian Angus and Sut Jhally (London: Routledge, 1989), 197.

24. Andrew Lycett, *Ian Fleming: The Man Behind James Bond* (Atlanta: Turner Publishing, 1995).

25. Gallagher, "I Married Rambo," 51.

26. Robert Warshow, "Movie Chronicle: The Westerner," in *Film Theory and Criticism*, eds. Gerald Mast, Marshall Cohen, and Leo Braudy (Oxford: Oxford University Press, 1992), 453–467.

27. Tasker, *Spectacular Bodies*.

28. Tasker, *Spectacular Bodies*, 8.

29. Tasker, *Spectacular Bodies*, 8.

30. Rick R. Altman, *The American Film Musical* (Bloomington: Indiana University Press, 1987).

31. Mark Twain, "Fenimore Cooper's Literary Offenses," in *Great Short Works of Mark Twain*, ed. Justin Kaplan (New York: Harper and Row, 1967), 169–182.

32. Frank Sanello, *Stallone: A Rocky Life* (Edinburgh: Mainstream Publishing, 1998).

33. Andrews, *True Myths*, 136.

34. Andrews, *True Myths*, 134.

35. John Fiske, "British Cultural Studies and Television," in *Channels of Discourse, Reassembled*, ed. Robert C. Allen (Chapel Hill, NC: University of North Carolina Press, 1992), 293.

36. King, *Heroes in Hard Times*, ix, emphasis added.

37. King, *Heroes in Hard Times*, 202.

38. Tasker, *Spectacular Bodies*, 7.

39. Schickel, *Clint Eastwood*, 280.

40. This quote is a part of the Rambo character's cathartic speech on the end of *First Blood*, raging against a society's hostility and hypocrisy toward soliders who were forced to fight a war they did not ask for and didn't believe in.

41. Gallagher, "I Married Rambo," 199.

42. Annette Hill, *Shocking Entertainment: Viewer Response to Violent Movies* (Luton: University of Luton Press, 1997).

43. Notable scholarship in the civilizing process includes works by Norbert Elias, *The Civilizing Process:* Vol. 1. *The History of Manners* (New York: Pantheon, 1978); Norbert Elias, *The Civilizing Process:* Vol. 2. *Power and Civility* (New York: Pantheon, 1982); Norbert Elias and Eric Dunning, *The Quest for Excitement: Sport and Leisure in the Civilizing Process* (Oxford: Basil Blackwell, 1986); Jib Fowles, *Television Viewers vs. Media Snobs: What TV Does for People* (New York: Stein and Day, 1982); Allen Guttmann, "The Appeal of Violent Sports," in *Why We Watch: The Attractions of Violent Entertainment*, ed. Jeffrey H. Goldstein (Oxford: Oxford University Press, 1998); Theodore D. Kemper, *Social Structure and Testosterone: Explorations of the Socio-Bio-Social Chain* (New Brunswick, NJ: Rutgers University Press, 1990).

44. Elias, *The Civilizing Process*, Vols. 1 and 2.

45. Short-term excitatory effects in viewers have been shown in studies by William Washburn Grings, *Emotions and Bodily Responses: A Psychophysiological Approach* (New York: Academic Press, 1978) and Daniel Linz, Edward Donnerstein, and Steven Adams, "Physiological Desensitization and Judgments about Female Victims of Violence," *Human Communication* 15 (1989): 505–522.

46. Kemper, *Social Structure and Testosterone*.

Part II

THE AUDIENCE

4

The Need for Speed: The Appeal of Fast-Paced Storytelling

I have a need. I have a need for speed.

—Tom Cruise, *Top Gun*

A lot of well-reasoned criticism of scholarship that deals with the viewers of violent entertainment has been raised because a lot of the standing research does not ask why the viewers turn to violence in the first place. Fowles states that "People who truly want to understand the role of . . . violence need to critically examine the role of this content in its many guises, in their own lives."[1] The "uses and gratifications" school, in fact, has turned its methodology to this problem in the past.[2] Cultural studies scholarship, in turn, when dealing with genres centered around violence, further calls for understanding a complex connection between audiences and violent entertainment, beginning with why the viewer selects a violent film to watch when there are others available. Simply asking a person "why do you like watching this" is an important first step toward seeing connections between identity and media text.

There is an interesting passage in Kermode's article on the horror film, analyzing the genre as only he, a lifelong horror fan, could:

> I remember forming a fleeting bond with a fellow movie-goer at a screening of *The Fly* at the Manchester Oxford Road Odeon in the 1980s when an onscreen doctor preparing to abort Geena Davis' insect foetus turned out to be director David Cronenberg. While everyone else cringed, the two of us chuckled smugly from opposite sides of the auditorium, like ships signaling each other in deep fog.[3]

As he elaborates on his enjoyment of the genre, Kermode goes on to point out the complex pleasures offered by a genre that others, those who do not watch it actively and do not understand it, dismiss as an aberrant, sadistic pastime of people who only enjoy seeing suffering, cruelty, and gratuitous violence. Horror, he argues, "demands to be read metaphorically rather than literally," and is a vehicle for the exploration of various contemporary issues, everything from the role of media in society and the media effects controversy to racial and class conflict, and so on.[4] Or, at least, this is how good horror works. Scholars of the genre, whether in literature or in film, have, of course, understood this for decades. Likewise, it is well known that successful science fiction uses its aliens and robots and extraterrestrial worlds for metaphorical explorations of contemporary social issues. As Newcomb and Hirsch explain, for a piece of entertainment to be consistently successful in garnering a mass audience, it must be rich, textured and on some level relevant to that audience's lives and experiences.[5]

Similarly, Kermode argues that a connoisseur of horror is also a discerning authority on the good and the bad, and talking to the viewers of the action film reveals how they approach the genre as an art form. The art form, in turn, consists of a body of films of varying quality. Asked to distinguish between the good and the bad, the action viewer will readily speak about the differences between, say, *Lethal Weapon* (1987) and *Action Jackson* (1988), *Mission: Impossible* (1996) and *Mission: Impossible 2* (2001), *Die Hard* (1987) and *The Taking of Beverly Hills* (1991), *Under Siege* (1992) and *Under Siege 2* (1995), or *Terminator* and *Terminator 2* (1984, 1991) versus *Terminator 3* and *Terminator: Salvation* (2003, 2009).

But the initial phase of understanding the action/adventure user's relationship to the genre has to begin with the very basic pleasures the viewing experience brings. Hill discusses her reasons for looking at avid viewers of ultraviolent films:

> There are more productive ways to debate screen violence . . . which will prove useful to those interested in the process of viewing violence. The question I want to ask is: why do people wish to see violent movies? It is only once we discover why watching violent movies is a popular leisure activity that we can begin to understand the complex emotional responses to viewing violence.[6]

Among the participants of this study, an overwhelming majority indicated the most basic enjoyment came from the fast narratives of the action genre. The pleasure of the constant speed and the pleasures created by seeing climactic action sequences are described by each of the interviewees, from the youngest to the oldest. These are the pleasures Tasker writes of when remarking about the "sensuous experience" and the "breathtaking nature of visual spectacle, or the feelings of exhilaration at the expansive landscapes in which the hero operates."[7]

However, as the following testimonials bear out, socialization also plays as much a role in developing tastes for media as the psychological appeal of the content itself. Each of the women I spoke to, save for one, Cindy, started watching action because at one point in their lives that was the only choice available. Growing up with a houseful of brothers, raised by a single father or an overbearing father, or dating men who would only watch action exposed these women to the genre and allowed them to develop a taste for it. Now, when they have a choice between action/adventure and some other, nonviolent or "feminine" genre, they still turn to the action film first.

Carl, a twenty-five-year-old college senior, speaks of both the pleasures of seeing the fast-paced movement, as well as displeasure when the action stops:

> You go in there and you know you're gonna get something exciting and you're not gonna be bored. For some part, some movies say they're action/adventure, but they end up being boring. So, in that matter, action/adventure, *Mission: Impossible*, things like that where . . . there's something going on in the movie that excites the fan or the audience.

With this initial answer to my question of why he likes action films, Carl, in fact, touches on several issues that keep reoccurring throughout the interviews, among both men and women, young and old alike: the importance of speed, genres most disliked because they are the opposite of action/adventure, and the hierarchy of pleasures to be offered by film entertainment.

Talking about "something going on" became a recurring phenomenon throughout the study. The phrase refers to how the viewers expect to see a film that is a collection of very fast-paced, climactic sequences, a quick cycle of urgent problems suddenly resolved through spectacular and unusual displays of violence, destruction, and special effects. A plot that is at the same time compelling, but not so complex as to slow the story by requisite stretches of expository dialogue, ties all of this together.

As I began all of the interviews by asking the interviewees to talk about what it is that piques their interest in a new film, they would all say that— along with favorite stars—the action sequences shown in television ads or theatrical trailers would be one of the most important factors in making that first impression. While the interviewees also prove to be the discriminating viewers described above, ready to talk at length about the types of action films they dislike, or films that did not live up to expectations because of weak plots or bad characters, the action promised by the ad is usually the first thing that marks a film as a potential option for viewing.

As Dwayne, a twenty-one-year-old undergraduate and professional wrestling enthusiast, explains, "Speed is important. Usually when you see it advertised, there's always that speed. Something always going on."

There are phrases the interviewees employ to describe the pleasure of watching the fast-paced narratives. Being "on the edge of your seat" is one of the oft-repeated remarks. The phrase, as a matter of fact, is a sort of marketing cliché for suspense films. Ads for action films often guarantee that the film will have the audience balanced on the edge of their seats with excitement. Similar phrases would almost always promise a physical sensation of some sort as well. The copy of the original *Die Hard*'s print advertising said the film would "blow you through the back of the theater." When asking the interviewees what the "edge of your seat" phrase meant to them, how they could describe the physical sensation they felt when watching a successful action film, I got replies explaining that being "on the edge of your seat" meant getting actively involved in a film, caring where the plot and the characters were going, and being made to care how the problems of the film were eventually resolved. As Carl explains:

> To me, it's when I sit there, sit through a movie . . . a lot of times you go to a movie and you feel like you're sitting there for two hours. With some of the movies that I've seen, the ones that I like actually, it doesn't seem like two and a half hours you're sitting there 'cause you're constantly waiting for something to happen. So you're sitting at the edge of your seat, just waiting for the next exciting thing.

None of the interviewees, however, talk about the importance of a surprise at the end of a film. Kelly, a nineteen-year-old college student, talking about enjoying *Fight Club*, came closest to touching upon the intrigue of the unexpected and how she enjoyed the *Sixth Sense*-like ending of that film, where it is revealed that Brad Pitt and Edward Norton are the same person. As an aside about Kelly and *Fight Club*, when I pressed her to reflect on the themes of masculinity in that film, she acknowledged them, but did not care as much about them as she did the action, the fight scenes, and the surprise ending. Kelly also adds, none too surprisingly perhaps, that one of the best films she has seen in the past several years is a German action film called *Run Lola Run*, a *Roshomon*-like story about several perspectives on a robbery gone wrong and a woman running through crowded streets to save her boyfriend from crime syndicate hoods. I add "none too surprisingly" because this film is almost physically exhausting to watch, with scene after scene of German star Franka Potente (Matt Damon's costar in *The Bourne Identity* [2002], and *The Bourne Supremacy* [2004]) sprinting through the streets. This film is action film pacing distilled to its basic essence. Jane, one of the graduate student interviewees, is another big fan of this film.

But the speed and fast movement of the narrative is a constant even across gender, racial, and national lines. It was especially interesting to listen to

Charles, an eighteen-year-old undergraduate and future pharmacist, originally from Africa, talk about the exciting pleasure of the genre. When talking about why he likes the action film, he became more animated than during the discussion of any other issue. As he said, "[the action film is] more like non-stop movement, not just one setting, [not just] people moving around slowly . . . things that catch my eye . . . more fast-paced . . . things happening. . . . Flash! . . . You know, it catches my eye . . . keeps my interest."

Reading this transcription of Charles's statement cannot adequately render his feelings toward the film. One must imagine him tensing, swaying back and forth in his seat, literally balancing on the edge of his seat, speaking the phrases in sudden exclamations, his tone rising with each phrase. When saying "Flash!" he is not conveying any literal explanation of what he saw, the importance of anything flashing on the screen, say like an explosion or bright special effect, but more like giving an exclamation like "wow," except the word "flash" better conveys that sense of speed and urgency.

During the discussion with Vipul, a twenty-three-year-old college student and economics major from India, there is yet another comparison between the speed of the action film and other genres he does not enjoy as much. For Vipul, of major importance is literal speed displayed on screen, not just the pacing of the story. He likes to see fast-moving hardware on-screen, planes and cars involved in chases and combat:

> Chases, car chases, or fighter jets in the sky chasing each other or something. Or fighting, fistfights or whatever. For some reason I really like movies like that. I would say more of chasing or fighting. You know, that keeps the movie interesting, not like other movies. . . . I like aviation and automobiles, those are hobbies that interest me, so I guess that's why I like the action-packed movies.

As Carl originally mentioned, the success of entertainment hinges on the satisfaction of the need for speed. The speed, in turn, is the antidote to boredom. A film that is "boring" is diametrically opposed to the action film, it is the type of film that does not bring pleasure to the high-using action-watcher.

Even among the older male interviewees, the very rapid pacing of the stories is a requirement. As Louis, a fifty-seven-year-old physician, explains his requirements for a good action film, if the pace is allowed to slacken, he becomes physically uncomfortable to the point of wanting to walk out of the film. He states, "I like it because it's fast paced, things happen quickly and I like the movement, the quick resolutions." When I asked him how he feels when there is a lull in the action, when the pace slows down, he said, "It becomes boring. I get tired. I get stressed and restless and I want to walk out."

Louis's boredom sets in when the resolutions that are important to him are not solved through a physical confrontation, a violent confrontation, a shoot-

out that makes it clear as to who wins and who loses. On the end of a gun-
fight, like in a spaghetti western or a *Dirty Harry* film with Clint Eastwood—
Louis's favorite actor—one combatant will remain standing and another will
be dead. This brings a clear resolution to the problem, albeit not an entirely
realistic resolution as Louis readily admits, but one without the sort of ambiguity one has to deal with in real life. As far as Louis is concerned, and all
the interviewees when it comes to the issue of boredom, a film is something
to invest time in to see an idealized version of reality. In Louis's case, when
that ideal is not achieved, when a problem is not solved through action or the
pacing is not as fast and as stimulating as he would like it, his admitted short
temper and impatience gets the better of him and he is tempted, as indicated
in the comment above, to walk out of the film or change the channel. In fact,
he jokes that very frustrating movie-going experiences were those where he
would have gotten up and walked out of a film but knew his wife wouldn't
have followed him. Furthermore, on the subject of his wife's entertainment
preferences, he is ready to compare his wife's genre of choice, the soap opera, as the direct opposite of what he likes in an action film. The soap opera,
General Hospital in particular, his wife's favorite, is something he actively
"despises." When asked why, he explains:

> Because it bores me. It has no end. You begin to watch it, you begin to spend
> time on a storyline that will never have a satisfactory conclusion. Then you real-
> ize that you wasted your time and it makes you angry.

This comment is especially interesting as it confirms, in proverbial chapter and verse, what analysts of the soaps have written about the structure of
that art form and the pleasures it creates for women and the way it generally
antagonizes men.

The action fan will require entertainment that involves characters, situations, problems to be solved that are not quite what he or she will see or ever
encounter in real life, yet one that bears some reasonable resemblance to the
real world. The importance here is that a quasi-realistic world must exist in
the action film, and that the protagonist should solve a problem in a way a
real person might fantasize about but could never bring him- or herself to
actually do. This, of course, lends itself easily to a "Walter Mitty" parallel,
one that numerous actions films very explicitly draw. For example, the plot
of *Sidekicks* (1992) involves a timid, weakling teenager who idolizes Chuck
Norris and deals with every stressful situation by fantasizing what it would
be like if his hero suddenly showed up and helped him. *If Looks Could Kill*, a
sleeper hit of 1991, deals with a "typical" goof-off high school kid (played by
21 Jump Street actor Richard Grieco who looked about thirty years old) on a
class trip to France getting mistaken for a spy, then accessorized for a world-

saving mission with a weapon-loaded sports car, James Bond gadgets, and a beautiful female sidekick. Even films aimed at much younger audiences, like the *Agent Cody Banks* films (2003, 2004), the *Spy Kids* (2001, 2002, 2003) films, or the *Harry Potter* series (2001, 2002, 2004, 2005, 2007, 2009), about kids being granted immense world-saving or supernatural powers, work on this same formula. Arnold Schwarzenegger's *Last Action Hero* again has a lonely kid (Austin O'Brien) dealing with mundane situations like a boring literature class by escaping into the daydream of an action film version of Hamlet, complete with Schwarzenegger in the title role and a clever tagline describing the film ("there's something rotten in the state of Denmark, and Prince Hamlet is taking out the trash").

A more controversial edge to some action films' Walter Mitty fantasies comes when the films are giving a more exciting alternative to problems that are very close to reality, problems solved in a boring manner in the real world. Many of these films are represented by a specific action film cycle of the early 1980s, very obviously inspired by the Iranian hostage crisis and the subsequent series of kidnappings and hijackings in the Middle East, if not the very aftermath of the Vietnam War itself. Here, films such as *Iron Eagle* (1986), *Red Dawn* (1984), *The Rescue* (1986), *Invasion USA* (1985), *Death before Dishonor* (1987), *Uncommon Valor* (1983), *Missing in Action I, II, III* (1984, 1985, 1988), and *Rambo II* had more potent and final solutions to national crises than the slow-moving, boring approach of diplomacy. In each film, the "diplomatic solution" always fails, prompting teenagers to steal planes and rescue their fathers from hostile foreign nations (*Iron Eagle, The Rescue*), loners beating back an invasion (*Invasion USA, Red Dawn*), maverick soldiers rescuing hostages (*Death before Dishonor*), or disobeying the government and rescuing POWs from Vietnam (*Uncommon Valor, Missing in Action, Rambo*).

These themes of the individual, the little guy, the Walter Mitty character, achieving something important is, in some way, inspirational to each of the interviewees. Over the next several chapters the comments on their readings of films may vary, but they all agree that the victory of an action hero can be read in a metaphorical way and looked upon as an inspiration. While they each say that they do not—and claim they never have—feel inspired by an action film to get into a fight or do something dangerous, they feel the victories of the action hero suggest they, too, can achieve some personal victory in one aspect of their lives.

Proving no distinction between the female and male interviewees in this case, Helen, a fifty-three-year-old divorced mother from Montana says:

> My first thought about September 11th was we need to send Rambo over there to respond for us. I got pretty upset when I heard Barbara Walters say Hollywood would have to rethink their attitude of presenting movies like *Rambo*

and *Die Hard*. Like I said to some of my friends, who agreed, seeing our action heroes kick some terrorist butt right now would really make me feel good. . . . Lets us pretend we were that hero and that is how we would handle it.

Generally, however, each of the female interviewees enjoys the noise and the speed and the pacing as much as the men do. One thing the two genders have in common with no variation is the need for constant visual and auditory stimulation throughout the film-watching experience. Helen also adds about her film preferences:

My father was a World War II buff and a big fan of John Wayne, so I grew up on war and western movies. I grew to enjoy them as much as he did. I like the excitement and fast pace of that type of show and I enjoy watching the bad guy get beat down or blown up. My favorite TV shows were *Gallant Men*, *Combat*, *12 O'Clock High*. As well as *Have Gun, Will Travel*; *Rawhide*; and *Wagon Train*. I should probably add I am a bit of a *Star Trek* fan as well. I always found mystery and chick flicks very boring.

Just as with the men, the pleasure of constant stimulation and a hyperkinetic pace is sought by all the female interviewees, young and old, irrespective of national or racial background. For example, Cindy, a twenty-three-year-old Caucasian undergraduate, wants, just like Carl, for the film to make her forget the passage of time as she gets completely caught up in the frantic crisis situations and rapid-fire violence. "I don't want to feel like I'm watching something for two hours," she says. "I want to be more like, WOW, that's two hours? I like explosions, effects, car chases, I like blood, I like gore, I like fight scenes, especially if it's a girl kicking a guy's ass."

In turn, Selina, a twenty-year-old African American undergraduate, also says that she likes the genre because "things are blowing up. Car chases. Typical run of the mill action movie [conventions]. . . . Yeah, liked *Fast and Furious*. I don't like slow movies. I like being stimulated. Kept on my toes. I can't stand movies that just drag for no reason." When I asked her how she feels when there is a lull in the action, she explains that such a slow point would almost always mean a flaw in the plot. The action plot should be simple and self-explanatory enough so the film does not need to pause too much for exposition. "I would feel annoyed [if there was a lull in the action]. If it was too easy to figure out, like if they set up the action but go back to retell how it happened."

Once again, an interesting point about five of the thirteen female interviewees is the influence of men in their entertainment and leisure activities growing up. Although this subject pool does not lead to any conclusive statements about the issue, which is beyond the scope of the study, it does make suggestions for future study. Kelly, a nineteen-year-old undergraduate; Helen; Connie, another nineteen-year-old undergraduate; Diana, a thirty-three-year-old mother and wife of interviewee Harry; and Stephanie, a twenty-four-year-old undergraduate and full-time mortgage company employee all tell stories of being the only girl in a family full of brothers or giving in to men's demands of which films would be watched on dates. Diana, when told that she does not fit the profile of most women after having explained that her first choice for a film is an action film rather than a romantic/relationship film, replied with "well, I'm not your typical girl." She also went on to explain that she first got hooked on action films when dating in high school. Boys she would date would always want to watch action films and, in time, she came to like the films. She especially began to like the *Indiana Jones* films because she found Harrison Ford attractive.

Connie, Kelly, and Stephanie all tell similar stories of being the only girl in the family and growing up playing the competitive, aggressive sports their brothers played—including wrestling and fighting where brothers had no qualms about knocking them around, "beating the crap out of [them]" as hard as they could each other—and watching action films because those were the films the boys wanted to watch.

Helen also tells of her early family life, where her father and brother were the strongest personalities in the family. For example, they taught her how to shoot firearms. But she had almost no part in the usual "feminine" pastimes of teenage girls coming of age, like concerns over clothes and makeup because her father would not allow it. Here, her story takes a darker edge, telling of her father's domineering control over her life and forbidding a lot of social experiences:

> I wasn't allowed to wear the "in" clothes or hairstyles, my father would not allow it. No makeup, no fancy shoes, no mini skirts, which was what everyone wore back then. I wasn't allowed to have kids over to the house, they made too much noise for him. Never had a birthday party, too much trouble and expense.

However, these five women, just like the other eight who do not claim to have had the masculine influence in the development of their entertainment tastes, make a similar claim to enjoying the same fast pace of the genre.

Therefore, as research on cross-cultural violence enjoyment previously suggested, people will consume violent entertainment all over the world with equal gusto and explain that it satisfies similar needs for excitement.[8] The participants in this study represent a variety of racial, ethnic, national, and age groups and articulate the same enjoyment of fast, "action packed" stimulation. Zillmann has summarized research looking for inherent psychological and evolutionary roots for the enjoyment of viewing violent happenings, and his hypotheses for this across-the-board attraction to a violent genre like action/adventure can range from a vestige of an archaic fight-or-flight impulse to curiosity driven by a prehistoric need to remain vigilant to threats facing one's community.[9]

One influential arousal hypothesis by Berlyne claims the attraction to suspense lies in its creation of an "arousal jag."[10] This hypothesis holds that suspense melodrama is comprised of sharply rising tension, followed by moments of resolution and relief. The spikes in action Berlyne terms the "arousal jag," followed by the satisfactory release of tension.

However, I am not ready to conclude that the arousal jag hypothesis best describes the role action movies play for these interviewees. From what they are saying, it seems like true suspense, a true worry over whether or not heroes will vanquish villains or whether or not heroes will survive, is never present for these people. Especially when it comes to series films, where the same hero returns over and over again and fights even more outlandish villains, the outcome of the films is never in doubt and the viewers are never looking forward to those post-jag tension-releasing moments. From what they are saying, explaining that they are looking forward to the high points and are bored by the moments lacking tension, I am not certain this hypothesis can be best applied to this group of action viewers.

The responses the interviewees give for their fundamental enjoyment of the genre best fit theories of a segment of the population who are naturally high sensation seekers, expounded on, for one, by Zuckerman.[11] For such people, Zillmann's work further elaborates, the excitement of a violent film or program is sought out as a remedy for feelings of boredom and a lack of stimulation, an attempt to create a state of "excitatory homeostasis."[12] While there is one interviewee, nineteen-year-old Brett, an undergraduate and martial artist, who compares the physical sensations of watching an action film to the excitatory pleasures of playing sports—"I've always been an athlete, someone who's always pushing myself and I like to have my heart beating quicker, and action movies do that"—in accordance with further work by authors such as Goldstein and Guttman,[13] the sensation-seeking pursuit of action remains a constant for every action viewer, even nonathletes. However, Brett remains the only interviewee who ties his sports experiences to the action film.

Erika, twenty-one, a lifelong athlete, describing herself as a "total jock," names specific films that come to mind when asked about what she likes and what she associates with the genre. However, she does not draw parallels between the films and sports. As she replies when asked about what the genre means to her, she says:

The first thing that comes to my mind is *Live Free or Die Hard*. That is like one of the best movies because . . . well, I love Bruce Willis, number one, but, well they all kind of blend together but there are like all these explosions and car chases and this and that running around, and they're fun and exciting and they have these side plots . . . but they're fun.

A vague parallel between the *nature* of the fast-paced action film and sports is drawn by Jane, twenty-seven, a graduate student and the only interviewee who admits to having thought about the roots of her enjoyment of violence. Of course, Jane's age, education (which extends to the Ph.D. level), and undergraduate studies in psychology set her apart from the average viewer and make her more introspective than the common viewer. She claims to have been an avid boxing fan for years, but stopped following the sport seriously after the well-publicized "antics" of Mike Tyson and Don King. They made her suspect that many of the fights might be fixed. The nature of sports, to Jane, is in their unpredictability. Generally, she explains, unpredictability is at the heart of all dangerous endeavors, "sports" like the Gravity Games and X Games and such "extreme" activities, because there is the constant possibility that the participant could fail, make a mistake, and get badly hurt. However, when the "antics" of Don King begin to suggest a fix, a predetermined outcome and the elimination of chance, the sport is immediately robbed of its appeal. In her eyes, and quite contrary to a interviewee like Louis, for whom the action film is successful when it is a ritualized meeting of expectations time and again, the good action film for Jane is an anarchic and unpredictable art form, similar in nature to a dangerous sport. In her words:

> Sometimes I wonder why I watch it because I think it's barbaric, but I do like it. Sort of not knowing what the outcome will be like is what keeps me addicted. I think I'm fascinated with violent sports . . . and to give away my redneck past, like I have this cousin who used to do cockfighting. [I like watching] Gravity Games, skateboarding where they can fall down and get hurt. I like pro-wrestling. Sometimes I like the pop culture thing that everybody likes.

Patrick, Carl, and Louis put an interesting value on the speed and stimulation of the action genre that is different from all of the other interviewees. All three give it a literal, dollar value. They have a personal rating system for what their money is worth when going to the theater or renting a video. Various pleasures given by films are attached with a monetary amount and excitement is the most valuable commodity. For example, in Carl's previous statement, he alludes to going to films with certain expectations, and when he pays for an action film, something that has been sold to him through advertising, he gets upset when that bill of goods does not include the kinetic, fast-moving action he was expecting.

Louis also very clearly articulates the same sentiments when he says that "for my money, don't waste my time with drama and love stories."

Patrick, a thirty-year-old computer engineer explains that "I'm paying ten bucks to get into the theater, so I don't care about the big love story of the day. I can rent that and my wife will like that."

In fact, the romantic drama is interesting in this study because for all, except Jane and Sam, the romantic film, the "date movie" or "chick flick," is diametrically opposed to the action film. All the interviewees dislike the genre because of its lack of movement, the slow pacing, too much dialogue, and the general feeling of boredom it inspires. Jane, interestingly, says that she understands the different appeal of the romantic film and can enjoy it for what it is. To her, the film has its place and to her the "date movie" is often pleasurable as just that, something to see with a romantic partner. Sam, the twenty-seven-year-old office manager from Chicago, explains that he is a film buff, a connoisseur of film art. He likes all movies, he explains, and he can enjoy every well-made film if it meets the intended goal of the genre.

Later chapters will deal in greater detail with various interviewees' regards for expressing emotion, indicating how many action fans are averse to an inordinate display of emotions and self-disclosure. This, in some part, may account for the antipathy toward romantic films. Romantic relationships require people to lay bare most of their emotions, to make themselves the most vulnerable, and romantic films deal with the problems and pain this can cause. Action adventure, more often than not, focuses on either the subjugation of emotion or the ability to ignore pain. Every interviewee, when asked if the romantic relationships in the action film were realistic, answered in the negative. However, they all said that it should not be. In fact, in action films, romance always happens quickly. The genre is a big believer in love at first sight. A man and a woman may be thrown together by circumstances and sex follows soon afterward. There are no complications regarding courtship, communication, determining if a couple is compatible, and whether or not they have enough "chemistry" or common interests.

In the following chapter, however, another paradox will present itself as action characters and actors can be carefully differentiated as being more or less emotional and communicative. Although each female interviewee, save for Jane, expresses a dislike for romantic melodramas, all of the women interviewees will also show greater fondness for those characters and actors who are the most expressive of their emotions.

The rest of the subject pool, while not so verbal on this subject as to need direct quotation, all gave answers to the effect of "the speed," "the impact scenes," "something going on," "the fighting," "the cars and chases," or the "excitement" as to what it is they automatically associate with the action genre.

TECHNOLOGY

The male interest in technology has long been a focus of sociological and anthropological research, not to mention a very fertile ground for comedians. The action genre's connection to technology is twofold. On the one hand, it utilizes the state of the art in current filmmaking technology; animated by cutting-edge special effects, shot on the latest digital cameras, optimally displayed on the most powerful speakers, high-definition screens, and projection systems. On the other hand, action films often involve technology in their plots.

The iconography of the genre often involves the melding of the male body with military technology.[14] At one point, the 1980s action epics like the *Rambo* series or Schwarzenegger's *Commando*, *Raw Deal*, *Predator*, and *Red Heat* were dubbed the "equipment movies" because they all had a requisite sequence of the heroes arming for combat, carefully readying the "equipment." These would be quickly cut scenes of hands loading guns, sharpening knives, or preparing explosives, often catching glimpses of a flexing bicep or glistening pectorals in the background. The ultimate melding of man and machine, of course, is Schwarzenegger's *Terminator*, the male body and the machine a seamlessly integrated whole.

That masculine power and virility, especially in times of peace and order, can be projected through inanimate objects, complex, powerful, and loud machines, and has had an interesting treatment by anthropology. As Lionel Tiger writes:

> Assertive young American males spend their money adding huge tires to their barely muffled pickup trucks . . . are decisively more likely to acquire and covet stereo equipment, often the louder the better. They pursue status, including sexual status, through objects that create noise. The industrial setting provides a handy tool kit for assembling a personal style. It recalls the bower bird, who collects trinkets, glass and bits of this and that to produce a seductive nest for females choosing a partner, as he perches expectantly on his real estate.[15]

The interviewees ignore the fact that many action films' thematic treatment of technology is ambiguous. For example, the dominant message of a typical James Cameron action film would go ignored. Cameron, in numerous interviews, has explained that the theme of society's overreliance on technology is something he likes exploring.[16] While he says he does not intend to do anti-technology films, he is interested in what happens when society becomes overreliant on it and the technology eventually goes haywire or breaks down. This theme is already present in his first major film, *The Terminator*. Here, the United States places its entire nuclear arsenal under the control of a single super computer that one day becomes self-aware and malevolent. The computer starts World War III, then begins manufacturing Terminators to hunt down the surviving humans. This theme continues in *Aliens* (1986), *The Abyss* (1989), in his script for *Rambo II*, which stresses the unreliability of military technology, and, of course, in his Oscar-winning *Titanic* (1997), where faith in technology and the "unsinkable" super ship leads to disaster. His fans at large, not just the participants of this study, no doubt ignore this message.

Of all machines, cars are usually the most important to men. Jeff, a twenty-three-year-old Asian American undergraduate, Steve, a twenty-two-year-old African American undergraduate, Ray, a nineteen-year-old undergraduate, and Cliff, a twenty-three-year-old bookkeeper all indicate that they can be enticed into seeing a new film—paying theater prices because they need to see the film as soon as it opens—if impressive sports cars are central to the plot. When talking to Jeff at length about *Mission: Impossible 2*, one of his favorite action films, I tried to press him into analyzing the themes of the film as he saw them. When I asked him if there were themes in the film that were personally important to him, he very promptly replied "yes." What were the themes? "The cars." Of course, "cars" are not a theme of the film, but he places such emphasis on their importance that he names them as a "theme." From that point, he gave a very lengthy thesis on the different types of cars used in the film, their capabilities, power, speed, and so forth.

Steve is an avid *James Bond* fan. After explaining how he was drawn to Bond because of his family's roots in Jamaica, home to Ian Fleming's vacation/writing home, he predictably talked about his enjoyment and envy of Bond's gadgets and cars. For him, how much of a role a really good car plays in the plot will determine how successful or unsuccessful the film is. He explained that he was upset by *GoldenEye* because they didn't give the customized BMW enough screen time.

Ray is also an avid car fan, but less ostentatious with his taste in vehicles. His favorite car is not a BMW or Ferrari or some such exotic piece of hardware, but the more attainable Toyota Supra. Therefore, *The Fast and the Furious* films were an easy sell for him. Here the plots always involved the outlaw world of street racing. The Supra was one of the prominently featured cars.

Cliff spoke of his enjoyment of *Gone in 60 Seconds* for the similar reasons. Aside from being a fan of Nicolas Cage, he wanted to see the film because he is a sports car buff. Seeing the exotic cars up close and in action sold him on the film. However, Cliff's enjoyment of action ties the genre to technology in another important way. He enjoys playing video games. The connection between video games and action films is a natural one, with many successful action films spawning game spin-offs for decades. With a game, one can exert a degree of control over the world on the screen. There is no vulnerability, no lack of power when playing the game.

As early as the 1980s, Atari had games based on both the *Rambo* and *Indiana Jones* series. In turn, games like *Super Mario Brothers, Mortal Combat, Double Dragon*, and *Street Fighter* were turned into action films in the 1990s. *Tomb Raider*, based on the phenomenally successful *Lara Croft: Tomb Raider* video games, was one of the biggest blockbusters of the summer of 2001, and so far there have been three successful horror/action films based on the *Resident Evil* video games. For Cliff, enjoying a good video game based on a film he initially disliked can help alter his feelings about the film. He explained that he would classify the *Star Wars* films as action, and he got to enjoy and eventually become a fan of *Star Wars Episode I: The Phantom Menace* (1999) because of the video game based on the story. Initially, he was offended by the film because so many of the less-than-admirable characters seemed to have racial and ethnic associations to him:

> Most of the accents that the characters had in the movie were noticeably from different parts of the world. Like Jar Jar Binx obviously had a Jamaican, Caribbean type accent . . . and the Chancellor? . . . one of the bad guys who were behind Palpatine were definitely Asian . . . but those two especially pretty much offended me the first time I saw that because I didn't understand why he, George Lucas, would even think to do that.

Playing the video game, however, where he was cast in the role of Obi Wan Kenobi, one of the main characters, was such an enjoyable experience that it made him reconsider the film. He saw the film a few more times after getting into the video game and he started following the storyline more closely, investing more attention in the plot and characters and growing more interested in where the promised two sequels would be taking the story.

Of the female interviewees, only two, Cindy and Kelly, were vocal about technology in relation to the action genre. After Cindy got a chance to rent the first *The Fast and the Furious* film, she raved about the cars used in the racing scenes. She had originally been looking forward to seeing it because of the cars—although did not see it in its theatrical release—and she said the film more than met her expectations. She especially liked the way special effects were used to enhance the racing sequences. These were sudden zooming effects where the camera seemed to x-ray through the body of the car and show the gears and pistons in action as the vehicles were pushed to their limit or given a super-fast boost of speed from nitrous oxide canisters. Although Cindy has no actual technical knowledge of or experience working on cars, Kelly's father is a mechanic and she grew up around cars. This, she indicated, gave her an appreciation of cars in films.

One woman who did have a personal experience with automotive technology but no particular interest in seeing it on film was Stephanie. Her father owns a garage and a junkyard and she grew up watching her father and brothers work on cars all the time. The equipment, technology, and cars in films hold no particular interest for her, however.

Only one of the female interviewees is a video game fan. Kathleen, a twenty-five-year-old college student in Wisconsin, is an avid video gamer, but not a particular fan of very gory action games. Although she had played the popular and controversial shooter's-point-of-view games like *Doom*, she is the biggest fan of *Final Fantasy*, the name of which was given to a computer-animated feature film in the summer of 2001. Although, she explained, the film had nothing to do with the game, she enjoyed both, but not because the film had that loose connection to her favorite game.

ACTION AS ART FORM

Sam, the self-described film buff who has taken film courses in a small college in his hometown explains that he is always mindful of the "classics" in action/adventure cinema. He calls Kurosawa's *Seven Samurai* one of the "quintessential" action films and appreciates the special touches Steven Spielberg brings to the *Indiana Jones* films. At the same time, he said that he stayed away from many of the major action releases of the past several years because too many things were retreads and repeats of ideas and formulas used before. In his words:

> New ideas are important. The recent films are cookie cutter films. Nothing is new. Pretty much a rehashing of everything that's come before.

What is important to understand throughout this work is that active action viewers like my interviewees have various qualitative scales and standards that guide the way they pick and choose among the action fare they will consume. As much as they like the speed and excitatory rush they get from the chases and explosions and shootouts, they will not indiscriminately watch just *anything* that contains violence. Very few mention directors they are fans of, and most say they are fans of specific stars. When speaking of action directors, the most prominent one specializing in an excessive over-the-top style of action is Hong Kong director John Woo, and he is the only one referred to by a few of the interviewees. Jeff, Vin, Sam, Dirk, and David are the ones who actively follow his work. But when it comes to actors, an active action viewer will prefer to see a Mel Gibson action film or an Arnold Schwarzenegger or a Sylvester Stallone film, rather than surf channels on television looking for a car crash or go to the video store and hone in on the racks of the action films. There are exceptions, of course, like Louis who will—with tongue in cheek, as if knowing that his responses will raise eyebrows—say that he used to go to the video stores and ignore everything but the action films. However, even he will say that he would always prefer to see a Clint Eastwood action film or, to a lesser degree, a Charles Bronson film. Thus, while these people have their attentions captured by the violence and mayhem of an action trailer, they know which films are the best and which ones are the worst examples of the genre.

Much like Sam, Brad, a twenty-three-year-old film student from Vancouver, explains that a very good contemporary action film will have the similar marks of a great filmmaker that a lot of classic cinema had. On his Web page devoted to *First Blood*, he displays essays he has written comparing the styles of Hitchcock and Kurosawa to *First Blood* director Ted Kotchef. He is a devoted Sylvester Stallone fan, explaining that Stallone's appeal to him lies in how Stallone seems more larger than life than other action heroes, but, at the same time, real enough to be believable. For example, he states "I was watching *Die Hard with a Vengeance* a while ago, and there is a shot where Bruce Willis is slammed against a metal grate underground. If Stallone was doing this, he would have let out a yelp of pain so sharp that we, the audience, would feel it too." He adds: "The primary thing that makes his films superior to any other films . . . is simply based on realism."

However, neither Brad nor any of the other interviewees are uncritical when it comes to their favorite stars. Brad, for example, does not devote a Web page to the second, third, or fourth installments in the *Rambo* series, which, in his opinion, do not measure up to the perfect balance of realism and hyperbole of the first one.

To each interviewee, just the correct shades of realism are important in action films. The sentiment is unanimous that action films are becoming too reliant on special effects. Even as they feel exhilarated by the speed, they all agree that the explosions, stunts, and special effects can overwhelm a film. Even the fans of technology can be pushed beyond their threshold when all character and humanity seem to disappear from a film.

Such is the very interesting case of Steve and the *James Bond* series. As mentioned before, Steve admires the BMW and looked forward to both *GoldenEye* and *The World Is Not Enough* because Bond drove the latest model BMW sports car. To quote him accurately, he says he has a "fetish" for the BMW. When the car was not featured as prominently as he would have liked in *GoldenEye*, however, he was upset and felt the film suffered because of it. When asked to give his impressions of the series overall, he argues that the newer *Bond* films are not as good as the classic entries with Sean Connery.

A big problem, he explains, lies in the stunts, special effects, and technology. "Too much technology," he says. "Too much explosions. You can't really follow the story because you get lost in all the action."

Overall, for an active action viewer, the films need to be *about* something. Although the following chapters will deconstruct the entire meaning-making process of the action film, it is sufficient to mention here that its devotees see the genre as art because it speaks to the human condition when crafted successfully. For example, Kathleen explains that in her eyes the action genre is about the measure of a person and how many challenges he can meet head on. "After entertainment, the depth of it is whether or not humans can rise to the occasion of these extraordinary, although fictitious, events."

This thematic analysis is very similar to Victor's, who explains that the good action film "is generally about a normal person who finds him- or herself placed in an extraordinary situation. They must overcome great odds in the face of adversity to resolve whatever conflict they face."

Something else that is common to all the interviewees but summed up well by Edward, the forty-seven-year-old former police officer and carpenter, is the idea that not only should the films, in part, show an ideal on screen, but they should also depict it in a way that the viewer can relate to. He explains:

> My test for good movies: some movies I've gone to and halfway through I even forget I am at a movie because it's almost like I'm living the experience of this person on the screen or they have something in common with or touches on something that I've done or experienced. Not just all this blowing up or somebody shoots a car with a bullet and the hood flies off—'cause that just doesn't happen—I think that's kind of insulting to somebody's intelligence.

David, a twenty-five-year-old physics graduate student, adds to this, explaining that even explicit, if not gratuitous, acts of violence need to be part of a meaningful whole for the viewing experience to be worthwhile:

> Also for certain types of films, they contain a form of mindful violence, rather than mindless violence. Like an action flick where people are just randomly killed for the sake of killing are rather dull. But when they're dealing with . . . when violence is justified or when it's necessary, or are there situations where there are no other options?

Interestingly, this aspect of reality is what all the interviewees attribute to their favorite actors and will argue is lacking in other major action stars. As Brad's comments demonstrate, he is a Stallone fan primarily because he sees Stallone as playing realistic characters. He does not much care for Schwarzenegger because his physique is so extreme that it takes away from the suspense of his films. As Brad sees it, there does not seem to be any danger that can be threatening enough for someone of Schwarzenegger's brawn to overcome. In his words, "in Schwarzenegger movies he is so large that virtually anything he does is done easily, where we will often see Stallone red in the face using every ounce of strength he has to accomplish something."

Louis, who several times stresses the fact that he is "fanatical" about Clint Eastwood and usually finds himself imagining how much better any other action film would be with Eastwood, explains that there is a "naturalness" about Eastwood that lets him relate to his characters in a way he cannot relate to other action heroes. There is nothing that Eastwood could do, he explains, that would look unrealistic or contrived. This is important for a successful action film in his opinion. In fact, he says that he does not consider Schwarzenegger a real action hero but more of a comedian. Aside from comedy, for him another grave offense for an action actor is showing too much "arrogance." For this reason, he explains that he does not like Stallone:

> There's this arrogance about him. I get this sense that he is looking down on everyone. I think it has to do with his mouth. There's this arrogant set in his mouth, like he's sneering at everyone because they're less than he is, inferior to him.

Anthony, a twenty-eight-year-old business executive, who is just about as devoted to Schwarzenegger as Louis is to Eastwood, also makes a comparison with Stallone and claims that he cannot take most Stallone action films seriously. All but *Rambo II*, he says, are so extremely "overdone" that he cannot relate to them. He *can* relate to Schwarzenegger, however, because of his—Anthony's—own unyielding devotion to working out. Stallone's physique and body-centered image, however, cannot turn Anthony into a fan because the unreality of his films overrides what admiration he might have for Stallone's bodybuilding regimen. When I press him about all the humor and comedy in Schwarzenegger films, he counters by explaining that he likes "Arnold's sense of humor" and that the movies are just fun.

All of the interviewees, in fact, when asked to discuss their favorite action actors, will ultimately qualify their fandom by claiming their favorite actor is in some way realistic and the actor's rivals are not.

An interesting point in the artistry of the action film must be made about the fans of the martial arts. Since a number of interviewees practice the martial arts—Ken, Dirk, David, Patrick, Cliff, Brett, Edward, and Ray—they are all interested in seeing various styles represented in film.

As David explains, being a black belt in ninjutsu, a green belt in jujitsu, as well as having tried various other arts over the years, he likes to watch martial artists on screen as a technician. This approach holds true for all the other practitioners. David's favorite artist is Jackie Chan, whose on-screen moves and stunts he finds "simply amazing." When I question him about how Chan's on-screen work is really more choreographed acrobatics than real martial arts, he explains that he is still impressed by the skill it takes to pull it all off. A very negative reaction can be elicited from David, however, when Steven Seagal is mentioned. I was interested in pressing this point because Seagal's publicity has often stressed the fact that he is one of the highest-ranking practitioners of aikido, that he trained for years in Japan, and was one of the most sought-out instructors of the art before turning to acting. Seagal was also infamous, at one point, for circulating rumors about having been a CIA agent and a counterterrorism expert. All of this annoys David, who points out that someone who knows martial arts well would recognize how Seagal's on-screen moves are not that realistic after all and that the CIA rumors are just silly:

> I don't like that attitude he has. He has scenes where he walks into bars and gets into big fights completely unarmed. That's just unrealistic. In real life he would be killed. Then he keeps using those wristlocks which are actually very difficult to do.

I asked him if Jackie Chan isn't even more unrealistic, and he replied, "But with Jackie there's no pretense to reality."

As a whole, Jackie Chan was the most popular martial artist for this subject pool. Jeff, who is of Asian ancestry and a fan of Hong Kong cinema, explained that he has been a long-time fan of Jet Li, the Chinese actor who was discovered by American audiences after appearing in *Lethal Weapon 4*. Li's first American-produced film, however, was badly marred for Jeff by the taint of computerized special effects. In *Romeo Must Die*, computer effects, which made the appearance of all the fighting sequences look very conspicuously fake, enhanced Li's moves. As Jeff explains:

> I can't understand why they would do that. He's one of the best martial artists in the world. He's like straight out of the temple. The computer effects take all of his real skills away.

SUMMARY

For the active viewer of the action/adventure film, the experience of the genre includes a number of basic pleasures it can bring to a viewing experience. To begin with, these people all appear to be the high sensation-seeking personalities expounded on by previous psychological research. However, as can be seen in the case of a number of the female interviewees, this high sensation-seeking drive may appear, upon first glance, to be a trait that can be conditioned in a person. These women enjoy action films today because this genre was primarily available to them growing up. They, just like all the other interviewees, explain that slower films are not stimulating enough, and they feel bored without the relentless pacing of action/adventure.

For a high sensation-seeking individual turning to films or television, the effort of sitting still in front of a screen can quickly lead to boredom and restlessness. The interviewees indicate that they will easily stop concentrating on a film unless the plot starts dealing with extreme life and death suspense. The fast-moving narratives, frantic excitement, and overwhelming visual spectacles that are the staple of action films are what hold the attention of such people and keep them stimulated.

At the same time, true fans of the genre will approach this entertainment with a discerning eye. They look at it as an art form. Many will have favorite directors whose work and style interests them. They all have favorite actors they feel they can relate to on some level. They will be looking for plots and themes that, on a metaphorical level, will attempt to make sense of some aspect of life.

As the following chapters illustrate, looking at a high action-user's relationship to the genre helps to make further sense of their own identities within an ever more complex modern social structure.

NOTES

1. Jib Fowles, *The Case for Television Violence* (Thousand Oaks, CA: Sage, 1999), 132.

2. Good examples of media reception and the uses and gratifications process can be seen in the following works: Karl Eric Rosengren, Lawrence A. Wenner, and Philip Palmgreen, *Media Gratifications Research: Current Perspectives* (Thousand Oaks, CA: Sage, 1985); Jennings Bryant and Dolf Zillmann, *Responding to the Screen: Reception and Reaction Processes* (Mahwah, NJ: Lawrence Erlbaum, 1991).

3. Mark Kermode, "I Was a Teenage Horror Fan: Or, How I Learned to Stop Worrying and Love Linda Blair," in *Ill Effects: The Media/Violence Debate* eds. Martin Barker and Julian Petley (New York: Routledge, 2001), 129.

4. Kermode, "I Was a Teenage Horror Fan," 130.

5. Horace Newcomb and Paul M. Hirsch, "Television as a Cultural Forum" in *Television: The Critical View* ed. Horace Newcomb (New York: Oxford University Press, 2000), 561–573.

6. Annette Hill, *Shocking Entertainment: Viewer Response to Violent Movies* (Luton: University of Luton Press, 1997), 1.

7. Yvonne Tasker, *Spectacular Bodies: Gender, Genre and the Action Cinema* (New York: Routledge, 1993), 6.

8. Dolf Zillmann, "The Psychology of the Appeal of Portrayals of Violence," in *Why We Watch: The Attractions of Violent Entertainment*, ed. Jeffrey H. Goldstein (Oxford: Oxford University Press, 1998), 179–211.

9. Zillmann, "The Psychology of the Appeal of Portrayals of Violence."

10. D. E. Berlyne, *Conflict, Arousal, and Curiosity* (New York: McGraw-Hill, 1960).

11. Marvin Zuckerman, *Sensation Seeking: Beyond the Optimal Level of Arousal* (Hillsdale, NJ: Lawrence Erlbaum, 1979).

12. Zillmann, "The Psychology of the Appeal of Portrayals of Violence," 110.

13. Jeffrey Goldstein, "Why We Watch," in *Why We Watch: The Attractions of Violent Entertainment*, 212–226; Allen Guttmann, "The Appeal of Violent Sports," in *Why We Watch: The Attractions of Violent Entertainment*, 7–26.

14. This issue is discussed by Susan Jeffords, *Hard Bodies: Hollywood Masculinity in the Reagan Era* (New Brunswick, NJ: Rutgers University Press, 1993) and Mark Gallagher, "I Married Rambo: Spectacle and Melodrama in the Hollywood Action Film," in *Mythologies of Violence in Postmodern Media*, ed. Christopher Sharrett (Detroit: Wayne State University Press, 1999), 199–226.

15. Lionel Tiger, *The Decline of Males* (New York: St. Martin's Griffin, 1999), 198.

16. Two good biographies of James Cameron are: Christopher Heard, *Dreaming Aloud: The Life and Films of James Cameron* (Toronto: Doubleday Canada Limited, 1998) and Mark Shapiro, *James Cameron: An Unauthorized Biography of the Filmmaker* (Los Angeles: Renaissance Books, 2000).

5

Mirror Image: Finding a Personal, Social, and Moral Identity in the Action Film

What does it take to change the nature of a man?

—Steven Seagal, *On Deadly Ground*

Contrary to the criticism of the fans of violent entertainment, asserting that the viewer performs little critical and analytical activity, speaking to the fans about the meaning of their favorite films reveals an ongoing attempt at the negotiation of identity, personal experiences, and values with the narratives of the films. How the men and women of this subject pool talk about the action film, or sometimes how they try not to talk about certain aspects, begins to appear, upon close scrutiny, to be interestingly gendered.

Talking to the study participants about how they see their lives and identities reflected in some metaphorical way through the narratives of the genre provided information that led me to divide the chapter into two sections. Asking them why the action film interested them, why the stories of this particular genre appealed to them more than other forms of entertainment, the participants attempted to explain that such films reflect the world as they see it. The social and political relations in the movies, they feel, are accurate representations of the real world, and the narratives revolve around an examination of value systems and questions of morality that is important to them. However, as the participants spoke, I began to recognize patterns of discourse that reflect issues at the heart of the gender and masculinity crisis debate. The first section of this chapter, therefore, reflects the moral orientation of the genre as some of the participants see it. How viewers identify with favorite films and favorite action actors, in the second section, demonstrates the extent to which various men and women feel comfortable *discussing* issues of identity, power, gender relations, and emotional vulnerability—all thematic concerns beneath the hyperbolic confrontation and contention of the action film. The male discomfort with disclosure, with admitting weakness, and allegiance with action stars who try to enact the same type of indestructible masculinity in real life is noteworthy.

VALUES IN ACTION

Although it is true that the fans are looking for an excitement arousal from the scenes of confrontation and destruction, violence alone does not create a pleasurable viewing experience. In great part, my interviewees seem to be in agreement with film critics who insist that special effects technology is gutting films of important plot and character elements. The technology of the action cinema is certainly appreciated by all of the interviewees, however, a lot of pointed remarks made it clear that it needs to share the film's time with plot and theme. The very meaningful narratives and statements they look for in the action film get lost when the special effects technology begins to overwhelm the story. As Dirk, the book editor, comments on the *James Bond* films he has loved since childhood, the first thing he would do to the films in a perfect world, if he could be granted some control over them, is to slash about half the budget of each of the new films. This, he feels, would force the filmmakers to put more interesting dialogue on the screen, more of the meaning and more of the characterization that had originally appealed to him in the *Bond* series.

Cliff, a twenty-three-year-old college graduate and bookkeeper, was one of the interviewees who was most verbal about the representations of personal identity and values in the archetypal action/adventure narrative, especially during our discussion of *The Matrix*, *Gladiator*, and the *Crocodile Dundee* films, all favorites from his youth. For him, the dramatization of the ideal male hero has to be linked to a code of honor that the hero is able to rise to, a code of moral conduct he devotes himself to no matter the obstacles stacked in his way.

In our lengthy conversation about *Gladiator*, with which he was very impressed, especially its bucking of many action film conventions, including expectations of a happy ending, he explained that the film's main appeal lay in its acknowledgment of the most universal concerns over justice. Looking at the hero's dilemma of being a wrongly accused man, he could see a larger-than-life reflection of some personal life experiences.

> Well, I've been wrongly accused, a lot of times, and he [the film's hero, Maximus] had to come back to prove himself and all of that. I don't have that, so I

think he had it a little better than me sometimes . . . [laughter] because sometimes I can't prove myself and the way he did . . . he got to prove himself.

The action film to Cliff, in general, is a morality play negotiating reflections of reality and images of an ideal world and the ideal behavior of people
trying to find the best in themselves. What makes a greater impact on Cliff
than the story of a person being able to overcome some epic obstacle—what
I assumed would be the case—is the story of a hero fighting to achieve a personal goal to be a better man. That better man, according to Cliff's standards,
is very close to the hero archetype in Joseph Campbell's famous comparative
mythology studies; a hero apotheosized by his road of struggles, ultimately
becoming a role model and servant for the greater social good.[1] For Cliff,
in fact, the idea of the hero being apotheosized into a better man, it must be
stressed, can be literally interpreted that such a moral man is a better *man*.
The ideal model of heroic masculinity, for Cliff, includes a man with a code
of honor and ethics superior to those of the average individual.

As I attempted to further gauge his impressions of Maximus (Russell
Crowe) and his fight to overcome injustice, Cliff insisted on turning the
conversation to *The Matrix*, explaining that perhaps that film's hero fighting
a constructed reality, a hegemonic computer's creation of a false consciousness, is something closer to a couple of personal realizations about how life
and experience are always relative. In his words:

> The whole movie was pretty much about computers and the whole world was
> within the computer. And, you know, it turns out that people really, the life that
> people think is real, is really within the computer. I found in my life that there's
> always something underneath.

The part of the film that explains how the deprogramming process could
only be tried on people up until a certain age made an impression on Cliff. In
the film, an expository sequence has hero Keanu Reeves receiving a tutorial
about the world as it truly exists after being awakened from his computer-
fed dream life. He is shown how humans are genetically engineered to be
bio-cells for a giant computer that has taken over the world. Feeding off the
energy created by living bodies, the computer, in turn, stimulates the brains of
its human batteries by implanting images about the lives they are living. According to Reeves' mentor (Laurence Fishburne), the system created by the
Matrix computer is such a perfect illusion "that people will fight to the death
to protect it." The mental connection to the computer can be broken while
people are young, but over time the program becomes so strong that its hold
can never be broken. Revolution, even against a computer overlord, is best
achieved by the young and idealistic.

When I asked Cliff to explain this in personal terms, he said:

> To me that totally makes sense, because if you believe something for so long and you find out that's not true, you still hang on to the way you used to think and think it's pretty much true, so I think a lot of things in the world are like that. Like [when] I found out that the quality of my high school education, how horrible it was . . . and the approach my high school texts came from were not wrong, but just not right. So I noticed that, in *The Matrix* it kind of helps you see stuff like that.

Asking him if the struggle of the Reeves character to fight such an overwhelming adversary, just like the hero of *Gladiator* taking on the emperor of Rome, is what makes the genre enjoyable, Cliff clarified that the struggle itself was not what made the films interesting. What is important in a good film, he insists, are the ends to which the heroes apply their victories. In both films, not only do the heroes win, but it is suggested that their triumphs will be leading to the downfall of an unjust system. This victory for the greater good is what Cliff terms the "hero aspect."

> What I mean is . . . the hero aspect. I would say that's more me. I would rather aspire to be the one that's helping people than, than more than I do in real life. Like I see those movies and it kind of makes me feel better because they help me see an episode where someone is helping do something that helps other people and I think to myself, you know, that's not so far fetched and maybe I can do some of that myself.

In fact, the most remarkable part of Cliff's interview is his attribution of the development of a personal set of values to the action genre. This admission came in our discussion of how realistic and how idealized endings of films can be. Here *Crocodile Dundee* came up in the discussion, a film Cliff enjoyed a lot when he saw it on television as a child, and a film where blue-collar romanticism is pitted against upper-class cynicism. In the course of the film, a protagonist (Paul Hogan) of no considerable material wealth, but an ample stock of charisma and action hero attributes of bravery, loyalty, and physical toughness, vies for the affections of a beautiful woman (Linda Kozlowski) engaged to a smarmy, pretentious business executive (Mark Blum). Naturally, the film concludes with the woman realizing that the salt-of-the-earth action hero is the better man. On the one hand, Cliff's own affinity for physical, adventurous outdoor activities like diving, the martial arts, and weight lifting made him immediately identify with Crocodile Dundee, but the film's criticism of pretentious, superficial material acquisition well jibed with his own value systems. He explains:

Even though she was in love with the rich man, she sees a different life and sees she wasn't happy with a life like that [materialism], that it was more superficial, like it was just about money. Like maybe being with the bushman she realizes that life could be more than money. Which I think is true and I don't really care that much about making money. I think I would rather do something else in life . . . 'cause most of the time when you make a fortune, you can't spend it because you're busy making the money, so it's a vicious circle like that.

When I ask him what general value systems he sees in action films, he replies:

It's interesting because I think I got my moral set from the movies. I grew up with the action movies, so I think the movies pretty much taught me that. Just general ideas like you help out others. That someone should help out those who are less fortunate.

These comments from Cliff are interesting because it might beg one to ask about his family life and upbringing. Although Cliff explains that his parents were divorced, he claims that they shared custody of him and he took turns living with both. However, he also said that he used to live a lot with his grandmother.

Cliff's analysis of and comments about *Crocodile Dundee* help illustrate the anthropological and sociological interest in aggressive entertainment and its implication for power and self-assertion among males in the postindustrial society. Especially when it comes to the issue of a man's attempts at securing positions of status, power, and reproductive opportunities, *Crocodile Dundee*'s class warfare for the affections of a woman is a perfect demonstration of the eminence/dominance dichotomy and the male paths to power. As civilized society works at orienting itself away from physical approaches to the attainment of power within the community, this theoretical dichotomy attempts to understand how the attainment of wealth and intellectual prestige become a male's path to a position of dominance and prime reproductive opportunities. The *Crocodile Dundee* plot clearly demonstrates that the postindustrial, information-based society (the woman for whose affections the bushman hero vies works for a major magazine, and her yuppie suitor is likewise of the media/information business sector—one of the magazine's top executives) makes the "eminent" executive the logical choice as a spouse for the female, while the physical bushman is a comic, disoriented outsider in the middle of New York City's overwhelming modernity. However, the film appeals to Cliff because it becomes a critique of the logical implications of the eminence/dominance dichotomy; the plot imposes morality upon the theoretical framework and suggests a higher standard by which a suitor's worthiness for female affection should be decided. The bushman might be a low-class throwback, but such intangible moral and ethical constructs as bravery, honesty, decency, and unpretentiousness prove a superior choice to the material, economic eminence of the yuppie magazine executive.

The "morality" of Crocodile Dundee, contrasted to the materialism of the yuppie competition for the woman's affection, is represented in a series of personality traits the two men possess. There is an egalitarian, populist appeal in Mick "Crocodile" Dundee's character. When he is introduced in the Australian Outback, his social circles include a pub full of rough-hewn, working-class types. In the wilderness, he is the honorary member of an Aboriginal tribe. Once he gets to New York, however, he is still able to move from one social circle to the next with ease and graciousness. He has no prejudices toward anyone, even as the woman journalist's high-class relatives and acquaintances treat him like a bumpkin. Of course, this is not the case with the magazine executive fiancé. As Cliff explained, this character is acquisitive for the sole sake of collecting money and social status. His impending marriage to the female lead itself is mildly suspect: as the woman's father owns the magazine, he might merely be seeking the marriage to gain more status and increase his power at the magazine. Dundee, of course, harbors no such ambitions and falls in love with the woman for her intelligence and self-reliance as she had impressed him early in the film by being able to hold her own in the dangerous Outback.

Cliff's comments are interestingly echoed by Steve, who explains that the action genre in general, aside from his enjoyment of and preference for the *James Bond* movies, is one he likes because there is a vein of reality in it that one can relate to, especially when it comes to its value systems. He explains that the outlandish and extreme plots of the *Bond* films are still a fairly recognizable rendering of the real world, especially real world problems like wars, terrorism, and government and big business corruption. However, when he explains that in seeing a "realistic" character like Bond—meaning realistic in the sense that he does not have superpowers and is not an alien or a robot or some such science-fictional entity—the films give that reassurance that real people can do what is right in the real world and that the real world's threatening problems can likewise be solved. Thus, for Steve, the ultimate manhood of the James Bond character is once again tied to his moral code.

James Bond is especially an important figure in this analysis, and why his fans enjoy watching his exploits is an important consideration. While fan community scholarship has previously focused on Bond devotees and shown a sizable female faction, that series does not have the female constituency among the participants of this study. The men who like Bond, among these interviewees, Steve and Dirk are the most avid fans, talk about the predictable cathartic enjoyment and fantasy-fulfillment pleasures of watching a character like Bond. Bond could almost be classified as the most extreme representation of all the classic masculine traits. Bond even contains both ends of the eminence/dominance dichotomy; he is someone who embodies both high-class, refined eminence *and* physical dominance. Bond is both well educated—several films in the series mention his Eton pedigree—and good with his fists in a fight. He is an erudite commentator on all things high culture like art, fine alcohol and food, state-of-the art cars and motorboats, *and* he appears to be an expert on an incredible range of weaponry, proficient in hand-to-hand combat, and unflinching when the situation calls for violence. When talking about the genre's depiction of masculinity, Dirk, in fact, admits that seeing such masculine perfection provides all the thrills of a typical *Bond* film. The ideal male, according to these films, in Dirk's words, is "an old fashioned and stereotypical [model]. A real man is handsome, wants sex and goes after it, handles himself well in a fight, drives well and has a sports car." Naturally, most of the *Bond* fans, Dirk adds, are men who do not and probably never will have most of these qualities. He displays his encyclopedic knowledge of *Bond* history and trivia by talking about Ian Fleming's relationship with 007, explaining that *Bond*'s own creator readily admitted that his hero was something even he couldn't ever live up to, a fantasy figure he would have liked to have been. "James Bond," Dirk tells, "is Ian Fleming times 100." Bond, actually, is about any of his fans times 100, if not more. So, through watching Bond, they can identify for about two hours with the perfect male they wish they could become.

Quite uncannily, however, Dirk does make claim to a number of Bond-like qualities. He makes his living through a pair of "eminent" professions; he works for the library system of a major Midwestern university, and he occasionally works as a book editor. He has studied various martial arts, often partakes in national martial art conventions and tournaments, likes outdoor activities like hiking and white water rafting, and he has served in the army special forces.

For Dirk, however, just as for Steve, or Cliff and his favorite action films, Bond's ultimate appeal is in his heroism. James Bond always rises to the most incredible challenges and takes on epic evil time and time again. He readily confirms Lycett's summary of the Bond character as being a decadent man who in a time of crisis is always able to make the morally correct choice and fight against the forces of evil.[2] In fact, when I discuss other forms of action entertainment with Dirk, he speaks very enthusiastically of his fandom of Asian martial arts and action films, especially John Woo's films involving baroque codes of honor and conduct among men locked in mortal combat. "In the John Woo films," he says, "there is always a strong message about what it is to be a man or what two men owe to each other. The bond between them. There is a good sense of honor among men." His favorite Hong Kong action star is John Woo repertory company regular Chow Yun Fat, who made his mark in the United States with *The Replacement Killers* (1997), starring with Mira Sorvino, *The Corruptor* (1998), with Mark Wahlberg, *Anna and the King* (1999), with Jody Foster, and in the third installment of the *Pirates of the Caribbean* (2007) films. Dirk explains that he has always seen Chow Yun Fat as the Chinese Sean Connery, a suave Bond-like ultra male.

Each of these interviewees' words, in turn, confirm Neal Gabler's analysis of the psychological and social appeal of archetypal action heroes and comic book characters, talking about how a hero's likability is rooted not only in his power, but also in the way that power is directed into action for a greater good:

> This idea . . . taps into one of the deepest satisfactions of moviegoing. Hollywood movies invariably celebrate individualism. Indeed, the star system is a tribute to it. But what makes a hero truly heroic—and what gives the audience its kick—is not simply that he stands alone. Villains, after all, often stand alone. It is that he deploys his individualism for the larger good, which is how the movies reconcile the American problem of self and society. Superman, Batman and now Spider-Man, not to mention John Wayne, Arnold Schwarzenegger and the Rock, are all nonpareil individuals who serve the community and do what in movies the community itself seems incapable of doing—namely, acting. Or put another way, they are both cool and good.[3]

I also mentioned to each participant that sometimes we can learn a lot about what someone likes by understanding what they strongly dislike. I asked them what types of action heroes they do not like or when do they see the protagonist of an action film badly written or rendered. Although almost all interviewees indicated in some form that a bad action hero is one who is unrealistically one dimensional, poorly individuated by the writers, or badly performed by an actor they dislike, Edward, a forty-seven-year-old carpenter and former Chicago policeman, and David a twenty-five-year-old graduate student, rate action heroes poorly if they feel that the hero's moral bearings and value systems are faulty. Both men indicate that it is correct to claim the action hero is a model of masculinity. However, they both say that for their personal enjoyment, the model of superior masculinity is ultimately defined by the hero's character, rather than physical abilities, toughness, or skills in delivering violence. Since both men are martial artists, Edward a black belt in hapkido and an assistant instructor in a Chicago area *dojo*, or school, and David is a black belt in ninjutsu, their very intense dislike of martial arts action hero Steven Seagal is fascinating and telling. It is especially noteworthy that both men feel that Seagal himself, the actor, possesses some serious character flaws that make it impossible to like the fictional characters he plays.

Edward says he cannot watch actors who appear to be too arrogant on screen, posturing and pretentious to the extent of displaying bad character. Interestingly, this is similar to Louis's dislike of Sylvester Stallone because of a perceived "arrogance." In Edward's case, the antipathy felt for Seagal stems from Edward's own training in the martial arts. Edward often tries to travel to Japan and Asia as much as his job schedule and finances allow, always with the aim of training with the top instructors in his art. Given this fact, I was surprised to hear how much he dislikes Seagal, especially since the standard format of Seagal's biography always includes information on how he moved to Japan as a teenager to study aikido with the masters and became the first Westerner to run a *dojo* in that country. Edward, however, focuses on arrogance he sees in Seagal, something that, in his perception, is inherent to Seagal's personality and seems to come through in all of his performances. This, in Edward's opinion, is counter to the values of the martial arts, against the values he is compelled to live by as an artist and the values he teaches his students. Edward readily backs up his perception of Seagal's arrogance by displaying a surprising level of pop culture literacy. He explains that he has read a lot of information confirming Seagal's character. Entertainment journalism, along the lines of programming like *Entertainment Tonight* or publications like *Entertainment Weekly*, has long run stories of Seagal's "difficult" personality and domineering behavior on film sets. The breakup of Seagal's second marriage was especially offensive to Edward. Seagal's marriage to model Kelly LeBrock, with whom he costarred in his second film *Hard to Kill* (1989), was tabloid filler for a while in 1996, due to LeBrock's claims of Seagal's blatant infidelity and physical abuse.

Second on Edward's list of disliked action stars is Stallone. Again, he senses pretentiousness and arrogance in Stallone. Edward is able, once again, to quote "behind the scenes" information about Stallone and the making of his films, and will quickly talk about how Stallone's films always need to exaggerate his height, to create a large on-screen image of an otherwise small (five foot seven inches) man.

Much like Edward, David explains that the martial arts are more than physical combat skills, but a value system for life. As I myself have trained with David in the same jujitsu *dojo*, I can personally attest to the value system aspect of the training. Here, rank advancements include a lengthy interview with the instructor, with the student explaining why he (or she) feels he should be granted a higher rank because he has improved morally and spiritually through the physical training regimen. Good martial arts films, as good action films in general, in David's opinion, are "mindful" rather than mindless, hopefully reflecting on some of the value systems he holds to be important. The interesting thing about David's application of martial arts values to action films is how his sentiments about Steven Seagal are almost identical to Edward's. Just like Edward, David dislikes Seagal's "arrogance" and is irritated by how Seagal "seems to think of himself as a god." "The martial arts," David explains, "should make you more humble."

While much has been made about postviewing sensations of aggressive feelings getting stoked, it is interesting how someone like Cliff explains that the identification he feels with the heroic men who do good and champion the causes of the underdogs and the weak, in turn, give him a good feeling after leaving the film. When recalling how he watched the *Superman* films—the 1978 and 1980 versions, both loaded with ample destruction—when he was young, he speaks of feeling pleasure at seeing idealism and heroism triumph. This is reminiscent of what has been termed the "moral monitoring" of a film narrative and its characters, with the viewer making judgments about the fates deserved by various characters throughout the story and enjoying sensations of suspense, as he will want to see a desirable outcome to the plot.[4] Although research has dealt with the short-lived aggression boost in some people after they had just seen a violent film, Cliff's testimony details an interesting postviewing effect to consider in the study of how the cognitive process is affected by a film.

How the high users of action talk about their favorite films, their favorite stars, and, essentially, what they are willing to say about each and how these fictional works fit into their lives can provide a glimpse inside people's personality and how comfortable they are talking about the heady emotions the action film deals with. All drama ultimately deals with conflict, but the action/adventure genre cuts to the core of issues like power and powerlessness, physical and emotional vulnerability, and values of right and wrong, good and evil. As the following section demonstrates, the films and actors certain people may gravitate toward can often reveal how much these interviewees are comfortable with acknowledging the importance and impact these issues have on their lives and identities.

As another reflection on the state of current action films, if not cinema in general, and the way films appear to be overwhelmed by technology and special effects, is the list of important action actors the interviewees chose to talk about. Even today, among many of the youngest interviewees who are in their late teens and twenties, the top action stars identified are the ones that came into prominence in the 1970s and 1980s: Clint Eastwood, Sylvester Stallone, Arnold Schwarzenegger, Bruce Willis, Harrison Ford, and Mel Gibson. Although a new generation of men with solid acting abilities are making action films in the 1990s and the millennium era, Nicolas Cage,

Keanu Reeves, Brad Pitt, Tom Cruise, Russell Crowe, Hugh Jackman, Vin Diesel, Matt Damon, and Ben Affleck being the most prominent ones, they are still not the first ones mentioned by the majority when asked to talk about the action stars that mean the most to them. One reason for this could be the fact that the Stallone- and Schwarzenegger-generation action films are readily available on television and are still being rerun with great frequency. The Turner basic cable networks, TNT and TBS, have a line of films they term the "Modern Classics" that are often run, among them the 1980s action films, such as the *Rambo*, *Indiana Jones*, *Die Hard*, *Lethal Weapon*, and *Terminator* series. But perhaps another reason the younger generation action heroes are not cited as all-time favorites might be because most of the new action stars do not have a strong signature action role yet, none of them have a *Rambo-* or *Terminator*-statured iconic character automatically associated with them, or because they do not do action films with great consistency. Of this new generation, only Hugh Jackman and his Wolverine role from the *X-Men* films (2000, 2003, 2006, 2009) and Matt Damon with his Jason Bourne character appear to be creating two new signature roles, yet neither of these characters is quite cemented in popular imaginations as icons the way Rambo or James Bond or Indiana Jones are. Moreover, because both Jackman and Damon regularly do a number of films outside the action genre, moviegoers might not yet see them as quintessential action actors. However, even when the fans are talking about the new action films, the similar concerns for a reflection of their lives and identities keep coming up.

HOW MEN AND WOMEN REFLECT AND DISCLOSE

Yvonne Tasker writes that one of the major misconceptions critics not well versed in the nuances of the action film have of the genre is that it is essentially an art form of unrestrained, out-of-control chaos and random violence. Looking at the narratives, and especially the action heroes and action stars, reveals a deeper concern with self-control, often the subjugation of emotions, vulnerabilities, and pain. As she is interested in the body-centered action films of the 1980s, films glamorizing the bodybuilder physiques of Schwarzenegger, Stallone, and their imitators and rivals, she points to the films as almost reflecting the very bodybuilding ethos of self-control in a paradoxical pursuit of the display of excessive masculinity.

> The visual spectacle of the male body that is central to muscular movies puts into play the two contradictory terms of *restraint* and *excess*. Whilst the hero and the various villains of the genre tend to share an excessive physical strength, the hero is also defined by his restraint in putting his strength to the test. And

it is the *body* of the male hero which provides the space in which a tension between restraint is articulated.[5]

The tensions between restraint and excess are present in most of the major
action films, in all films foregrounding strong male heroes, not necessarily
only the films of Stallone, Schwarzenegger, Vin Diesel, or large-muscled,
bodybuilder heroes. Self-control, restraint, coolness, and stoicism are also
major thematic concerns in the films of the less brawny action stars like Clint
Eastwood, Bruce Willis, Nicolas Cage, Chuck Norris, Steven Seagal, and
the James Bond films. What my discussion with the interviewees uncovered,
however, is the extent to which the fans see the differences between how
much or how little restraint of emotions different action actors "typically"
are willing to display in their films. Some of the interviewees will, in turn,
display different levels of emotional disclosure than they are willing to give.
The interviewees' allegiance to favorite action actors is a fascinating reflection of this ability to disclose.

Most interesting are the correlations I was able to draw between disclosure
and the fans of Sylvester Stallone, Clint Eastwood, and Arnold Schwarzenegger. In general, fans of Stallone seem to be more verbal about their private
lives, the emotional and social turmoil in their lives that they hope the action
film will help moderate. In contrast, fans of Eastwood and Schwarzenegger seem to value the restraint and guarding of emotions. Several such fans,
especially the Schwarzenegger fans, indicated they value emotional restraint
and shun disclosure so much that they were often difficult to talk to during
the more controversial and personal parts of the interview. This, however, is
not the case for all Schwarzenegger fans, as Patrick, a computer engineer and
fan of Schwarzenegger movies, was consistently one of the most articulate
members of the subject pool. Similarly, Louis, a committed Eastwood fan, was
very verbal and forthcoming about what his favorite films mean to him. Of the
other interviewees, Mel Gibson fans are generally less reticent about emotional
disclosure, as is the case for Harrison Ford fans. A notable fact about the interviewees and Steven Seagal is that he has no committed fans in this subject pool,
not even among the martial artists. As a matter of fact, Steven Seagal seems
to be almost unanimously disliked by the martial artists, except for Darren, a
twenty-four-year-old graduate student with some training experience in kung
fu. However, even Darren's sentiments for Seagal are nowhere near that of a
fan. He explains that he takes Seagal on a film-by-film basis, judging them on
the strengths of the plot, stunts, and action, not because he has any particular
affection for Seagal and either his on- or off-screen persona.

To illustrate the difference between levels of emotional openness and
restraint, it is interesting to begin by looking at interviewees Helen and

Louis. What makes these two testimonies particularly interesting to analyze are the negotiated—when not outright oppositional—readings they often make of their favorite films' themes. For Helen, the best action films are those starring Sylvester Stallone, especially the *Rambo* trilogy. Louis is a self-described Clint Eastwood "fanatic." As I probed their readings of their favorite films, it was very obvious that they watched the movies because of moral underpinnings they attributed to both films. However, recalling much of the critical analyses of the films, as well as the respective stars' and filmmakers' discussions of their work published over the past several decades, I was becoming more and more interested in taking note of how these two fans were not always reading the stories' dominant messages. The messages they interpreted in their favorite films were very much in line with their own social and political identities and viewpoints, messages they swore the films were clearly representing. However, most importantly, it is fascinating to see how much of themselves these two people are willing to reveal and when one of them becomes reticent to "get in touch with his feelings."

As alluded to in Chapter 2, Helen sees action films as a type of cathartic antidote to the frustrations of current world events. She explained as much in her comments about how pleasing it would be to see another installment in the *Rambo* series where the hero goes to Afghanistan to "kick some terrorist butt." "We could use a few of these heroes in real life," she says, "to take down the drug dealers and the dictators. The law sure doesn't do it. Send a few like Rambo or the Terminator out and let them do what needs to be done."

However, Helen also explains that she is an action fan, especially of Stallone, because in these films she can see both fictional characters and a real life celebrity whose values and experiences she can see as a reflection of her own life. In the *Rambo* films she sees a modern-day version of the John Wayne action films she grew up on. When I eventually present her with the argument that in many ways Rambo is also the antithesis of John Wayne, she very strongly disagrees. However, her personal identity negotiation through her films is something interesting to consider.

Helen's fandom of Sylvester Stallone is very typical of the core Stallone fan constituency. With Stallone's rise to stardom in the *Rocky* films, his image has been cemented as the perpetual underdog, the disadvantaged outsider battling to overcome odds, a long-shot overcoming epic obstacles to prove himself despite the fact that no one wants to give him an opportunity. Stallone's own off-screen persona has also been constructed as a real-life version of the *Rocky* story. To this day, despite the fact that almost since the early 1990s he has been trying to change his image, almost all Stallone interviews and career retrospectives begin with a retelling of his disadvantaged life since early childhood.

As Faludi remarks before her lengthy series of interviews with Stallone in *Stiffed*, the fight to change his image is now a *part of* Stallone's image. But the Stallone biography is still generally told in a Rockyesque narrative: born with severed facial muscles that created his drooping mouth and slurred speech, growing up in a troubled household with an abusive father (the line "you weren't born with much of a brain, so you better use your body" from *Rocky* is supposedly autobiographical), being a taunted outcast in school because of his looks, speech, and odd name, to growing up to be a theater student actively discouraged from pursuing the profession by his professors, to writing *Rocky* in three days and rising to overnight stardom.

Many of Stallone's most devoted fans will always profess their devotion because they claim they too have suffered through various disadvantages in life and were inspired by Stallone's own life story, or his films, to persevere and believe in themselves. The participants in this study who profess to like Stallone more than other action actors all tell a similar story; they all admire him for the values of perseverance, the ability to come through in moments where overwhelming odds are stacked against him. They all like him for that quality of vulnerability in his characters, ones who may always triumph and win on the end, but ones who are not invulnerable to begin with. In fact, the pain and suffering Stallone is willing to admit to helps accent the victories he achieves. For much of his career, Stallone very skillfully stuck to this theme in his films, offering various versions of underdogs triumphing despite the odds. When commenting on why Stallone was interested in the adaptation of David Morrell's novel *First Blood* (1972), a project that had languished in Hollywood for ten years and had, at various times, been considered by almost every major leading actor, he explains that he basically saw the book as a Rocky story.[6] The fact that at one point or another almost every person can feel like the world is against them, like they are not good enough, or are unfairly ridiculed and persecuted by the world at large, must be responsible for Stallone's success. Perhaps it is also at the root of why those same fans often have difficulty accepting him as anything other than an underdog.

When talking about her interest in Stallone, Helen also draws parallels between her own life and Stallone's. Although not directly claiming achievements and victories because of being a Stallone fan, she explains that a Stallone hero is the type of person she can fantasize about becoming.

I guess it would be more apt to say the action hero is what I wish I was. Strong and sure of themselves, always knowing the right thing to do. And that is not me. I guess I would say I relate a little more to Sly himself. As I understand, he was given a hard time about the nerve damage to his face that causes his droopy eyes and the slur in his speech. And I understand his father was quite mean to him and tore him down a lot.

As her comments in the previous chapter indicate, Helen's own relationship with her father was strained. The domineering behavior she experienced in her own home with a father who attempted to control every aspect of her life leads Helen to see a mirror image of her own life in the very unique connection between art and artist that comprises the Stallone persona.

As Helen further details her own troubled adolescence, she explains that the kind of life she had growing up is one that she found mirrored in Stallone films, creating the fascination and attraction for her:

> I was always the kid everyone made fun of because she was ugly and fat. . . . Didn't have any friends, ate alone in the cafeteria. The last one to be picked for anything in gym because I was so bad at everything. Afraid to raise my hand in class, afraid that I would have the wrong answer and the class would laugh at me, so I sat in back in the corner and kept quiet and always made sure I was the last one to leave the classroom to avoid being picked on. It wasn't until I reached junior high that I learned if I stuck up for myself they would leave me alone. After I mustered enough courage to deck a couple of the bullies when they cornered me I found out they would leave me alone. I got a reputation for being tough and most began to step aside when I walked down the hall. They didn't mess with me any more. I managed to hide the fact that I was scared to death. But I have always had a pretty low self-esteem. So I guess you could say the action films let me pretend I was strong and confident. They are my "Calgon, take me away" kind of thing.

Helen's fan fiction, of which she shared a copy with me, a sort of treatment of how she envisioned a fourth episode in the *Rambo* series, is a further step in creating her idealized self through the genre and inserting it into the *Rambo* mythology. The work is a lengthy outline of a story, highlighting the major characters, detailing the major plot points and offering bits of representative dialogue from several key scenes. The most important aspect of the story, however, something that will be looked at once more under the examination of gender issues of the genre, is the female love interest she creates for Rambo.

In many ways, Helen's "Rambo IV" treatment falls very neatly into Henry Jenkins's typology of fan fiction.[7] This is interesting since, as discussed previously, there is little organized fan activity among action fans. Among the Stallone fans there is no fan fiction activity, although many of the fans have ideas about how both the *Rocky* and *Rambo* series should be continued. For years there was a very strong consensus among the fans that neither of the series ended correctly with what appeared to be their final installments. For nearly two decades, it looked as if *Rocky V* and *Rambo III* would definitely be the last entries in the two franchises, and fans were especially angry with *Rocky V*. Essentially, the series's devotees were upset with the protagonist losing everything and winding up in the same slum neighborhood where the series began, only with a symbolic victory suggesting that a triumph of character and the spirit is more important that material possessions. By the early 2000s, Sylvester Stallone had started publicly acknowledging that he understood the fans' anger over *Rocky V*. By 2006 he declared that the need for a correct ending to the *Rocky* series had prompted him to go back to the character and make *Rocky Balboa*. In the case of the *Rambo* films, many fans simply wanted the hero to have an ongoing series of adventures, perhaps as a grungier version of James Bond, taking on epic world perils. In 2008, fans saw the release of *Rambo* and heard of plans to add a few more sequels to the franchise.

In Jenkins's analysis of fan fiction, viewers writing their own versions of their favorite films or television shows grants them a sense of power over the text, a power to reorder the "universe" of their entertainment, where they "pull characters and narrative issues from the margins; they focus on details that are excessive or peripheral to the primary plots but gain significance within the fans' own conceptions of the series."[8] Helen's "Rambo IV" falls under the categories of "expanding the series timeline" and "personalization"[9] in the terms of Jenkins's typology, in whole revealing more interesting information about Helen's own personality and range of activities between preferred and resistant readings of the *Rambo* films.

Helen's plot recycles elements of the first three *Rambo* films, but does so in a way that points out the general misreading of the films by their critics. The protagonist she retains from the first three films is the same reluctant fighter, rather than the aggressor of critiques. As author David Morrell has commented, "what critics don't understand is that Rambo really hates war,"[10] and Helen's story displays this very understanding. In expanding the series time line, focusing on aspects of the story ignored by the films, essentially a concluding statement about the character, Helen strives to end the story with Rambo leaving the battlefield behind for good. "I would want a happy and peaceful ending for our hero," she explains. "As it stands now, we don't know where he is, what happened (after the ending of *Rambo III*), did he come full circle? Has he found his peace? We need this to be answered for all the Rambo fans out there." Her story begins with Rambo wandering into a small town in Montana, similar to the opening of *First Blood*, and attempts to settle down by taking a job as a handyman on a woman's horse ranch. Soon enough, however, his former commanding officer visits him to ask for help in rescuing hostages in a Middle Eastern country, similar to the plot of *Rambo II*. On the mission into the Middle East, however, things go awry and Rambo gets captured, reminiscent of a capture sequence in part three. Also reminiscent of both parts two and three, the government betrays the hero, abandoning him in hostile territory. When the horse rancher, Christine, hears of this, with whom Rambo had become romantically involved before taking on the mission, she demands that the commanding officer, who is about to stage a rogue rescue attempt, allow her to go on the mission and fight to free her lover. At the end, both Rambo and the hostages are rescued, with Christine fighting alongside the men, and the saga ends with Rambo retiring to the horse ranch for a life of peaceful domesticity.

In the ending of Helen's "Rambo IV" treatment, points for uncanny prescience must be given to her. The ending of the 2008 *Rambo* film also involves the hero coming back to the United States and going home to his family's horse ranch.

The addition of the Christine character is what Jenkins terms "personalization," sometimes referred to among fan communities as the "Mary Sue" story. This is where a female writer will either center the story upon a new female addition to the regular cast of characters, or, at least, make that new character very important to the accomplishment of the plot's main mission. This character, of course, is autobiographical. Often she will have a romantic relationship with the hero. The "Mary Sue" story's origins are in fan fiction about an attractive young recruit on the Enterprise in *Star Trek*. Such young recruits will have a romance with Captain Kirk. Christine is a representative of Helen within the Rambo universe. Just like Helen, Christine is a horse rancher and shares values most important to Helen. For example, cruelty to animals is something Helen very vehemently condemns, and in one of the passages of representative dialogue, Christine warns Rambo that he will immediately be fired if she sees him beating or mistreating the horses. Christine, soon enough, has a romance with Rambo and in the end she becomes instrumental in saving his life and completing his mission.

But Helen also explains that Christine is that idealized version of herself she looks for in the generic action heroes. Christine has all the attributes Helen had wished she had but didn't feel she actually possessed:

> I do have a small ranch and I do all my own chores, including hauling the winter hay and repairing things. But that is about where the similarity between me and Christine ends. She is the strong, pretty, slim person I never was. Someone like Rambo would never even notice me.

It is also fascinating how another way Helen identifies with Rambo was a source of very intense controversy at the height of the films' popularity. As noted previously, an escapist action film's use of Vietnam as a central theme drew a great deal of critical condemnation, prompting attacks much the way *Pearl Harbor* was condemned for finding its entertainment in real life tragedy. Helen, in turn, says that she was drawn to the films because of her brother's experience serving in Vietnam and the war's long-term impact on him. Her brother was a special forces operative, as is the Rambo character, serving two tours of duty during the war and having been awarded the Bronze Star. Within a year of coming home, however, he committed suicide. In Helen's words, "We don't know exactly why, but we do know it had to do with something that happened while he was in Nam. So I do have a soft spot for Vietnam vets."

In such an instance, a preferred reading of the text is very much in effect, a fan like Helen seeing the movie as a reverential treatment of the Vietnam experience rather than exploitation. Although not an entirely unbiased source, novelist and American literature professor David Morrell has commented on his experiences with veterans and Rambo after the films, especially the second one, became a pop culture phenomena. As he writes in the foreword to the 2000 reissue of his novel, *First Blood*, until the controversy the films generated, his book was used in high school English courses as a cultural history of the war. Similarly, in his narration of the DVD release of *First Blood*, he indicates that the mental breakdown sequence at the end of the film prompted a number of veterans to write him and express appreciation of the story (even though the concluding breakdown sequence was written entirely for the film by Stallone and not in the novel). Although, again, not an unbiased source, Morrell was also quoted by Faludi in *Stiffed* as being ambivalent about many aspects of the film, especially the media labeling the films right wing. Although not voicing any pointed critiques, the liberal Morrell has mentioned that he always would have liked his character's new audiences to better appreciate its roots in a book intended as an anti-war commentary.

Where Helen's use of the films becomes oppositional, however, is in regard to their politics. She sees the films as conservative social commentary, as is the entire action genre, in her opinion. While on this point a large segment of the academic critical community would agree with her, she likes the films *precisely* because of their perceived conservative slant. In her eyes, the action films speak to a sense of disorder and chaos in the world, like crime running rampant and going unpunished because of liberal courts and laws. As she explains, the state of affairs around her gives her a feeling of stress and outrage, something the action films offer a symbolic solution for:

It is certainly true that there is not a lot of justice these days. All you have to do is look at the court cases to see that the criminal almost always wins in one way or another. If they are tried and found guilty, they usually get 10 years with 5 suspended, which means they are back on the street in 3. And while they are in prison they have some pretty good conditions as far as I'm concerned. TV, movies, good food, dental and medical care and they even get conjugal visits with their wives and girlfriends. Whatever happened to bread and water and the chain gang? Human rights people argue prison is a terrible place to be. They should be. We should make it as miserable in prison as we can. And when you get ten years you serve ten years. I believe the action films mirror our frustration with the system and look at it as the way it should be.

In light of these statements, it is interesting that Helen is not a Clint Eastwood fan. These sentiments of a lax criminal justice system are at the core of the *Dirty Harry* films, yet Helen does not care for them because of Eastwood's presence in the lead role. She explains that she has not liked his persona or performances in anything he has done since he first appeared in the *Rawhide* television series.

However, what I found particularly interesting was Helen's statement that the action films of the 1980s and 1990s, especially the *Rambo* series, are a continuation of generic traditions set by the action films she had grown up with. She says the comparisons are easy to draw between *Rambo* and John Wayne's westerns and war movies. Having knowledge of the genre as an active viewer myself, I disagreed with this point. The *Rambo* films and their treatment of Vietnam, to me, always stood as exemplars of the genre's movement to a disaffected nether region of the political spectrum. I agreed with Roger Ebert's assessment of the ideology in the films as "neither right-wing nor left-wing but coming from a paranoid wing of American politics that believes the soldiers were not allowed to win the war."[11] The novel, *First Blood*, had a story of a showdown between a disaffected, mentally unbalanced young soldier and a small town sheriff who harasses him because he does not like the length of his hair. What the book does, however, is constantly shift between Rambo's viewpoint and that of the sheriff, concentrating on how they are both right and wrong to a certain degree in the conflict, yet too stubborn to compromise. Their battle escalates until they both end up dead at the end of the story. As Morrell stresses in his introduction to the book, and once again in his DVD commentary and in his interview for Faludi's *Stiffed*, this conflict was supposed to represent the division of the culture over the war, with Rambo representing (ironically) the radical, disaffected left, and the sheriff standing in for the pro-establishment, pro-war right. Where neither side was willing to give, warned the book, one had the prescription for riots, violence, and hatred. Although the film put all the emphasis on Rambo, and Stallone crafted the screenplay to make it a Rockyesque story of an outnumbered underdog fighting against odds, it also tried to hedge its politics about what it said about the war. On the one hand, it implies that the war was not worth fighting and that Rambo himself would not have chosen to go had he been given a choice. On the other hand, it also argues that the soldiers were not allowed to win because of misguided policies from Washington. Film critics have pointed to the irony of Reagan's tacit praise of the second film, even though the story's villainous government bureaucrat has a photo of Reagan prominently displayed in his office. But I found the use of Vietnam in the first three films as a motivation behind the themes of government betrayal fairly typical of that era's action films. As David Denby wrote about 1980s action films in *New York* magazine:

> They make contact with a stratum of pessimism that runs very deep in this country—a sort of lumpen despair that goes beyond, or beneath politics. In these movies, America is a failure, a disgrace—a country run on the basis of expediency and profit, a country that has betrayed its ideals. The attack is directed not merely at liberals or "permissiveness" but at something more fundamental—the modern bureaucratic state and capitalism itself.[12]

Action films after Vietnam seemed to be declaring that there can be no clear-cut defense of the system, of the status quo, the government and institutions of law and justice. As Desser remarks, the new template for character and plot developments in the post-Vietnam action film includes the protagonist's background training as a killer for the war, a moment of betrayal by the government, and a legacy of slow-festering rage he calls on when needing to muster the will to fight enemies.[13] In very clear opposition to the tradition of the John Wayne action films, where the status quo and the system were unabashedly championed by each hero Wayne would play, the post-Vietnam action film, leading into the 1980s, the 1990s and even 2000s, displays a clear distrust of and hostility to the status quo. The action heroes here are mavericks who regularly need to break rules, if not commit outright illegalities, to defeat enemies because operating within the system would accomplish nothing.

Key here are the *Dirty Harry* films where in nearly each installment the hero solves his cases after being put on suspension or forced to take a vacation to be kept away from a case. His methods are deemed politically damaging to the department or to the mayor facing reelection and, thus, need to be constrained in some way while the rest of the legal institution pursues the politically correct method of handling the high-profile cases of each episode. In this, the films seem to imply that justice can no longer be achieved through the system because it is so hopelessly corrupt or inefficient. Now a hero who has a personal code of honor needs to act on his own, take matters into his own hands to affect justice, often fighting a dual battle against the principal villains and institutional representatives of the very society he tries to protect. In the ad campaigns for *Dirty Harry*, the protagonist was placed in a moral gray zone, referred to as a hit man for the law. His capacity for destruction and brutality are just as great as the villain's, except his violence happens to be directed at a different target. Of important note here is that before Clint

Eastwood, John Wayne himself was offered the nihilistic *Dirty Harry* script. Wayne turned it down, because of its dark pessimism.[14] However, earning the film its independent, outsider stripes is the fact that Robert Redford was offered the role but turned it down because of political reasons, too, troubled by the film's attacks on Miranda rights, then Paul Newman turned the film down because it conflicted with his own liberal sensibilities. A balance seemed to be struck with the teaming of liberal director Don Siegel and libertarian Clint Eastwood. In both Schickel's biography of Eastwood and Don Siegel's autobiography, it is claimed that never during the production of the film did the two have any political discussions. In his narrative on the DVD edition of *Rambo II*, director George P. Cosmatos similarly argues that he and Stallone never worked on crafting the film with any overt political statements in mind. Nevertheless, on this issue, Desser should also be given credit in his analysis of martial arts action films when he writes that "genres are said to be popular precisely because they answer, within structured fantasy, social, historical, psychological, or cultural issues within the culture that produces and consumes them."[15] Thus, whatever Eastwood, Siegel, Stallone, and Cosmatos might go on record as saying, especially in the wake of blistering controversy, it appears that in the social and political climates of the 1970s and 1980s, there could only be limited acceptable archetypal variations filmmakers could use to craft their action stories in order to stay relevant and profitable.

Another noteworthy theme of the action film's disaffection and anti-authoritarianism is its similar hostility toward business. Just as much as villainy comes from government institutions, it is also embodied in the corporate power structure. This is often seen in films with futuristic, science fiction elements. The *Alien* films, the *Terminator* films, the *Robocop* trilogy, and *Total Recall* are the most successful of such films, although there are scores of smaller pictures where the future is in the hands of despotic, corrupt mega-corporations. These films, set in the near future, play out on a stage of global and interstellar capitalism. Where the corrupt big government bureaucracies of old leave off, equally corrupt corporations take over in thwarting justice and opposing individualistic, disaffected heroes with personal codes of honor.

However, returning to Helen's viewing experience, Stallone films, like the *Rambo* trilogy, or something like *Cobra*, where the leitmotif of antagonism toward authority is accented with Stallone punching out a member of the police brass in the final moments of the film, are perfectly reconciled with the Wayne tradition of authoritarian action films. This, in part, is rooted in the conservative mantra of opposition to "big government." Although it is obvious that Helen ignores the issue when it arises in the *Rambo* films—instead concentrating on what, to some, might seem like superficial similarities between Stallone and Wayne, like the fact that both are "silent strong types that you certainly do not want to cross"—when I press her for an analysis, she replies that Wayne's authoritarianism only extends to local institutions, not federal ones. As she explains:

> I disagree that you cannot compare the scenario of *Rambo II* to John Wayne movies. The difference between Wayne and Rambo was Wayne's government and authority was more local than federal. That was the way it was back then because of the vastness of the country. Big Brother hadn't closed the gap yet. But if you compare *Rambo II* to *Chisum*, or even *Sons of Katie Elder*, you see a lot of the same elements, or at least I can see them.

It is likewise obvious that Helen ignores Wayne's war films, in all of which he was a high-ranking officer charged with turning boyish subordinates into men by integrating them into the military hierarchy as efficient, obedient soldiers. It is interesting to note that she chose to compare the military-themed *Rambo* films to Wayne's westerns rather than his war pictures.

Another interesting interviewee whose testimony is worth giving closer consideration because of his active reinterpretation of the text is Louis, the Chicago physician. He explains that a major appeal of the genre lies in its value systems and moral commentary on current social issues. He admits to having a short attention span and a lack of patience for entertainment that does not immediately engage him with its fast narrative structure. But he also talks at great length about the genre's moral underpinnings.

> To me an action film, a good action film, is one where there is a clear resolution, a resolution where good triumphs, where justice triumphs. For an action film to end correctly, good has to win over evil, it has to win clearly. You should be told clearly what happened. That the hero won, that he overcame the opposition, that he defeated, that he shot his enemy, which brings the film to an absolute conclusion.

This moment in the interview, in the opening few minutes when I wanted to get to the basic question of what it was about the action film that Louis liked more than any other genre, immediately intrigued me because of the unequivocality of his statements. The lack of ambiguity he seemed to be preferring throughout his entertainment interested me because film criticism usually, even by fan communities of lay persons, presents that such films are the most interesting where the filmmakers are able to play with, able to manipulate, viewers' expectations and surprise them with new twists on the old archetypes. Usually, a film where ambiguity, where there are moral gray zones, exists indicates a more sophisticated, more intelligent film. Louis, however, seems to dislike exactly this type of ambiguity. I found that fascinating. As he started talking about Clint Eastwood and why he considers Eastwood superior to all action heroes, I was intrigued even more, knowing

Eastwood films well myself and enjoying them precisely because I found a depth of ambiguity, shades of moral gray areas more sophisticated in them than in many other action films. How it was possible to see two different Eastwoods, I realized, contained the key to understanding how Louis negotiates the viewing experience with his identity.

Much is hinted at by Louis's commentary about the importance of a closed text in the action film:

> I like it [the action film] because there is always a resolution. Because they never leave it up to you to figure out and decide according to your own philosophy, which can go in one way or another way. To me a movie should always have one meaning and it should be clearly resolved.

In this statement one can see the appeal of the moralism of the genre mentioned before. Although stylized and postmodern in its mannered execution, the action film can also take very positivist attitudes when it comes to the metaphysical nature of good and evil. Louis likes the genre for this reason, seeing it as a reflection of his own value system when it comes to crime and punishment. These are sentiments very much in line with the law and order conservatism discussed by Helen. When I press the issue that such clear resolutions do not reflect the real world, where justice is, most often, not so easily achieved, Louis counters with his preference for entertainment that presents the world's most *idealized* version:

> Yes, we all know that the real world is not just, but it should be and the good action film will, for that hour and a half or two hours of my time, will give me a version of the world as it should be. Of course, I don't feel that people should be shooting each other in real life, but I would like to see more of good winning, more justice being done. The action film will show me results, a type of outcome we can try and achieve, a possibility even as we know most often in the courts those who are better connected, richer, more powerful will come out on top. But the action film shows me what I want the world to look like.

However, aside from these statements, I wanted to ask Louis what kinds of films he most definitely dislikes. I wanted to press him to be very specific about the kinds of things that antagonize him in a film because of what he told me when he agreed to the interviews. He had, at that point, made a quick comment that he likes suspense and excitement for his movie-going or cable-buying dollars, and the action genre is the one that most delivers the goods. Mention of "suspense" now intrigued me, because I was beginning to feel that his strong aversion to ambiguity might suggest that true suspense is something he does not really like. After having completed the interview, having asked every question I wanted, I still feel that way.

As discussed previously, Louis does not like "melodramas," love stories, dramas, and he especially hates soap operas. These are genres that bore him. However, as discussion came around to the violence of action films, of which we will talk at greater length in Chapter 9, there were several interesting things he said about genres and situations he intensely dislikes seeing. He does not like very grotesque horror films, explaining that slimy, gory monsters and mutations and scenes of dismemberment turn his stomach. He also very strongly dislikes psycho films and slasher films. He explains that he "hates" seeing films about people being terrorized, especially women and weak characters who cannot defend themselves. Trying to recall such films, he explains that they always consist of long, drawn-out scenes of characters getting tormented and victimized, having no recourse against their assailants until the very end of the film.

As previously revealed, for some interviewees the control of emotion seems to be important, and Louis's preference for Clint Eastwood films and hatred of psycho films seem to reveal that very same aversion to revealing weakness and the possibility of a loss of control. Despite talking about enjoying "suspense" in the action genre, Louis, in fact, seems to be using the action genre as an antidote to the suspense and uncertainty of real life. In a slasher or psycho film, the narrative is focused on a very "real" character, a person of average physical skills, an every-man or every-woman, not an ex-commando, cop, toughest fighter, or undisputed fastest gunfighter on the draw. The ordinary characters are suddenly met with an extraordinary challenge: getting assaulted by a homicidal maniac of superior skills and strength. In the course of fighting for their lives, they first reveal their weaknesses, the fact that they can break down, buckle under stress, cry and feel despair, before finding a hidden reservoir of strength and defeating their opponent. Externalizing emotion, mainly fear and admittance of weakness, is a main part of the slasher/stalker/psycho suspense genre. In contrast, the action film is founded on the supreme control of emotions. Humor creeps into the genre when action heroes respond to moments of epic stress and challenge with a wisecrack. Nothing shows more control than the ability to crack jokes in moments where real people would be paralyzed with fear. Clint Eastwood has made cool, cutting remarks in each of the *Dirty Harry* films since the beginning of the series. Even earlier than that, in his star-making role in *A Fistful of Dollars* (1965), he comes to the climactic showdown with the toughest opponent not only with steely resolve, but a taunt for the rifle-packing villain: "You said that if a man with a pistol met a man with a rifle, the one with the pistol would be a dead man. Let's see if that's true." It can, essentially, be argued then that a major appeal of Clint Eastwood action films may lie in their lack of suspense. The fact that an Eastwood character will easily survive every violent challenge is never in question.

Stephanie, the twenty-four-year-old college student and mortgage company employee, is the one other interviewee who seems to echo the kind of strong dislike for ambiguity Louis speaks of. When I tried to get her to explain why she likes films where she knows how the story will end, she explained that she watches the films to see *how* the story gets to that conclusion. She did add, however, that she does not care for Eastwood at all.

However, to give the analysis of Louis's personality more weight, it should be noted that there are a number of Eastwood films he has not seen and has no interest in seeing. Essentially, Louis is the kind of fan action actors who want to broaden their images after enough violence and destruction dislike very much. Louis does not want to see Clint Eastwood in anything other than action films and westerns. As Eastwood had tried for a long time to broaden his image past that of an action hero—only succeeding over the past two decades—he has both directed and starred in a number of nonaction films. Among these were *The Beguiled* (1971), a psychological thriller about a wounded Civil War soldier recovering in/trapped in a women's school; *Breezy* (1973), about a middle-age businessman falling in love with a young hippie girl; *Honkytonk Man* (1982), about an alcoholic country singer; *Bird* (1988), about jazz saxophonist Charlie Parker self-destructing with drugs; and the love story *Bridges of Madison County* (1995). Louis has seen *White Hunter/Black Heart* (1990), where Eastwood plays John Houston filming *The African Queen*, but "didn't really care for it." And he "never had the patience" to watch *Play Misty for Me* (1971), a thriller where Eastwood is terrorized by a psychopathic ex-lover. Interestingly, and tellingly, Louis is not a big fan of *Tightrope* (1984), an Eastwood crime thriller. Here, the Eastwood hero is thrust very far into the moral gray area as a detective whose own dark sexual compulsions are unleashed during the investigation of serial slayings of prostitutes. For a lengthy stretch, the film goes as far in upsetting audience expectations as to suggest that Eastwood himself might be the killer.

Just as in my interview with Helen, my discussion with Louis quickly provided the opportunity to ask questions about his interpretations of major Eastwood themes. These were themes I felt he was interpreting differently from the movies' dominant meanings. Essentially, he argued, as had Helen, against the deeper shades of moral grayness in the Eastwood films. I presented that in the history of the action genre, it was Clint Eastwood himself who signaled a major change in the thematic and moral complexities of action films. With Eastwood's rise to stardom in *A Fistful of Dollars* in 1964, film historians see the advent of a new generation and new sensibilities in action cinema; a movement from the John Wayne, World War II generation's action films, war films, and westerns to the baby boomers' films with Eastwood's morally complex antihero in the *Man with No Name* trilogy.

Louis's interpretation of Eastwood's rise to stardom acknowledges a change in styles, although not a change of moral sensibilities. A big difference he sees is between acting styles. He readily agrees that one can see the passing of the proverbial torch from one generation to the next, but mainly in terms of acting style. As he explains:

> I like Clint Eastwood because . . . he doesn't look like he's acting. There is a perfect naturalness in his performance. . . . I don't like melodrama, I don't like love stories, I don't like an actor posturing for a camera like he knows he is putting on a performance. I saw a lot of John Wayne's films and I didn't like him because he always looked like he was *acting* like he was the most important man on the screen. He had to be the biggest one on the screen, the most important one on the screen, everyone had to be smaller than he was, everyone had to look up to him, everyone had to immediately fall in love with him, and he looked like he was always aware of where the camera was and he was playing to that. He always had to have this sly little smirk on his face. He was this larger-than-life symbol, this symbol of Hollywood to the world, and it made his performance seem forced and unreal. You never see this posturing with Eastwood.

Louis sums up perfectly the change in generational attitudes:

> With the John Wayne films you had the films of my father's generation. They were more open to that posturing, that melodrama, that saccharine, open display of emotional extremes. What I really like about Eastwood is the way he looks so completely natural on screen, so perfectly at ease in every situation that he looks almost bored by what's going on.

My conclusion with this passage also includes the hypothesis that the preference for Eastwood's emotional reserve is more a personal reflection for Louis than solely a generational identification with a new actor rising to stardom in the mid-1960s. I was also suspecting that he might be erroneously attributing certain old films to John Wayne, especially when speaking of the open display of emotions. A major aspect of the Wayne films, to cinema historians and cultural critics at least, is Wayne's stoicism.

What Louis does not see in the Eastwood films, however, is a character of greater moral ambiguity than the typical John Wayne hero. Louis acknowledges a difference in acting styles, but he does not believe that the sort of ambiguity he dislikes in film is very much a part of the Eastwood persona and the typical Eastwood films. Being a fan of the spaghetti westerns myself, and having read a great deal about their making and director Sergio Leone's approach to the subject, I wanted to present Louis with some "possible alternate interpretations" of the films and see what he thought of them.

Looking at Italian director Leone's treatment of the generic western subject, then talking to Louis about the circumstances in which he first saw the
films during his youth, brought another interesting wrinkle to the issue. Leone
was an Italian who brings a European's eye and cultural background to the
quintessential American genre. Louis saw the films in Hungary, very eagerly
offering that his preferences for the American action heroes were shaped by
his life in a communist country. He feels that the totalitarian, socialist, col-
lectivist state fostered a need to revolt. Such a society's only outlet for one's
pent-up frustrations was in the cathartic pleasure of watching individualistic
heroes of the American westerns and action films. As he explains:

> What you have to understand is that life under communism is like life in a slave
> labor camp. Your life is not your own, you don't have an identity, you don't
> have a will of your own, you're a part of the state and you never have a voice
> for dissent, to disagree, to protest. That's why we loved the westerns and the
> *Dirty Harry* films and the *Kojak* films on TV, because in these films the power
> was in the hand of the individual.

Leone's take on the western genre, as documented by film historians, had
been shaped by his fondness for American literature before World War II,
then his experiences meeting American troops during the war and seeing a
lot of Hollywood films afterward. Leone always felt that the typical Hollywood western film unduly romanticized the harshness and brutality of the Old
West and unduly romanticized the American character. During World War II,
Leone had been greatly disillusioned by actually meeting American soldiers.
The idealists and heroes of the literature he had read about turned out to be no
different from soldiers anywhere else in the world. They could be as brutal,
as cynical, as dishonest as any man could become in times of war and hardship. Leone's approach to the western genre was to strip away the sentimental
American tinsel from the stories of the frontier. In Leone's films, the difficult,
merciless frontier lands could only be survived by the toughest, most brutal,
the most cynical of men. Leone's westerns are infused by the coldest of old
Italian philosophies, they are steeped in Machiavellian amorality. In a Leone
western, the law of the jungle rules and heroes survive by being more efficient killers, by being more ruthless and amoral than their opponents. Moral
superiority in itself does not save a man's life in a Sergio Leone film.

What created controversy at the time, however, mainly among the American critics, was the apparent removal of all moral grounding from the typical
Sergio Leone western. The protagonist in *A Fistful of Dollars* is little more
than a bounty hunter riding into the middle of a feud in southwestern town
because he knows there is money to be made in the mayhem. His motivations
never seem to go beyond making money, never include any transcendent

greater good to be achieved by the speeding up of the self-destruction of the two warring families.

When I presented this analysis to Louis, with the suggestion that perhaps the film's "new generation" message might be that simple, black-and-white notions of morality are as passé as John Wayne's posturing, he replies with his own analysis to point out how "obviously" the postmodern view misses important details. When I suggest that the beginning of the film—where the Eastwood character needs to ally himself with one of the two sides in the battle and makes his choice simply based on which of the two is stronger—is yet another argument against the moral orderliness of the black-and-white, right-and-wrong world, Louis again counters by explaining that there is a more complex logic at work in the script. He points out that one of the first scenes is of the thugs of one family shooting at and startling Eastwood's mule. Since this challenge cannot go unanswered and Eastwood guns down the thugs, he, essentially, no longer has the choice to start making moral distinctions between the two sides. Eastwood could not join the gang that is now minus four members because he needed to answer an insult. Furthermore, Louis explains that there is a very clear moral grounding to the story in a family Eastwood helps escape the anarchic town. Here, a wife and mother of a small child is forced to provide regular sexual services for one of the two gangs, with her peasant husband unable to do anything about it. Eventually, Eastwood frees her from bondage and lets the family slip out of town under the cover of night. It is interesting that Louis puts a heavy emphasis on the scene, even recalling that the film begins with Eastwood noticing the situation and deciding that the family needs to be helped. In fact, the film begins with a scene of the gang members taking the woman from her home, chasing her crying child away by shooting at his feet, and Eastwood calmly watching the scene and walking past.

Eastwood's remarks about this in an interview, here quoted from Schickel:

> Our hero's standing there and he doesn't do a thing. You know, your average western, the hero's got to step forth and grab the guy who's shooting at the kid or something like that. But this guy doesn't do anything; he turns and rides away. And I thought, that is perfect, that's something I've always wanted to do in a western.[16]

Selective memory and perception interestingly come into play when we discuss Eastwood's Oscar-winning *Unforgiven* (1992). With this film, critical praise and awards were lavished on Eastwood precisely because of the film's revisionist messages about generic codes of honor, violence, and morality. This film is an interesting contrast to *A Fistful of Dollars* because it begins with a world that tries to function according to moral tenets of right and wrong, transgression and punishment, rather than the Machiavellian chaos that rules the stage upon which *Dollars* plays out. However, as the film unfolds and the main characters' personalities are taken apart layer by layer, all pretenses of ordered, righteous violence and revenge are steadily deconstructed.

Predictably, Louis says that for him there is no message of deconstruction or critique as he is enjoying the narrative. When I ask him about the point of the film's "heroes" being a group of indiscriminate killers who only by happenstance find themselves taking on an execution job that could be justified, who would just as easily agree to kill innocents if the price was right, he argues that there is no indication in the film that this is so. However, in fact, there *is* and I quoted lines from the climactic showdown of the film. Here, Eastwood is squaring off with Gene Hackman's character as a corrupt sheriff and Hackman accuses him of being an assassin who killed women and children when he dynamited a bridge years ago and killed a train full of innocent travelers. Eastwood's reply is a cold "That's right, I've killed women and children. I've killed just about anything that walked or crawled at one time and now I'm here to kill you, Little Bill." Louis says he cannot remember that line. Of importance to him, however, just as in the case of the family in *Dollars*, is the fact that the overall mission of the main characters—no matter how amoral they may be—is just.

In the course of our discussion, Charles Bronson also came up. Louis told me that perhaps after Eastwood, Bronson was one of his very favorite action actors through the 1960s and 1970s. The reasons he cites are very similar to Clint Eastwood's appeal. Bronson is just as natural in front of the camera. His performances, as Louis perceives, lack melodrama and pretense. Perhaps as is the case with Eastwood—minus Eastwood's experimental forays into dramas—Bronson is also an actor who looks *so* natural and untroubled in the most extreme scenarios of violence and mortal danger that he appeals to Louis's preference for the complete subjugation of weakness. With Bronson I was interested in how Louis reconciled films like the *Death Wish* series (1974, 1982, 1985, 1987, 1994), where the main character was a vigilante, *The Mechanic* (1972), where Bronson played a mob hitman, or *The Evil That Men Do* (1984), where he was a government assassin. Repeating the same reasoning as in the case of *Dollars* and *Unforgiven*, Louis explained that ends to which each of the Bronson assassins applied their skills were just. Good had triumphed over evil in all of the films.

Louis also explained that he likes Bronson's family orientation. "Family is important to me," Louis said, "as is a strong marriage." Louis always liked the way Bronson made most of his films with Jill Ireland after they were married. That professional union always signaled a solid marriage for him. Louis also added that he was always a Paul Newman fan because of the stories he heard of Newman's strong marriage to Joan Woodward. It is a refreshing change of pace, Louis said, from all the other tawdry stories of celebrity divorces and affairs.

Looking at interviews with Louis and Helen, one can see a good demonstration that value system and life-experience negotiation with the action film can be observed in the most colorful fashion when listening to people explain why they are drawn to the action actors they like the most. The testimony they give about their favorite actors amply illustrates how individuals gravitate toward those narratives and personalities they see embodying their own life experiences. As can also be observed, when the image on the screen may not perfectly mirror a person's professed worldview, they can creatively interpret thematic, visual, and plot cues in films to reconcile themselves with the film.

I also do not think that the gendered nature of emotionally open and emotionally restrained testimony from Helen and Louis is completely coincidental. The manner in which one is very frank about his or her life's difficulties can explain why that person turns to action films because of the restraint and lack of ambiguity that falls along traditional gender lines. The female is willing to be emotionally open, while the male values restraint and control—despite the fact that he can quite eloquently and fully explain why he likes restraint. I began this section by mentioning that various action stars have fans among these interviewees who gravitate toward them in correlation to how open or closed they are with their commentary, and it bears adding now that none of the women profess any committed fandom for either Eastwood or Arnold Schwarzenegger. While there are five women, Helen, Kathleen, Amy, Stephanie, and Jane, who rate Stallone as a first-choice action favorite, there are also two women, Erika and Diana, who say they very much dislike him because they feel he is a bad actor. The female interviewees rate Mel Gibson, Nicolas Cage, and Bruce Willis as the top three favorites. This presents what could possibly be an interesting paradox; these same women, except for Jane, also told me that they do not like romantic films, relationship-focused "chick flicks." These three stars, however, are the ones who take most of the forays outside of the action genre, often doing very intense, emotional dramas, sometimes romantic comedies. It also bears recalling, however, that most of the women who like action films say they became fans because they grew up under such circumstances—in families full of brothers, dating men who only watched action films—that they had little choice but to be entertained by a steady diet of action films. The one exception is Cindy, who has one female sibling. The phenomenon of most women preferring a more emotionally open action hero could hypothetically mean that while a woman can be exposed to nothing but a certain genre for years, until the form, tempo, and thematics of the film become habitual and expected, a woman might also be more naturally inclined toward a preference for emotional access and disclosure. For men, Mel Gibson, Arnold Schwarzenegger, and Jackie Chan are the top three favorites, with Bruce Willis often getting a mention as someone whose films they will see based on the overall appeal of the story, rather than because of Willis himself.

It should also be mentioned that the male fandom of Jackie Chan is almost unanimous, except for Louis. Although none of the men said Chan was their first choice favorite action star, they all explained that Chan's physical prowess, the fact that he is always touted as doing his own stunts and he supposedly always comes close to at least one fatal injury in every film, makes him a curiosity.

However, two sources of commentary about Chan are worth analyzing here, as they bear interesting reflection on male film-watching. Other than Louis's negative impressions of Chan, Darren also explains that he can take Chan only in small doses, seeing an occasional film with him, but somehow remaining at a distance from the films. Apparently these two interviewees have problems with Chan because of the emotional intensity reason, but come at the issue from apparently opposite directions.

Louis, who values the ultracoolness of Eastwood and Bronson, explains that he gets irritated with what he sees as Chan's hysterics. He says that every time he comes across one of Chan's films shown on cable, he "can't exactly decide where to place him on that spectrum spanning from Bruce Lee to the Three Stooges. But probably closer to the Stooges than Bruce Lee." Louis prefers the Eastwood and Bronson heroes because they seem to be completely sure of themselves in every situation, because they always look like they are more than ready to rise to any dangerous occasion, and he explains that in Chan he sees a person who appears—either as a part of his act, or perhaps because of the way he might really feel about his action hero status—as bumbling and ill at ease. Louis explains that he has heard the basics of Chan's career, that after Bruce Lee's death, Chan quickly fell into a position where he was looked at as Lee's rightful successor as a martial arts star. However, Louis says that when he looks at Chan, he can't help but feel that he is looking at someone who seems almost stunned by the fact that he somehow wound up playing the hero of an action film. Similar to his comments about John Wayne, Louis says that Chan looks too much like he is acting, that he is deliberately playing to the cameras. The ultimate mistake Chan makes, however, as Louis sees it, is that in too many scenes he makes Louis feel like Chan almost wants to smile at the silliness of the things he has to do for the camera. Clint Eastwood, on the other hand, is the perfect action hero because he avoids any hint that he might not perform his duties on screen with complete unflappable seriousness and self-confidence.

Although Louis sees Chan as being hysterical, unrestrained, and unsure of himself, Darren explains that his main problem with Chan is that he cannot feel like he can relate to Chan's characters in any realistic, human level. For Darren, that personal identification, that experience of shared identities, is impossible to achieve when watching a Chan film. Darren explained this, as I mentioned some facts about Chan's life from his 1998 biography, *I Am Jackie Chan: My Life in Action*, that Chan "cowrote" with journalist Jeff Yang. Darren seemed surprised when I mentioned that Chan is married and has a son. He was most surprised when I told him how the book details Chan's confessions of having been a spoiled playboy of sorts when his success first overwhelmed him. That is very difficult to imagine, Darren says, because of one of the most annoying and unrealistic aspects of the characters Chan plays. Frankly, Darren comments, he had often wondered if Chan might be gay, as he appears to be completely asexual in "every single film" he appeared in. He points out that in all of Chan's Hong Kong films—structurally quite different from his Hollywood films like the three *Rush Hour* (1998, 2001, 2007) films—he always has two very attractive female costars. However, "he has absolutely no sexual chemistry with either one." This, in fact, is quite an accurate summary of the archetypal Hong Kong Jackie Chan film. In those films, Chan almost always plays a bumbler who somehow winds up in the middle of a criminal plot and defeats his opponents because his ineptitude winds up giving him an unpredictably dangerous edge in all of the confrontations. In the course of the story, he gets partnered with two women, one of whom is intelligent and competent in the martial arts, the other of whom is a broad, hysterical bimbo stereotype. The trio eventually demolishes its way through an unlikely set of confrontations to defeat an arch-villain. In the course of the plot, exactly as Darren summarizes, no romantic relationship of any sort develops between Chan and either of the women. Even in those films that end with a vague suggestion of a future relationship, their interaction throughout the story completely lacks any sexual tension.

Why is this lack of sexuality, lack of any semblance to adult human feelings and relationships, as is the case in Chan's Hong Kong films, only open to conjecture? Chan's biography does not mention it. His films were always made with an eye toward a broad international release—in fact, by the time he broke into American distribution, he was already a major star in Asia, Australia, and Europe—the accent on violence, however comic, is understandable; violence is universal and does not require the translation of large amounts of dialogue. However, sex is always a valuable commodity in the border-crossing films. Why Chan's films never include suggestions of a love triangle or a ménage à trois, even if mined for comedy, as they could help the films' box-office ratings, is a mystery. In several interviews Chan gave during his rise to fortune in the United States in the mid-1990s, in response to the Americans' squeamishness about media effects, he quickly, and rather evasively, explained that his films are really live-action cartoons made with the family in mind.

Although it is understood in communication, psychology, sociology, and various interpersonal relations research that men are generally more reticent to discuss or consider the messy details of romantic and deeply emotional issues, the wide appeal of Chan's live-action cartoons among the male interviewees might be rooted in the films' very lack of anything resembling a mature adult relationship. When men watch one of Chan's films, they can be sure that they are never assaulted by a sudden subplot of a couple analyzing their relationship, coming to terms with feelings or romantic problems of any sort.

At this point, recalling Dirk's and Steve's comments about James Bond, it begins to appear as if the men in this group prefer their entertainment to deal with emotional/romantic/relationship-oriented themes in either of two ways: to ignore it completely or to offer an extreme fantasy version of it.

Just as Cliff explained how he was fascinated by Russell Crowe's character in *Gladiator* because he felt he had similarly been a victim of false accusations and persecution, and Helen is drawn to Sylvester Stallone because she feels she had some of the similar struggles as Stallone, action heroes, generally, can become extremely successful embodying universal conditions, experiences, and aspirations, especially experiences related to hardship and suffering. Men and women, in turn, might react to heroes who handle it by bearing their pain and vulnerability on their sleeves before striking back in spectacular revenge, who coolly dismiss the hardship and handle armies of oppressors with the sort of disinterested calm one would show mowing one's lawn, or by being so invulnerable to the pain as to laugh it off. The depictions of the hero as the sufferer or the hero as embodiment of cool, larger-than-life invulnerability respond to two of the most universal experiences or aspirations. Stallone seems to be the most successful when he suffers. Both his *Rocky* and *Rambo* series are replete with Christ imagery. Clint Eastwood is as cold, detached, and invulnerable as most people wish they could be during life's crises. Even when Eastwood very quietly, deftly directs his own stories to carry on a dialogue about, if not critique of, the contradictory and oppositional natures of heroism or masculinity, he can be read perfectly straight by those who want to believe in the reality of the invulnerable male hero. His precursor, John Wayne, was as invulnerable, large, and sure of himself as American audiences wanted to be sure of themselves and the rightness of their country's power in the post–World Way II era. But another universal concept the hero may embody is rebellion, and when an actor does this perfectly, the hero as the outsider, the one going against the grain, standing alone in a nimbus of moral strength and superiority against the oppressive strains of conformity and tradition; stardom and fan worship can follow, even if sometimes for just a little while. From James Dean to Marlon Brando, Steve McQueen to Paul Newman, and the roguish scoundrels that made Harrison Ford a star in the *Star Wars* and *Indiana Jones* films, the dangerous rogue helps give audience members fantasy representatives for the times they feel like they are apart from society at large, feel alienated from the status quo, or just like to fantasize about the attractive appeal of being the one who stands apart, the one who is not following the crowd. The rebel in films is also one who is ready to display pain and emotion. Perhaps none too coincidentally, women have always been fans of the classic rebels like Dean, Brando, and Newman. But aside from true disenfranchisement and alienation, no one likes to think of themselves as a "follower," as being "average" or "conservative." Being the "other" has its special appeal, its own ego gratification, and a couple of the younger interviewees mentioned the appeal of an action hero carefully cultivating his rebel image.

Ray, a nineteen-year-old undergraduate, and Vin, a twenty-one-year-old undergraduate, both talk about life-shaping experiences as newcomers to American culture. Ray is originally from Poland but lived part of his life in Greece before moving to the United States with his mother at age thirteen. Vin is originally from Costa Rica and vividly recalls his youth as a marked outsider, especially in school. Both young men explain that action films focusing on the otherness, the outsider status, or a displaced rebel hero defying conventions have a special appeal to them. Both, in turn, are fans of Vin Diesel.

Ray explains that he especially likes the original *The Fast and the Furious*. As I asked him to comment about favorite films that have themes relevant to him, he referenced *Furious* as a film he had just seen and had sought out to see because of the race cars. He discussed how he was interested in the cars and the racing in all of the four *Furious* films, but the ones starring Vin Diesel made an impression on him on a level beyond the visual excitement of the cars he likes. As the plot of the first films deals with an undercover cop (Paul Walker) infiltrating the street-racing gang, I first had the impression that Ray was focusing on the cop's character. Ray even explained that he usually has a wary, cautious disposition when meeting new circles of people, and the themes of deception, infiltration, subterfuge, and broken trust in the film were intriguing to him. They stem, of course, from his immigrant past, moving between three vastly different cultures as he was growing up. Although he likes the strong action hero males dealing with concepts of alienation in a film's metaphorical text, he does not need these heroes being superhumanly stoic. When I asked him if he could relate to the character of the cop mainly, as I assumed that the identity of an immigrant who needs to establish himself in a new culture would be easily negotiable with that of the cop trying to work his way into the culture of car thieves, he explained that the Vin Diesel character was the one he felt more of a bond with. He explained that he understood my point and why I would think he identifies with the cop, but the Diesel character's outlaw status, his rejection of society and conventional rules, made Diesel more of a representative of the marginalized.

When I explained to Vin that identities will be protected in this book (mentioning that he will be given a new name in the book), he told me that he would especially enjoy it if he knew he would be named after Vin Diesel. However, as "Vin" talks about his life experiences that shape his preferences for heroes, for him a more hyperbolic, superhuman hero is required, one who likes to venture into the world of bodybuilding.

Diesel, aside from the first and fourth *Furious* films, also starred in *xXx* (2002), along with a number of underperforming films like *A Man Apart* (2003) and *Babylon A.D.* (2008), and began his career ascent after Steven Spielberg noticed an independent film he had produced, written, directed, and starred in at the Sundance Film Festival. Spielberg expressly wrote a minor role for him in *Saving Private Ryan* (1998). Afterward, Diesel attracted attention and began establishing himself as a lead actor in the role of an anti-hero in the well-regarded 2000 science fiction film *Pitch Black*. There he played a dangerous, masked, straightjacketed convict reminiscent of Hannibal Lecter. But this same character, Riddick, becomes the unlikely savior of a band of space travelers stranded on a desert planet. Diesel's Riddick exudes charismatic cynicism and rebellion, a character he has explained in interviews as representing "anyone who's been ruled out or given up on." His most memorable line from the film is a response to a question from a religious pilgrim member of the stranded travel party. When the pilgrim implores why Riddick refuses to believe in God, he corrects with "Think someone can spend half their life in the slam with a horse bit in their mouth and not believe? Think someone can start out in a liquor store trash bin with an umbilical cord wrapped around his neck and not believe? . . . I absolutely believe in God. And I absolutely hate the fucker." In *The Fast and the Furious*, Diesel is the archetypal likable rogue, a dangerous outsider who is wanted by the law and possesses a heart of gold. His criminality, making money running illegal races on the nighttime streets of Los Angeles, becomes justified halfway through the film as he explains how his father's life was destroyed by an unscrupulous partner in the legitimate racing game. He had been let down by the dominant, naive value system of the culture that claims honesty and decency are rewarded by the fates ordering the universe, then adapted his own code of conduct. He avenged his father's death and chose to prosper outside the rules of society, making his money in street races. This later helps him provide for his new "family," comprised of his sister and loyal gang members, literally putting food on the table they peacefully share each day, even saying Grace before eating. In *xXx*, Diesel's third most successful role to date, a cross between the *Dirty Dozen* and James Bond, he is once again a criminal, forced by the government into becoming a spy on a dangerous assignment in order to pay his debts to the system whose rules he had been breaking all his life.

As I was discussing different action heroes with Vin, explaining how I found it convenient to dichotomize heroes into either loners/outsiders or ones who work in teams, have partners, or are a part of the system, like nonrogue cops, spies, and soldiers, I wanted him to tell me which type of hero he generally finds more interesting. The loner and outsider is closer to his tastes, he explained, being able to relate to such characters in light of his immigrant background. Going to school as a young boy who had just come over form Costa Rica had often been difficult, having been forced to endure racial taunts.

> Through grade school I got tortured a lot because some of my "friends" [noteworthy here is his pause, ironic smile and accent put on the word "friends"] found out that I was Costa Rican and they would go off on calling me monkey and banana boy and all these things and every day I would sit there and think about how one day . . . not get revenge but stand up to them and kick all their asses. But you know that never happens now, does it? You just carry it on your back until you can finally put the bag down.

Although not professing a significant identification with Stallone's suffering characters, even though he has seen all the major action films from the 1980s, Vin explains that other than the loner hero, he likes heroes who endure hardship before striking back at their oppressors. Judging from his own tormented childhood, this is understandable. In his own words:

> What I like to see in a movie is when they keep beating a guy down and then he just . . . mentally, you know, snaps. Like in the *Patriot*, there's that point when they hit a turning point and nothing can stop them. So that's pretty fun to watch.

A second dichotomy I wanted to discuss with him involved the physicality of the action heroes. I asked his opinion about action heroes either falling into the body-centered, muscle-fetishized camp of Schwarzenegger and Stallone or the less physical, leadership, personality, quick-witted camp of Mel

Gibson, Bruce Willis, and most of the new generation of action actors like Nicholas Cage, Keanu Reeves, and Ben Affleck. Although hesitant at first, slowly giving both types their due, Vin eventually leaned toward the physical side of the dichotomy. This, however, was something I expected, given the fact that as I sat down for the interview with him I noticed that he must be a regular weight trainer himself. Wearing a tank top during our discussion, his defined muscularity was visible. But his was not the blunt, hulking muscularity of a football player or someone who does a lot of straining manual labor and develops a utilitarian amount of brawn. Vin had the lean, defined muscularity of the gym, of the specialized exercise equipment designed to isolate muscle groups and develop them to their aesthetic best. In analyzing action heroes, he quickly told me that Arnold Schwarzenegger was his favorite, having seen *Conan* (1981) when he was a child and having been impressed, first and foremost, by Schwarzenegger's size. Picking Vin Diesel as his favorite of the late 1990s, millennium era of action heroes is not surprising since Diesel is the most muscular of the young crop. He easily rivals Stallone at his peak of muscularity, and most of Diesel's action films have dutifully fetishized his body. In each of his action films, his shirts were often removed, unbuttoned, or extremely tight for maximum display.

In light of Vin's looks, I found it interesting to note, although not entirely surprising, that he does not claim to be athletic in the sense of participating in organized team sports. He claims to have taken part in some intramural basketball games when in high school, although infrequently and he was never on any sports team. Literature on the psychology and culture of bodybuilding generally emphasizes the individualistic orientation of the sport, mainly attracting people who do not like to have their identity get lost within a group. Former professional bodybuilder and Cuban expatriate Sergio Oliva had, in numerous articles through his career, explained how he had been drawn to the sport in his youth, but could never find the outlet to train and compete in his homeland because Castro had declared bodybuilding and its aggrandizement of the individual antithetical to Marxism. Schwarzenegger's own 1983 autobiography, *Arnold: The Education of a Bodybuilder*, recalls how as a boy he was involved in various team sports like soccer, but did not like the fact that victories would be attributed to the team dynamic and there was little opportunity for individual recognition. But analytical, academic literature also mentions the sport as part power compensation for those who feel disenfranchised or unable to fit into conventional standards of appearance. Notable are works by Klein and Heywood.[17] Their books detail how the majority of male bodybuilders are of blue-collar backgrounds, taking working-class, traditional reverence for strong masculinity to its fringe extreme, and how female bodybuilders are generally of upper-class, college-educated backgrounds with body-image problems who choose to rebel against images of hegemonic femininity. As Fussell's 1991 autoethnographic book *Muscle: Confessions of an Unlikely Bodybuilder* concludes, the statement that a person who trains his or her body with weights wants to make to the world is that the body is designed to be a "silent, raging scream of descent," a declaration that "more than anything in the world, no matter what it takes, I do not want to look like you, I do not want to be like you, I do want to *be* you."[18] An interesting dimension of this issue is the phenomenon of muscle as not only physical, but also psychic protection. Explaining his own attraction to sport when he felt weak and vulnerable on the streets of New York, Fussell writes:

> It was in the aisle, in this store, in September of 1984, that I finally caught the "disease." Here it was I came across *Arnold: The Education of a Bodybuilder* by Arnold Schwarzenegger. A glimpse of the cover told me all I needed to know. There he stood on a mountain in Southern California, every muscle bulging to the world as he flexed and smiled and posed. Just the expression on his face indicated that nothing could disturb this man. A victim? Not bloody likely. As for his body, why, here was protection, and loads of it. What were these great chunks of tanned, taut muscle but modern-day armor? Here were breastplates, greaves, and pauldrons aplenty, and all made from human flesh. He had taken stock of his own situation and used the weight room as his smithy. . . . Nothing else had worked for me. The Harvard Club tie and The New York Society Library card had done nothing to ward off attack. . . . By making myself larger than life, I might make myself a little less frail, a little less assailable when it came down to it, a little less human.[19]

That Vin should also be a fan of an actor like Schwarzenegger is not too surprising, as Schwarzenegger, much like Eastwood, represents the complete subjugation of weakness, self-doubt, and vulnerability. I was expecting him to profess a stronger allegiance to Stallone and the types of beaten-down characters he specializes in, but the fact that Vin does not may yet again be telling of his personality. Some people can more easily express their inner turmoil and may perhaps be able to stand a more frequent cinematic representation of it. Schwarzenegger fans, I have come to believe after these interviews, do not want to be reminded of their weakness. In many ways, Schwarzenegger is very similar to Eastwood. Just like Eastwood cracking dry one-liners, from as far back as *A Fistful of Dollars* to the famed "go ahead, make my day" quip as Dirty Harry, Schwarzenegger is so immune to such human flaws as fear and pain that he makes cutting, ironic jokes in the most perilous of situations. That Vin should also be an avid Vin Diesel fan is again logical. Although not as stoic and robotic as Schwarzenegger, Diesel's power and self-control are displayed in his muscular body. His ethnic looks, according to his publicity, also made him something of a cipher, an open text for his fans who apparently always ask what nationality and ethnic background he comes from. So far, he has played characters ranging from Italian and Cuban to Puerto Rican and Jewish. Reportedly, his loyalists, on occasion, share fan fiction about him over the Internet. Diesel's well-guarded, secretive background and exotic looks serve as a sort of human inkblot test fans want to see their own fantasies in.

In fact, as my interviews progressed, I began to realize that the level to which self-disclosure and emotional access manifested in interviewees could be well tied to their preferences for action personalities. Clint Eastwood and Arnold Schwarzenegger, for example, seemed to be the actors of choice for people who valued emotional restraint more. As evidenced in Louis's comments, the stoicism of Eastwood characters seemed to reflect the value they placed on the control of emotions. As evidenced by Helen's disclosure, on the other hand, Sylvester Stallone fans place more of a concern on the display and discussion of feelings. Examining how much of their personal backgrounds these actors have publicly discussed and the manner in which they have discussed them reveals striking differences, something critics have not been discernible enough to always recognize. Although all of these actors have been spoken of as extensions of their characters, analysis has generalized them all as propagating the image of invulnerable, indestructible, and impenetrable masculinity. I believe this is not the case and their respective fans have always been aware of it. The fans, in my experience with this study, also reveal quite a bit about themselves, as we can see through Louis, Helen, Ray, and Vin so far.

When I brought up the issue of gravitating toward action stars based on emotional accessibility to Kathleen, a twenty-five-year-old art student and avid Stallone fan, she quickly agreed with my hypothesis. She explains:

> I think my feelings on that are similar. . . . He [Stallone] often plays this very strong, very masculine character, and yet he is like a teddy bear underneath it all, with a heart of gold. He is not afraid to cry, which is very unusual for playing a tough guy, or just being a guy, period.

This helps support the audience research statistic stated earlier about a large female constituency for some of Stallone's films. Here Kathleen is referring to the ending of *First Blood* and a scene in *Rocky III* (1982) where Stallone's characters break down and cry. As Stallone himself remarked about the female fans of Rambo: "It's amazing, like 82 percent [of females] wanted to go back and see it again. Even though it's a war film, it is kind of a sensual film. The character is one of those misunderstood types that I think you can feel maternal toward, in an odd way."[20]

But the remarkable thing, to a point, is that Stallone's biography and the anecdotes he tells about his early life are very frank about his struggles and repeated failures. Although to a degree this is a shrewd publicity move, through vulnerability tying Stallone's real persona to that of his larger-than-life fictional characters who become heroic by adversity, the image of the real man is likewise lifted to heroic status by implying he has overcome obstacles just as epic. Nevertheless, comments like the following are noteworthy in light of how other action actors talk about their backgrounds. Speaking of his relationship with his father, Stallone says:

> My father was an extraordinarily exacting man, and if what you did wasn't a photocopy of the way he did it, then you had no abilities and had to be chastised and corrected. And quite often the correction was, you know, shocking. He made me feel extraordinarily inept. . . . Why can't you be smarter? Why can't you be stronger? . . . I didn't have one virtue. He never said he was proud of me. He was very judgmental, and I was always being judged guilty.[21]

On his self-image growing up, he says:

> I was not an attractive child. I was sickly and I even had rickets. I was scrawny, my mouth went to one side. I was like a poster boy for a nightmare. In a contest between me and a bulldog, you'd say the bulldog's better. My personality was abhorrent to the other children, so I enjoyed my own company and did a lot of fantasizing.[22]

Although many celebrities romanticize their early struggles, Stallone's own hardship, going back to life in a dysfunctional family with an abusive father, is starker, more discomfiting than the usual tales of waiting tables and washing cars before discovery and stardom. It is also a sharp contrast to life stories about Eastwood and Schwarzenegger.

Eastwood's image of coolness and stoicism extends from his fictional characters to real life due, in large part, to his very private personality. He might not talk a great deal about enduring struggles and early failures because he is often reticent talking about *any* part of his private life.

Schwarzenegger's on- and off-screen persona, however, is a melding of fictional superman and real life superman due to one of the most well-calculated public relations campaigns a major star has ever coordinated. His fans, in turn, at least those represented in this study—save for Vin, up to a point—appear to be similarly cool to the idea of any complete emotional release when it comes to talking about the meaning the action film brings to their lives.

I summarize here the circumstances surrounding two Schwarzenegger biographies for the information they present and the controversy surrounding one of them as Schwarzenegger himself took issue with the content. The first biography that attempted an in-depth look at the star's life and the publicity

ng years before I went back to school and I am elf-discovery. *Rocky* helped me with that . . .

machine that framed his image was the 1991 book *Arnold* by British journalist Wendy Leigh, which had a very short shelf life. Critical reception of its research methodology and presentation was cold, on the one hand. On the other, the Schwarzenegger managerial machine, coupled with the Kennedy family legal muscle, had, allegedly, bombarded it with everything from libel threats to attempts at purchasing the publisher until its author became a media pariah. Further allegations went that journalists realized they would either have future interview access to Schwarzenegger if they decide to shun Leigh, or they went ahead and gave Leigh interview space and airtime and risked alienating Schwarzenegger. The book's printing of kiss-and-tell information by his various former lovers and allegations about his father's Nazi past were objectionable to the actor and apparently, according to Nigel Andrews's 1996 book *True Myths: The Life and Times of Arnold Schwarzenegger*, an affront to an image-making industry he constructed around himself that functions to create an on- and off-screen superman.

The thesis of Andrews's work is that perhaps outside of Madonna, there is no other contemporary star who is more of an unknowable commodity than Arnold Schwarzenegger. His career is a testament to superb public relations image construction, sometimes through anecdotes of the actor's life that are so wildly over the top as to paint him as nothing less than truly superhuman. This, however, has apparently been Schwarzenegger's compulsive drive even before he started playing superheroes on screen. An odd case Andrews recalls involves information Schwarzenegger gave in a series of interviews for the 1977 documentary *Pumping Iron*. The commercially and critically successful documentary about professional bodybuilding was what first gave Schwarzenegger notice outside of the bodybuilding community. His natural charisma and several outlandish statements made on camera let him stand out among all the bodybuilders profiled. The most outlandish of statements, but one that would long be a part of the Schwarzenegger legend, were his claims about how he reacted to the news of his father's death. Schwarzenegger, with stunning, straight-faced earnestness, explains that when he was in the final phases of conditioning for a Mr. Olympia contest—the Super Bowl of professional bodybuilding—a time when he needed to block out all distractions, he had to block out the news of his father's death and keep on training as if nothing happened. Explaining how he had to tell this to his mother, he claims "I understand what she had to have been going through at that moment, her husband dying, but that was a time of preparation when I had to ignore everything. So I told her, I'm sorry but I can't come home for the funeral." What will always be remembered, of course, Andrews writes, are Schwarzenegger's words and his cool, nonchalant delivery. The fact that his story was soon enough proven false—actually, Schwarzenegger is on record stating several different versions of his father's death, and to this day no one is certain which one is correct—is usually not remembered. The effect it had was the creation of the image of someone who is completely impervious to the emotions and pains of mere, fragile mortals.

Another legendary, oft-quoted, part of the Schwarzenegger interviews for *Pumping Iron* were his claims that the pains and strains of the gym gave him as much pleasure as sex:

> The greatest feeling you can get in the gym . . . is the pump. . . . It's as satisfying to me as coming is, you know, as having sex with a woman and coming. So can you believe how much I'm in heaven? I'm like getting the feeling that I'm coming in the gym. . . . I'm coming at home, when I'm backstage pumping up and when I pose in front of five thousand people. . . . So I get the feeling that I'm coming day and night. I mean it's terrific. So, you know, I'm in heaven.

This image of superhuman toughness is something action fans either *want to* identify with or they find so unrealistic as to be off-putting. Kathleen was willing to disclose very personal information about childhood hardships and traumas that let her identify with Stallone's struggles. The ability to cope with hardship and her present career plans, Kathleen states, can be tied to her fandom of one action star, but the ridiculous invulnerability of the other she could never relate to. Speaking of her identification with Stallone, she explains:

> My life isn't nearly as traumatic as his . . . but yes, a few similarities stick out. I was made fun of in school, too, but not because of anything physical, or concrete problems I had. I was and am vocally gifted, and so at age six, I started auditioning for plays, something most kids don't even give thought to considering. . . . Most kids concentrated on sports and cheerleading, something I ignored. I was also poor, but probably not to the degree that Sly was. We did and will still visit St. Vinnie's [a thrift shop] for clothes. . . . When I was eight, I also had to endure a personal tragedy. My grandfather, whom I was very close to, died very suddenly at age sixty-nine. Thus began the downward spiral into depression, self-hatred, and an unknowing need to express grief that I'm still fighting the aftereffects of today. . . . Third and fourth grades are still almost a complete blank. I spoke little, and withdrew into fantasyland, my imagination, while still doing speeches and being in public plays. I also developed nervous habits and wore braces and headgear for my teeth. Thus, kids just thought I was weird. . . . Cartoon characters became my friends, and I'd create scenes for myself.

In her adult life and the choice to pursue art as a future career, she once again credits to her fandom:

> After I graduated, it was three long years before I went back to school and I am continuing my journey of art and self-discovery. *Rocky* helped me with that . . .

now I'm getting back into acting. . . . All I did as a kid was pretend and make up stories that I told myself. When I heard about Sly writing *Rocky* and all that, along with a bit of his biography, I saw and felt something very familiar in that. That pain, the loneliness, that continuing struggle was something I was instantly in sync with. The fact that he is an artist and writer too just got me more intrigued. Here is someone who went through similar crap that molded him and basically carved him into who he is today, and he made it. And he went through worse than me, so I know I can make it, too.

Schwarzenegger, however, she has a harder time identifying with and, she explains, only in his later films like *End of Days* (1999) can she start to warm to him because of the emotional vulnerability he is able to portray.

Kathleen is also one of the only two women who are fans of Jackie Chan. The other woman is Ruby and she explains that she basically likes to watch Chan's stunning acrobatic and martial arts skills. Kathleen, however, explains that while appreciating Chan's skills, she became a big fan after reading his biography. The lengthy section of the book dealing with Chan's difficult childhood touched her. In disturbing detail, Chan tells a very long story of having been separated from his family at age seven, then raised in the brutal China Drama Academy that gave its headmaster the legal right to train and discipline the students to the death. Kathleen explains that she admires Chan's strength and perseverance, much as she does Stallone's, and his ability to achieve the success he did despite all the adversity in his life.

Before commenting on how Schwarzenegger's fans position his work in their lives and how they reconcile it with their identities, it is also fair to mention that there is a degree of the "deconstruction programme" Andrews attributed to Stallone at work in Schwarzenegger's films as well. As Louis mentioned that he cannot take Schwarzenegger seriously, that he looks at the actor as more of a comedian than a true action star, the humor, the ironic one-liners that are Schwarzenegger's trademarks always seem to signal to discerning viewers that all the ultrastoic machismo going on in the films need not be taken seriously. On an ironic note, critics who say they find Schwarzenegger's films more palatable than Stallone's usually say that is so because Schwarzenegger can make fun of himself whereas Stallone is always deadly serious. Writes Nicolas Kent in his 1991 companion piece to his acclaimed documentary, *Naked Hollywood*: "Sylvester Stallone is in trouble because, unlike Schwarzenegger, he has never learned how to spice his action-adventure movies with self-mockery. Audiences either take him as seriously as he takes himself or they laugh *at* him, not, for all that he might wish it, *with* him."[23] Stallone might cry and bleed, suffer and reveal that he has weaknesses, but it is an exercise that ultimately apotheosizes him. At the end of the torment, he emerges as a mini-god. Schwarzenegger might be able to overcome armies of killers, alien monsters, even a gun battle with Satan himself, a clever pun capping each confrontation, but it all serves to maintain an air of absurdity about the situations.

Perhaps the lack of such humor, an inability to raise the absurd, was what hurt other body-centered action heroes who tried emulating Schwarzenegger's career since the mid- to late 1980s, even into the 1990s. The most notable of such failures—although certainly not the only one, with second place going to Dolph Lundgren, Stallone's opponent in *Rocky IV*—was Jean Claude Van Damme's tenure as action star. As if trying to combine the most effective elements of both the Stallone and Schwarzenegger personas, Van Damme readily talked about growing up a weak, bullied child who turned his life around through bodybuilding and the martial arts, moved to the United States, and, against tremendous odds, achieved action film stardom. Unfortunately, critical fan opinion quickly decided that in place of Schwarzenegger's sly, self-deprecating humor and charisma, all that came through a Van Damme film was a tremendous sense of ego and self-importance. Rosanna Arquette, his costar in *No Place to Hide* (1993), was reported to have said that "Jean-Claude is his own biggest fan."[24]

Whether it is because Schwarzenegger fans insist on focusing on the emotion-burying, stoic essence of his films, ignoring the "deconstruction programme" of the humor that could actually be critiquing machismo, or because they feel the humor helps further suppress the emotion that betrays weakness, getting the sort of self-disclosure the most avid Stallone fans can offer is not as easy with the Schwarzenegger devotees.

My interview with Anthony, a twenty-eight-year-old business executive, was as interesting as the one I conducted with Vin. He recalls being a Schwarzenegger fan since his teens, idolizing the actor for his physique and dedication to bodybuilding chronicled in such magazines as *Muscle and Fitness* and *Flex*, and for Schwarzenegger's business savvy and success as an unlikely politician. Although Anthony has a successful career in the business world, he is also an avid weight trainer himself, explaining that he "fanatically" devotes time, even on the most hectic work days, to at least an hour in the gym. He explains that in college the first thing he attached onto his dorm room wall was a Schwarzenegger poster.

Getting Anthony to talk about the feelings and emotions he invests in film, as well as the more controversial topics of masculinity and gender conflict—as will be in full evidence in the following chapter—was not so easy, however. The most striking feature of the experience of interviewing Anthony is his energy going into the interview, then the sudden reticence displayed when it came to talking about identity and emotional disclosure.

In the beginning of the interview, Anthony could be described as being of high spirits, full of enthusiasm and quick wit. I was invigorated at the idea of getting a lot of easy, clear, and well-expounded-upon information out of him, as he is an intelligent and well-schooled individual. However, the beginning of his interview could also be described as being cocky, if not verging on condescending. He was quick to crack jokes about fuzzy-headed, egg-headed academics spending their time and energy on something as trivial as action films. In some parts he gave replies in a voice imitating Schwarzenegger's accent.

One aspect in which Anthony was very different from all the other interviewees was his claim that he makes most of his film-watching choices based on reviews. None of the other interviewees said this, instead talking about being attracted to a film based on the excitatory pleasures promised by trailers or because a film had a favorite actor, was made by a favorite director, or the plot sounded interesting. In this subject pool, the action film seems to be the ultimate critic-proof film. This is not the case with Anthony, however.

As I discussed Anthony's film-watching with him, it became obvious that there were several very important intervening factors that have affected his film-viewing habits in the past several years. He explains that his job is so demanding that he has very little time to watch films. When he does spend his money on films, he wants to make sure they are worth seeing and he now—as opposed to his teenage years—checks what critics are saying. He is also involved in a "serious" relationship with a woman who does not like action films. He explains because of this they often see films he does not like: "touchy feely movies" and "chick, relationship movies."

When I wanted to talk about how he selected the films he saw or was considering seeing, he explained his ritual of turning to movie reviews. At this point of the conversation, I was again getting the impression that there was a considerable touch of elitism to the information he was disclosing. This impression, of course, was built on his throw-away comments about the egg-headed academics who "actually" spend time studying something like the media. Although he does not claim to watch "art house" films, Anthony does say that he likes what he calls "cerebral films." These, apparently, are superior to his girlfriend's "chick movies," yet still within mainstream genres. He likes to watch intelligent action films and he likes mysteries. He explains that if he is considering seeing a film, he would first turn to the movie reviews in Friday's section of the *Wall Street Journal*. He highly endorses that newspaper for reliable reviews and analyses of films.

Anthony's all-time favorite action films are the *Indiana Jones* series and the *Terminator* films. Of the other 1980s action films, he claims he usually liked the first entry in a series, then got ever more turned off by the subsequent sequels. He explains that *First Blood* was a good action film, but the second and third entries into the Rambo trilogy were inferior. This he soon qualifies, though, adding that perhaps the second *Rambo* film was made the only way the subject and the character could have been approached in a sequel. The third film, however, he says he felt was very bad and a waste of his viewing time. The fourth film, he says, greatly improved on the series after the hyperbole and unrealistic action of *Rambo III*. Similarly, he claims that he enjoyed the first *Die Hard* a lot and the first *Lethal Weapon* a lot, but their sequels were poorly made. When he explains how these films were getting worse with each entry, he certainly is in agreement with the critics, and I myself concur in my own capacity as a fan, except Anthony's early explanation, giving so much credit to critics' judgment, starts to make Anthony's own sentiments suspect here. Listening to him talk, I was beginning to worry that he is completely removing himself from the topic and letting the critics speak for him. Of further frustration was his speaking style at this point, where his replies were quick and glib, appearing thoughtless in too many instances. As I started getting replies to my questions that didn't seem to want to go beyond few-word answers, like "no," "yup," "didn't like it," and "hate it," I realized that I needed to begin insisting that we stay on each question for an extended amount of time and press him to articulate his feelings more fully.

As will be the case in the following chapter, where Anthony's penchant for replying to sensitive and controversial questions by quoting what critics *would* say or what the "typical academic types" would say, his aversion to talking about emotional topics was obvious. Although when I insisted on getting answers, he would eventually articulate his feelings with thoughtful commentary, but by that point the glibness, the slickness was gone and he would often look rigid, self-conscious, and uncomfortable.

Anthony's likes and dislikes can easily be characterized. He likes fast moving films, films he deems "intelligent" and "cerebral," and he very much dislikes slow, emotional, "touchy feelly" romantic and melodramatic films. His favorite action stars are Arnold Schwarzenegger, Harrison Ford, Mel Gibson, and Clint Eastwood. With Ford and Gibson, however, he quickly qualifies that he does not like their romantic, melodramatic films. At the time of the interview he recalled that he had just seen *Random Hearts* (1998) with Ford and "hated it." I wanted to clarify the plot and the reason he might have disliked the film as, once again, he was not very willing to say more about it than "hated it." As I asked him if this was the Ford film that had a suspense plot but was really more of a love story, he confirmed it quickly and said that was exactly why he hated it.

His commentary about why he specifically liked Schwarzenegger explained that he was a fan of the focused, single-minded characters the actor played on screen, a quality Anthony was certain was an extension of Schwarzenegger's real life personality. In Anthony's words, Schwarzenegger has a "decisiveness of action, willingness not to compromise. I work with a lot of shady type characters, so someone who is firm, but veiled in the persona of a machine, I think is good." In one sense, as Anthony explained that he tries to be as driven in both his weight training program and in his professional life, his identification with Schwarzenegger and the values he sees the actor embodying become obvious. However, it is also important to note that the real life manifestations of on-screen personas are so important to Anthony that he likes Schwarzenegger because he believes the screen persona might be close to the real thing. Again, having for years studied the "real" Schwarzenegger's involvement with bodybuilding, as documented on the pages of the *Muscle and Fitness* and *Flex* magazines, Anthony, no doubt, feels the connection between the fictional and the real is very solid.

He makes similar comments about Eastwood, that he likes the way the real Eastwood and the characters he plays seem to be very close. Here, making a joke about his strange television watching habits to illustrate how his hectic professional life leaves very limited amounts of time for entertainment, he tells me that once he actually had his television on a "Classic CSPAN" broadcast where they were rerunning Carmel city council coverage from the late 1980s, when Eastwood was the mayor.

> I'd put him right beside Arnold because he always played strong characters with a lot of backbone. Physically, ethically, morally. When you see him on the city council coverage on CSPAN, the personal character comes through the same way. It's really great to see because what you see in his movies is exactly what he's like in real life. It's great! Dirty Harry runs the city council. He's exactly the same way in real life.

Anthony, apparently, very actively seeks out certain reserved, strong representations of masculinity because he believes such modes of behavior are useful and preferable in real life. He seems to want to confirm this by gravitating toward the work of actors he thinks are close in real life to their fictional alter egos.

Although interviewees like Anthony demonstrate that personality traits, such as the degree to which they feel comfortable seeing intimate emotions displayed, discussed, and dealt with, are often reflective of the films they watch, having an overwhelming concern about issues of control and weakness is not necessarily a concern for all interviewees. Many fans turn to the action film because they feel the narratives reflect lives they have lived—in a metaphorical sense—just as Ray and Vin talk about their immigrant background, because the films are in line with their moral and ethical value systems, and very often because the films reflect the way they see the world and social and governmental institutions operating. The interpretations the fans make of the narratives, the themes, however, can still be found across the spectrum of scholarly identified levels of activity, negotiation, acceptance, or rejection. Other fans can also take a type of detached, connoisseur's, expert's stance back from the film, looking at it as a broad art form and appreciating it as such.

One of the most fascinating interviewees takes the art connoisseur's distance from the genre and is able to give large-scale analyses of the history of the genre, of the virtues and pleasures offered by various action subgenres. Patrick, thirty years old, is a computer engineer and also an aspiring writer who admits to having dabbled in screen writing and attempted to sell video game scenarios to game manufacturers. Thus, the critic's eye Patrick is able to cast at the action film, the way he is able to judge various films in the context of a larger scope of art, is understandable. Although he, too, says that he gets pleasure out of the speed and excitement of the action film, he also indicates that good action films will also be as thematically and morally complex as possible. Although he explains that for his money he does not want to see "the big love story of the day," he is, in fact, expecting that action films delve into characters' psyches, which should be as complicated as possible. "What I really hate," he explains, "are characters that are cardboard, that are one-dimensional." For him characters that are caricatures, that are unoriginal, the ones that feel like the writers and filmmakers gave very little thought in constructing, are not interesting:

> There always has to be something on the other side, just like a good villain has to have . . . if you don't give him a reason why he has to drive this bus full of school children off the side of the road, it's completely brainless. The other side of the coin is true. You know, Mel Gibson from the *Patriot*. Here you have this guy . . . who's trying to get away from his past in the French and Indian war when he lost his mind and butchered people. That's how the movie starts, actually. [Pausing to recall the actual wording of Gibson's narration in the beginning of the film.] "I always feared that the sins of my past will come back to haunt me." It has to have that second dimension of the flawed hero because you don't have any people who don't have at least a few flaws.

It should also be noted that Patrick is interesting in terms of seeing someone for whom strength and power are not a means of repressing emotion or weakness or the complications and insecurities of life. Strength, power, and the ability to control circumstances, at least in the physical sense, are easily Patrick's most obvious attributes. Standing at least six feet and three or four inches tall, Patrick has been involved in sports in one way or another for much of his life. He had always been very athletic in grade school, high school, and college. He had played soccer, football, weight trained, and has a black belt in jujitsu, a sport he has trained in for nine years. The weight-training regimen has very obviously marked itself on Patrick because his tall physique is extremely imposing; his shoulders wide, chest massive and barrel shaped and hands that can ball into hammer-like fists. If not for a very jovial disposition, he would be quite an intimidating man. As will be evident in the following chapter through his comments on the meaning of masculinity, Patrick can be surprisingly critical of the stereotypical concept of macho, of the need to use strength as a means of control, or the suppression or hiding of emotions. As we will see him elaborate in that chapter, a bad action film for him is one where masculinity is used to "prove" things, prove points, settle scores, prove one's worth and toughness. He, instead, likes films where characters change by learning something about themselves.

When I try to bring the focus to the body-centered versus personality/intellect/charisma/leadership-centered heroes, he explains that he prefers the thinking action heroes more than the flexing or fighting ones, the ones for whom the body has been fetishized to bring attention to and "prove" their toughness. When I mention that this is interesting in light of his own athleticism and involvement with a martial art, he explains, quite concisely and humorously, that everything is a matter of perception and relativity:

> You have to come to my home town to really understand. It's like one of my friends . . . said, "jeez, you really do come from a land of giants." I'm like medium, medium small in my town. The average shoe size on my soccer team when I was a junior in high school was a thirteen. We had some very big gentlemen and ladies in my town. I don't know why, but we do. But especially growing up, throughout high school, I was very much on the smaller side, so I had to use my brain in a lot of cases, or my mouth, to get myself out of [possibly violent] situations. When I went out into the larger world, I found out there were quite a few people I could step on if I needed to, but I don't need to.

Patrick also says that he enjoys a number of Arnold Schwarzenegger's films. However, he says that he likes these films for their humor, but a very precise type of humor. The eye he casts toward the humorous situations, the jokes in a Schwarzenegger film, are of the art form aficionado's knowing, analytical gaze. He enjoys picking up on the knowing, self-referential post-modern form of the Schwarzenegger humor, the humor that, as mentioned before, is hinting that all of the action and mayhem and hyperbole happening on screen should not be taken very seriously.

For example, he explains how he watches and enjoys *Predator*, one of his favorite action films. For one, he likes the fact that it has science fiction elements, that Schwarzenegger's antagonist is an alien from outer space. Patrick is also a science fiction fan, so he appreciates the science fiction crossover into the generic action plot of commandos going on a mission. The humorous aspects of the film, however, have to do with the cast. To Patrick, this is a commentary on Schwarzenegger's career, as several of the most prominent and colorful members of the commando team are played by actors who were in previous Schwarzenegger films. In fact, actors Bill Duke, Jesse Ventura, and Sonny Landham are all veteran villains, having appeared in some of the standout examples of the genre in the 1980s and 1990s. *Predator* contributed Ventura's one-liner, "I ain't got time to bleed," which he later enjoyed quoting during his run for the Minnesota governorship. When it comes to the film's machismo and posturing, of which there is plenty in the opening of the film, with Schwarzenegger and Carl Weathers (Apollo Creed of the *Rocky* films) sizing up each other's grip upon a handshake, Ventura spitting tobacco, and Shane Black (the film's most odd bit of casting: Black is the screenwriter behind *Lethal Weapon*, *The Last Boy Scout* [1991], and later Geena Davis's feminist action film *The Long Kiss Goodnight* [1996]) cracking jokes about his girlfriend's genitalia, Patrick's analysis is also unique. He explains:

> The reason that I like that one is that despite his physical size, they put something against him that his physical size isn't going to help him with. I mean, he gets to flex his muscles and run around without his shirt on through the whole movie, but it's really his brains that beat it [the predator].

For Patrick, essentially, the action film does not seem to be a symbolic exercise in the control and suppression of emotions. He is not interested in statements about manhood being proven through stoicism. He appears to be looking at Schwarzenegger as an action comedian, but, unlike Louis, Patrick truly likes the actor and his films on that level.

Patrick's view of all the major action heroes seems to be influenced by his analysis of character creation, acting, and storytelling. In fact, he does not profess strong allegiance to any one action actor and does not seem to be as strongly connected to a specific personality like Louis or Helen or Vin or Anthony appears to be. Patrick, instead, determines the quality of individual films based on his own criteria of what it takes to tell an effective story. But it must be mentioned that Patrick does, most often, seem to favor Mel Gibson over other action stars. He uses Gibson's films as the best examples of how a good action film should be constructed. He does not, however, appear to have a connection to Gibson on such a personal level as to say he feels his own life, experiences, and value systems are mirrored in Gibson.

Of course, what should also be added at this point is that Patrick's reasons for not admitting that the action film's narratives of overcoming suffering, struggle, and obstacles are resonating with him so deeply as they do with

Kathleen or Vin or Helen might be because he might not have traumas so intense to order his life around. He volunteers no information about personal trauma, so we can choose to take his words at their face value. However, again, as will be evident in the following chapters, Patrick does appear to be judging the genre on how thoughtful and complex an approach it gives to ruminations on the nature of manhood.

Interestingly, other interviewees who also are not fans of extreme displays of machismo, especially the muscle flexing for its own sake, are other athletes like Brett, David, Edward, Carl, and Cliff. As Cliff and Carl both train intensely with weights—Carl's sport used to be Olympic-style weight lifting—the lack of importance they place on the exhibitionism of the hyperdeveloped bodybuilder hero is noteworthy. Both say they are interested in the films for their themes, plot, overall artistry, and statements made, rather than heroes who are able to out-macho all their opponents.

Again, with such data we can ultimately take people's testimony at their face value and accept the fact that some individuals might not be drawn to sports and competitive endeavors to strictly prove points, even scores, or seek some psychological redress for personal hurts in the past.

For example, Jeff, a twenty-three-year-old undergraduate and active martial art film watcher and Jet Li devotee, explains that he does not consider himself a very macho individual and does not feel the need for physical posturing and aggression. "I'm not an aggressive person," he insists, "actually I'm quite timid." In fact, Jeff does not look like an athlete at all and is not physically imposing or muscular in any way. Although we cannot know if physicality, or its lack thereof, or aggression and physical conflict has ever been an issue in his life, one thematic problem he seems to be considerate of, critical of, when talking about films, is the race of major characters. As Jeff is of Chinese American ancestry, it is worth noting that in the case of martial arts films—without admitting to making his choices consciously—he lists only Asian actors like Jet Li and Jackie Chan and says he particularly likes to follow the career and films of Hong Kong director John Woo. He explains that he is also a fan of major American actors, particularly Tom Cruise in action roles like the *Mission: Impossible* films and John Travolta when he plays either action heroes or action villains.

As I had some vintage action film fan magazines, a biography of Jackie Chan, a biography of Sylvester Stallone, and some still photos from several *James Bond* films and *Armageddon* on hand when talking to Jeff, I wanted to show him several of the pictures when we were discussing the body images of action stars. Although he quickly declared that he prefers the action hero who handles his challenges more through personality, wit, and cunning, rather than his objectified muscles and body, the most noteworthy part of his examination of the pictures was a displeasure with scenes from *Rambo II* and its Asian villains pictured.

SUMMARY

Interviewing these study participants about the action film's metaphorical connection to experiences and values governing their lives reveals a selection process of films that is often very precise and serves the fulfillment of various personal goals. But, most importantly, when the interviewees talk about the films they watch and actors they are fans of, we can see clues emerging about their own personalities.

Having seen that the true heavy viewers of the action film will discerningly pick and choose what they want to see, the testimonies of the interviewees in this chapter help give a glimpse of why they might be gravitating toward certain films and action stars. It is true that the high user will watch a lot of action films with all of the major action stars, perhaps settling for actors and films and themes that he or she does not deem to be the best of the genre, simply to fulfill that need for the fast moving, highly-stimulating narratives. However, as the testimonies here gave evidence, a true fan of the genre is a devotee of films of a certain theme or certain actors because such themes and stars reflect their own self-image and personalities. Preferences can also often be classified along gender lines, and these interviewees demonstrated some classic gender differences in perception, attitude, and communication styles.

The self-control, restraint, and stoicism in the face of crises, hardship, and distress that the action film glamorizes are attractive to men who find self-disclosure and the discussion of emotional issues difficult. The fans of Clint Eastwood and Arnold Schwarzenegger especially demonstrate this here, as they discuss how their favorite star embodies the virtues of emotional reserve and self-control. Emotional openness, however, varies in action films and certain stars and certain fans deal with it in a variety of ways. For example, talking to Vin Diesel fans or Sylvester Stallone fans, or even fans of Mel Gibson or Nicolas Cage or Bruce Willis reveals that not all fans require emotions to be denied through stone-faced stoicism or laughed at. The films of these actors more openly admit the male capacity to have emotions and feel weakness. Discussing this with their fans reveals people who find it easier to talk about emotions. Perhaps not coincidentally, the female participants in this study more readily line up behind these more "sensitive" actors.

The next chapter, however, will reveal how the adversity, the pain, and the challenges the action hero has to be man enough to overcome are often metaphors for current social stress factors tormenting them exactly for being men. The same stoicism that men admire and wish to imitate, however, may also keep them from addressing their problems in a more organized, public manner.

NOTES

1. Joseph Campbell, *The Hero with a Thousand Faces* (Princeton, NJ: Princeton University Press, 1972).

2. Andrew Lycett, *Ian Fleming: The Man Behind James Bond* (Atlanta: Turner Publishing, 1995).

3. Neal Gabler, "Inside Every Superhero Lurks a Nerd," *New York Times*, May 12, 2002.

4. Studies on identification with characters in fiction and the interpretation of moral messages can be found in Paul E. Jose and William F. Brewer, "Development of Story Liking: Character Identification, Suspense and Outcome Resolution, *Developmental Psychology* 20, no. 5 (1984): 911–924; Barbara J. Wilson, Joanne Cantor, L. Gordon, and Dolf Zillmann, "Affective Response of Nonretarded and Retarded Children to the Emotions of a Protagonist," *Child Study Journal* 16, no. 2 (1986): 77–93; Dolf Zillmann, "The Psychology of the Appeal of Portrayals of Violence," in *Why We Watch: The Attractions of Violent Entertainment*, ed. Jeffrey H. Goldstein (Oxford: Oxford University Press, 1998), 179–211; Dolf Zillmann and Joanne Cantor, "Affective Responses to the Emotions of a Protagonist," *Journal of Experimental Social Psychology* 13 (1977): 155–165.

5. Yvonne Tasker, *Spectacular Bodies: Gender, Genre and the Action Cinema* (New York: Routledge, 1993), 9.

6. Frank Sanello, *Stallone: A Rocky Life* (Edinburgh: Mainstream Publishing, 1998).

7. Henry Jenkins, *Textual Poachers: Television Fans and Participatory Culture* (New York: Routledge, 1992).

8. Jenkins, *Textual Poachers*, 155.

9. Jenkins, *Textual Poachers*, 163, 171.

10. Laurent Bouzereau, *Ultra Violent Movies: From Sam Peckinpah to Quentin Tarantino* (Sacramento, CA: Citadel Press, 2000), 150. Morrell's impressions about Rambo as a cultural icon and some of the misinterpretations of the character are cited in this book's chapter on the Rambo films.

11. Roger Ebert, "Review of the film *Rambo: First Blood Part II*," in *Roger Ebert's Home Movie Companion* (Kansas City, MO: Andrews McMeel Publishing, 1992), 452.

12. David Denby, "Movies: The Last Angry Men," *New York*, January 16, 1984.

13. David Desser, "The Martial Arts Film in the 1990s," in *Film Genre 2000: New Critical Essays*, ed. Wheeler Winston Dixon (Albany: State University of New York Press, 2000), 77–110.

14. Emanuel Levy, *John Wayne: Prophet of the American Way of Life* (Metuchen, NJ: Scarecrow Press, 1988).

15. Desser, "The Martial Arts Film in the 1990s," 103.

16. Richard Schickel, *Clint Eastwood* (New York: Alfred A. Knopf, 1996), 145.

17. Alan M. Klein, *Little Big Men: Bodybuilding Subculture and Gender* Construction (Albany: State University of New York Press, 1993); Leslie Heywood, *Bodymakers: A Cultural Anatomy of Women's Body Building* (New Brunswick, NJ: Rutgers University Press, 1998).

18. Samuel Wilson Fussell, *Muscle: Confessions of an Unlikely Bodybuilder* (New York: Avon Books, 1991), 19, 192.

19. Fussell, *Muscle*, 24–25.

20. Frank Sanello, *Stallone*, 148.

21. Sanello, *Stallone*, 16.

22. Sanello, *Stallone,* 16.

23. Nicolas Kent, *Naked Hollywood: Money and Power in the Movies Today* (New York: St. Martin's Press, 1991), 108. Emphasis in the original.

24. Marshall Julius, *Action!: The Action Movie A-Z* (Bloomington: Indiana University Press, 1996), 225.

6

Man Talk: Managing the Modern Male Identity (Crisis) in the Genre

There's something about maniacs messing with good men that always pisses me off.

—Louis Gossett Jr., *Iron Eagle*

When I mention that my primary field of media research involves action/ adventure films, it often invites commentary and input, usually from those who do not like the genre. Often the commentary from men who do not like action films is tinged with a rarefied air of condescension. They do, however, understand that at the core of such films is the issue of masculinity, and they feel the films are speaking to the masculine condition. Usually, however, they do not like what is being said, or claim they cannot or do not need to relate to discourses on machismo. These men claim they do not like to tie masculinity to narratives centered on violence, and they are not interested in displays of toughness because they do not feel powerless or disenfranchised in a way so as to need a movie-screen–sized morality tale of power. But one particularly useful and interesting commentary or critique that I received from a fifty-five-year-old woman several years ago has stuck with me. As our discussion wandered onto specific action personalities, she explained that she cannot understand the reason for the success of the genre, especially as some of its most prominent figures are people like Arnold Schwarzenegger. She explained that she found him unattractive because of the extreme bodybuilding physique. Sylvester Stallone's looks are an improvement, she said, but not by much. Such a muscular physique is way beyond fitness, she said, it is on the level of grotesque. She said that she won't watch a Schwarzenegger film because he is not the sort of "female's ideal" the male stars were when she was young. She explained that actors like Paul Newman and Cary Grant, whose films she grew up with and still loves, were her favorites because the men represented that ideal a woman wished a man could be: they were handsome, confident, and suave.

This was certainly interesting because she was suggesting that a male actor could not be a success unless women would validate his work. I thought the commentary was on par with suggesting that a female performer should not be successful unless she is of *Playboy* specifications and her work was oriented to please men. While I can understand why she likes the sort of star that she does, I also recognized that she does not understand the real reason behind Schwarzenegger's success. As a matter of fact, many people do not, and they do not understand the success of the late 1960s to millennium era line of action heroes. Schwarzenegger is not the icon that he is because he was a female's ideal, but because he is a male's ideal. As a matter of fact, the same can be said for Stallone or Eastwood or Jean Claude Van Damme or Steven Seagal or Vin Diesel. Although Stallone might have had a sizable constituency of female fans, women, for a time, were drawn to Van Damme's films because of his *GQ* looks, and Mel Gibson always had a lot of female admirers, but the stars who shaped the modern action film were primarily speaking to men. Although this is undergoing a transformation today, with Tom Cruise, Brad Pitt, Nicolas Cage, and Matt Damon becoming the new A-list of action, for the participants of this study, the quintessential modern action heroes are men who speak to the problems, insecurities, and longings of men.

Clint Eastwood gives one of the best explanations for the male's ideal action hero. At the apex of his career as a top box office action hero in the late 1960s and early 1970s, with a line of successful westerns and the *Dirty Harry* films to his credit, he had often explained that he knew full well that his core constituency were young men, guys with a high school education, a menial job, people who do not have much of a say in society. Eastwood added that his films are enjoyed by the kind of aimless young men he used to be, working various odd jobs before getting his acting break. These are the young men who wanted to go into a theater for an hour and a half and get a vicarious thrill out of seeing someone who can talk back to authority, who makes his own rules, who lives by his own code of conduct and ethics, because the real world will seldom give anyone the opportunity to do that.

> My appeal is the characters I play. A superhuman character who has all the answers is double cool, exists on his own without society or the help of society's police forces. A guy sits in the audience, he's twenty-five years old, and he's scared stiff about what he's going to do with his life. He wants to have that self-sufficient thing he sees up on the screen . . . but it will never happen that way. Man is always dreaming of being an individual, but man is really a flock animal.[1]

The hero who provides these vicarious thrills is one in the middle of a narrative about power, about a man getting power, regaining power, exercising power for a higher cause of justice that is falling by the wayside in modern society. Action heroes of the mold Eastwood's characters come from, or Arnold Schwarzenegger's characters, or those of Stallone or Bruce Willis, have more pressing issues to attend to than impressing women with their suave manners. As a matter of fact, the women of the universe these characters inhabit do not impress easily with confident, strong masculinity. The women of that world are not looking to be rescued, they are looking to run the world. The staggering muscularity of Schwarzenegger, therefore, or that of Stallone or Vin Diesel, the martial arts mastery of Steven Seagal or Chuck Norris, or the stone-faced stoicism and quick draw of Charles Bronson and Clint Eastwood are not meant to make women swoon; they are made to make men fantasize about inhabiting the personas of these characters, to have the larger-than-life power it takes to overcome all obstacles around them, to single-handedly battle armies of antagonists. These attributes are the armor Fussell saw on Schwarzenegger, the flesh and blood armor that renders the man invulnerable against the attacks of modern society, that renders him larger than life, superhuman, and, at the same time, less human.[2] These action heroes need to prove they still have a place in this world. The best way they can do it is when a threat presents itself, when through brute power, ultrahuman stoicism, and the ability to take pain where mere mortals break down, they assert themselves and prove their worth, if only for a short while. In just as many films, the action hero tries to prove not just his worth to the world at large, but that his life, as a whole, had some meaning that is worth remembering, worth passing on to his offspring. Action heroes try to hold on to their families that are either in a crisis because of them or faring well despite them. They are desperately trying to disprove statements by Eastwood himself when he says:

As far as the tormented male thing goes, maybe I'm interested in it because it's an obsolete thing—masculinity, I mean. There's very few things men are required for, except maybe siring. I guess I'm interested in the insecurities that keep outsiders outside.[3]

To many of the male fans in this subject pool, the crisis of masculinity lies in the paradoxes and contradictions between what a man needs to do, what a man is expected to do to fit in, the legacy he will try to leave for the future through family and children, and how he is regarded and treated for it in return.

Such readings are very astute because they accurately put the finger on why the era spanning from the 1960s to the late 1990s created underappreciated heroes from Dirty Harry to Rambo to Bruce Willis's John McClain, the hero of the *Die Hard* series. In *The Presidio* (1988), a cop action thriller, Sean

Connery, playing a career army officer, has a reflection about how soldiers are always treated in all societies. They are like a big, ugly, vicious dog, he explains, something you let out of the basement when you think your house is in danger, but once the threat is gone, you want to hide it away as quickly as you can because you are ashamed of it.

The one constant among the testimonials coming from each of my interviewees, even those who have some very fundamental disagreements about the nature of masculinity, is they feel the action film takes on the issue of masculinity in a twofold approach: it first glamorizes male strength, then shows its anachronistic shadings in the modern world and asks if it is worth reproducing for future generations. The genre keeps tensions alive, it implies men are standing on thin ice today, no matter how many times they might rise to the occasion and destroy terrorists, drug lords, or gangs of assassins. If anything, the action film, in the eyes of this subject pool, does not show men regaining lost ground, no matter how much they might try, but rather buying a moment's reprieve from being rendered completely obsolete. In turn, if they are very lucky, they are deemed worthy of a second chance by a girlfriend or wife and have a future with their children.

Interestingly, some of the most thoughtful testimony on the topic explains that the best of the action films will explore the duality, while the worst the genre has to offer simply deals with men proving how tough they are or how tough they can be "when pushed too far."

Patrick, the thirty-year-old computer engineer and Schwarzenegger fan—only as far as enjoying Schwarzenegger's self-mockery—says that for him the genre is interesting only as long as it is self-reflexive. A good action film has to ask questions about itself, it needs to examine the role of masculinity in society and the future of masculinity. He states that certainly everything the genre is criticized for is represented in many films, although not in the ones he will spend time watching:

> There is a common problem in the media. Just pointing to a problem and having a one or two word reduction to it. Like, oh, it's a testosterone flick and shrug it off. But there can be so much subtlety inside. It's like saying, "it's a film." Or "it's a color film," or a "black and white film."And [yes] there are boatloads. . . . I'm just amazed at how much money goes into bad films.

But, since Patrick explained that he does some writing of his own and he has been serious enough about it to try submissions to some publishers, I ask him to elaborate further. This he does very clearly:

> By and large, the bad ones are varying things like you gotta be tough, you have to be strong, and you basically have to pommel someone to prove yourself. The

better ones are more about . . . case by case . . . they're more about learning to
deal with different aspects of masculinity.

When I ask him what he means about "learning," he explains that the learning and discovery of an action hero is his coming to grips with aggression.
This aggression, in Patrick's opinion, is an inherent part of masculinity, and
one must either learn how to control it or channel it into positive action in
times of danger. Patrick often brings Mel Gibson up as a reference point in
our discussion, so when I asked him about what he would use as the perfect
exemplars in the Gibson oeuvre, he quickly points to *Braveheart* (1995) and
The Patriot (2000). Both films, in Patrick's opinion, are the two sides of the
same coin. At the time *The Patriot* was released, critics indeed needled it as
being "*Braveheart* in 1776." In fact, both films *are* similar. They both involve
men who would rather stay out of a conflict that is escalating toward war. But
with the loss of a loved one, the family is thrust into a crisis, they are pushed
over the brink, they strike back in revenge and wind up being a figurehead in
a revolution. In *Braveheart*, Gibson's new bride is murdered, spurring him
to rebel against the tyrannical British rule of Scotland. In *The Patriot*, the
murder of one of his children leads him into the rebellion against the British
colonial government. "There is a huge masculine undertone to those films,"
Patrick says, especially how a man's capacity for violence affects his relationships with those around him. "The two core elements in those films are how a
man is related to a lover, a lost love, and how the man is related to his family."
It should be noted, though, that *The Patriot*, generally regarded as a paler
imitation of the Oscar-winning *Braveheart*, begins its story by establishing
that the capacity for violence and the ability to degenerate into the most brutal
and sadistic of killers is very well a part of the Gibson character's personality. As Patrick very accurately observed in the previous chapter, the narration starting the film is key. There the Gibson character explains that during
the French and Indian War he had a breakdown, lost all his inhibitions, and
took part in vicious massacres of captured enemy soldiers, soldiers who had
surrendered and laid down their arms. Now as a family man, a single father
raising a houseful of kids, he tries to reconcile the two parts of his personality. Or, more like it, he is fighting to suppress his violent side, struggling to
keep hidden the violence that has been a part of him. No matter the cause, no
matter the circumstances under which the violence was carried out, civilized
society will not condone a man raising children to be tainted by such acts of
brutality. While the *Braveheart* protagonist rises to the challenge, takes up
arms, and fights for a just cause, the hero of the more glossy, more stylized
The Patriot is a darker character to begin with. Masculinity and violence are
linked from the outset in the second film, and the capacity to do violence is

not something that comes about as a result of happenstance, a dark turn of fortunes. This inherent violence, however, is something Patrick approves of when looked at through the analytical lens of a film. It defines what he means by a character going through a "learning" process:

> Aggression . . . not really violence, but aggression . . . is part of masculinity. Violence is a part of the world, but aggression is a part of masculinity. . . . Part of the whole kit and caboodle. Dealing with that is a core problem. There have been a lot of action films that have dealt with it in a different way. Finding yourself and things, subtler things. You don't really hear a lot of things about women traveling to Tibet to find themselves. This isn't something they do, this is a male, you know, thing. So a lot of action movies, especially when the main character is going through a transformation to learn. The bad ones it's more a man trying to prove himself. The good ones, it's a part of him trying to come to grips with his personality.

Patrick's observations about the masculinity of the genre are very much in line with film and literary criticism charting the classical social and philosophical tensions in American adventure stories, traced as far back as books and films about the frontier. In fact, according to the history or the archetypal American adventure, "classical" masculinity, or "old-fashioned" masculinity, was at odds with the greater society, the civilized social order, even in the olden days.

The archetypes were cast in the novels of the first James Fennimore Cooper's "Leatherstocking" novels. The supreme hero, a character of faultless moral bearings, physical strength, combat skills, and unflinching courage, was a man at odds with the civilized world. Civilization, in the Cooper novels, is a realm of the female and that of too many effeminate men, corrupt men, men who compromise, who are weak and are traitorous. Although the men of the civilized colonial world are not exclusively villainous, none of them could ever measure up to the physical and moral stature of the outsider hero, Hawkeye. One does not need to look too closely to draw parallels between the Hawkeye character and the Bruce Willis protagonist in *Die Hard*, or Rambo for that matter. Hawkeye's tight bond with a Native American partner is likewise echoed in dozens of modern "buddy" action films, the white hero partnered with a minority sidekick. Such literary conventions first moved to the movie screen with western films, which, in turn, as Tasker posits in her action and masculinity analysis, would eventually give up many of its archetypes to the action/adventure film once the "Old West" failed to hold the interest of audiences.[4] However, through the history of American dramatic art, femininity and masculinity, community and individuality, the wilderness and civilization were always the most important thematic oppositions explored. They were always the polar opposites, inexorably linked and dependent on each other, yet ultimately always irreconcilable. The wilderness and individuality, the realms of primal masculine physicality, the American adventure story always presented, were naturally to be replaced by forces of civilization and community, progress, and the realm of the intellect, the feminine. Warshow summarizes his analysis of western film archetypes and yet another important western dichotomy, the geographic dichotomy pitting the East against the West:

> Very often this woman is from the East and her failure to understand [the Western hero] represents a clash of cultures. In the American mind, refinement, virtue, civilization, Christianity itself, are seen as feminine, and therefore women are often portrayed as possessing a kind of deeper wisdom, while the men, for all their apparent self-assurance, are fundamentally childish. But the West, lacking the graces of civilization, is the place "where men are men"; in Western movies, men have the deeper wisdom and the women are children.[5]

The tension, however, at least in the western, is rarely left in equilibrium, the balance does not last. It is a historical art form, and we know the days of the Wild West were brief. The wilderness, where the male penchant for aggression and physicality, individuality, and rugged self-reliance thrived, was overcome by progress and civilization.

An ironic state of progression from one world to another is best seen in John Ford's westerns. Ford likes documenting historical progress from wilderness to civilization, the masculine to the feminine. But he dramatizes the irony in male heroism, protecting the very progress that will bring about its own obsolescence. When Ford teamed with John Wayne for some of his most memorable westerns, one of Wayne's favorite themes was also added to the mix: that of the strong, masculine father figure attempting to secure his legacy through his sons. Since this father-son theme was present in the westerns Wayne made with Howard Hawks, as well as many of his war films, metaphorically handled as Wayne played the team leader/father figure molding immature boys into men, the theme is definitely a Wayne favorite, not just a Ford construct. In Ford's westerns, though, heroism is seen in the protection of the community and the securing of the future of the family. The most extreme masculine traits of aggression, skills with guns and fists, are put to the service of protecting the community. But once the community's threats had been eliminated, ironically so, too, a world comes to an end where the strong male is needed, the legacy of his rugged traits not entirely secured for the future. In these films, the strong male is left but to wander away into the archetypal sunset at the end of the film.

The best example of this statement is framed in the final shot of Ford's *The Searchers* (1956). Here, once the outmoded Wayne hero's job is done (whose expiring shelf-life is clearly established throughout the film), he cannot join the community he just helped. His young sidekick (Jeffrey Hunter), whom he drove and bullied throughout the film, we can guess, will, no doubt, *not* continue in his image. So Wayne turns and starts walking into the distance. Besides being framed by the camera itself, the audience sees him framed in a doorway, the camera on the inside and Wayne walking away into the wilderness on the outside. However, the interior of the home now overwhelms the composition on the screen—civilization overwhelming wilderness. In the windowsill sits a potted flower, another favorite Ford image of civilization: the garden, the image of domesticity. As the camera draws backward and Wayne keeps shrinking, so the interior of the room grows, the image of civilization overwhelming the last tiny glimpses of the wilderness surrounding Wayne on the outside. Eventually the door closes, the metaphorical door of civilization, modernity, female supremacy closing on the masculine wilderness.

Similar in some ways to this and noteworthy is the ending of John Sturges's *The Magnificent Seven* (1960), where the progress from the masculine code of the gunfighter in the wilderness to the feminine world of domesticity is presented in harsher tones and the traditions of one generation of rugged fighting men is not kept alive in their "offspring." However, the ending of Sturges's film implies that the new world is not entirely so pure, even if the progression from one to the other may still be the natural evolution of human society. Here the gunfighters save a town the audience is never entirely so sure is worth saving. As a matter of fact, the heroes of the film might not be so sure the peasants they fight for are that worthy either. However, as gunfighters, as people schooled in the hard, masculine ways of violence and killing, they take on the job of ridding a Mexican village of a gang of marauding bandits because there is nothing better they, the gunfighters, can do with their time or skills. One of the most ironically humorous scenes in the beginning of the film has Steve McQueen considering what else he could do, other than work as a hired killer. He was told by a man in another town that he could have a prosperous future as a "crackerjack clerk" if he took advantage of the opportunity. Thus, with nothing better to do, they head to Mexico and fight for the peasants, despite the fact that their employers betray them several times. Eventually, all but three of the gunmen get killed. The ending, however, sets the world of the gunman side by side with that of the "civilized" peasants. Here, the civilized side is a field being worked by the peasants. The field, ready to be picked of its harvest, is clearly feminine. It bears new life. Then, one of the gunmen (Horst Buchholz) actually starts to look at the peasant life longingly, especially since he had been attracted to one of the peasant girls. He considers laying down his gun, and soon enough he does so. He hangs it up on a fence post and joins the girl picking crops in the field. This gunfighter, most importantly, is the youngest member of the group, commonly referred to as "The Kid." He is the next generation of men, he is the future, whereas the other two survivors are older, weathered, leathery gunmen, too old for anything other than to ride away into the distance and obsolescence. When one of them looks at the peasants and says, "so, I guess we won," the other replies, "no, we didn't win. We lost. They [the peasants] won. We always lose."

In several key ways, this film is an important precursor to *The Dirty Dozen* in 1965, both films about misfit males on the fringe of society. On the one hand, the male characters are marginalized in the beginning of both stories since they possess no other skills besides the worst masculinity is capable of: aggression and the ability and willingness to kill. On the other hand, they become the saviors of society in a sense, or a small community representative of the larger civilized society as a whole. In *The Dirty Dozen*, the marginalization of the main characters is the most extreme: they are a motley collection of convicts during World War II. Their crimes represent some of the worse brutality men can commit. Some are murderers, others thieves, thugs, and sex offenders. However, at the height of the war, they are given a chance to redeem themselves by going on a suicide mission behind enemy lines. In essence, the Allied cause, the free, democratic, civilized world now needs these thugs and brutes to survive.

In *The Dirty Dozen*, however, the continuity of a tradition, the metaphor for securing the future of rugged men through "offspring" of some form, is no longer even a feasible question. Although celebrated in the course of the film for what they can achieve for the rest of civilized society, the men here become expendable, they *must* become expendable and die for the sins that put them in prison in the first place.

Sam, a twenty-seven-year-old film buff, remarks about the significance of this. Sam likes old movies, and he explains that even the older action actors, men who were in their prime as tough guys in the 1960s, are his favorite action heroes. He is also a fan of *The Dirty Dozen*, and in terms of the masculinity crisis theory, he believes the plot is very significant in its use of the convicts. He explains that they represent all strong, hard masculinity run amok, yet at the same time they display traits that society cannot afford to completely eradicate. Civilized society may *want* to destroy these traits, declare them obsolete, yet it can never afford to do so. Such men may be locked away from the world under normal circumstances, hidden from the world as best as possible, just like the big, ugly guard dog Connery talks about in *The Presidio*, but the world still cannot go on without such men. Even the most extreme masculinity, the form of masculinity an enlightened society overtly tries to wipe out, Sam interprets, must sometimes be called upon to actually save it. However, seldom are these characters redeemed by their deeds, seldom are they given the chance to reintegrate in society, to bond with family and influence the future through children.

As Sam is a devoted Stanley Kubrick fan, he draws a comparison to *A Clockwork Orange* (1971). He feels *Orange* is likewise exploring the paradoxical issues of masculine strength, aggression, and violence and how far an enlightened society should go to condemn it and control it. Here, tampering with the male psyche and "natural" behavior, even if it can sometimes manifest itself through nothing less than the most repulsive acts of brutality, has side effects just as dangerous as unchecked aggression. Once a person cannot call upon the instinct for violence, he remains a potential victim of not only all the other violent threats of the world, but the specter of state repression. One of the many wickedly ironic twists of the story takes place after its anti-hero Alex (Malcolm McDowell), a sadistic thug and rapist, gets his brain reprogrammed. Once Alex has been pacified by the reprogramming, one of his former victims, a political activist, wants to (unknowingly) use him as a campaign platform against the government's authoritarian policies. It seems, the film wants to argue, that if a society could truly be pacified, what would its citizens be able to do to prevent a repressive, fascistic regime from taking over? If the people would be incapable of even considering anything violent, would their fate be no different from that of cattle at the mercy of their overlords?

It is interesting to realize that as popular entertainment chooses to explore the "enlightened" vilification of hard masculinity, it rarely ever warns of what might happen if all those supposedly anti-social traits would be completely eliminated, as *A Clockwork Orange* does. What would indeed happen if strong masculinity could not replicate itself and set a legacy for the future? Although action films, according to critics and its fans represented in this study, have masculinity at their core, they have never presented a vision of all the worst of men being eradicated. If anything came as close as *Orange*, it was science fiction once again: an episode of the original *Star Trek* series, titled "The Enemy Within." If Nathanson and Young's 2002 work on the negative images of males in the media is to be given its due and their thesis accepted that the same characteristics that popular culture criticizes the most about masculinity is the same as what it attributes to images of evil and demonic beings, then the evil of "The Enemy Within" is masculinity at its extreme. Here, the story has Captain Kirk split in two by a transporter accident, with one part being purely good and the other wholly evil. The evil half is the personification of aggression, the impulse for violence and lust. It is strong masculinity taken to its extreme. Naturally, Kirk's crew quickly wants to destroy this evil incarnation. However, what they begin to notice is that the "good" half is not entirely right either. The "evil," they realize, came from within him, was always a part of him, and now as the "evil" is separate, what is left behind becomes ever more indecisive, weak, lacking motivation, passion, or bravery. In essence, if a purely biological parallel is drawn, the "good" Kirk appears as if he had been castrated. The "evil" aggressiveness in him resembles a pure distillation of testosterone.

Patrick likewise remarks that he, too, has seen it as significant that so many times action films find their heroes in prison in the beginning of the story. Masculinity is no longer just objectionable, such a metaphor says, but it is to be treated like a contaminant, a hazard to society that needs to be locked up. However, suddenly an impossible mission must be accomplished and men in prison are the only ones who are able to get the job done.

Patrick is definitely correct in claiming that there are unusually high numbers of criminal heroes and prisoner heroes. *The Dirty Dozen* itself spawned an entire war film subgenre about misfits and criminals being rounded up into the most proficient fighting unit that can accomplish a crucial mission. By the late 1970s, even television followed what in 1965 was a terrifically controversial premise. Producer Stephen J. Cannell's action series *The Black Sheep Squadron* involved a more sanitized collection of "screwballs and misfits," biding their time in a special unit until they would be court-martialed. In the meantime, of course, they became known as "the terrors of the Pacific," winning the battles no one else could. Later, in the 1980s, at the height of the popularity of special forces Vietnam vets as heroes films, Cannell repeated the criminal-hero formula with *The A-Team*, its outsider-male-as-last-resort theme summarized in each episode's introductory narration: "In 1972, a crack commando unit was sent to prison by a military court for a crime they didn't commit. These men promptly escaped from a maximum-security stockade to the Los Angeles underground. Today, still wanted by the government, they survive as soldiers of fortune. If you have a problem, if no one else can help, and if you can find them, maybe you can hire the A-Team." John Carpenter's cult action/science fiction film *Escape from New York* (1981) begins with a criminal (Kurt Russell) getting recruited to save the president, the opening scene of *Rambo II* has its hero being retrieved from a federal prison for a mission few others have a chance of completing, and, among legions of similar films, *Demolition Man* again has a once-convicted cop emerging from a cryogenic prison to save a feminized society—in the words of a criminal (Wesley Snipes), "a pussy-whipped, Brady Bunch version of itself"—from an ultra-violent killer.

Patrick then explains that one of his favorite films is *Virtuosity* (1995) because of the harder-edged approach it takes to the male-marginalized-through-criminal metaphor and that male's relationship to a single mother

who almost becomes his love interest. Here, yet another convict emerges
from prison because he is the only one who stands a chance of catching a
super villain. As the film is a science fiction/action hybrid, the criminal is
very literally "super." He is a computer hologram's personality named SID
6.7 (Sadistic, Intelligent, and Dangerous), who gets programmed into the
body of a nanotechnology android (in the form of Russell Crowe) and goes
on a killing spree to fulfill his original programming. Outfitted with the psychological profiles of history's most brutal serial killers and dictators, the
hologram was made to cause mayhem as a virtual reality simulation used to
train cops. Now with SID on the loose, the only one who stands a chance of
stopping him is imprisoned cop Denzel Washington, supervised by, naturally,
a woman (Kelly Lynch). In addition, the female supervisor is a successful
single mother doing very well raising her daughter on her own. What makes
a great impression on Patrick is the fact that the cop is very much guilty of
everything he was charged with, and the way the Washington character's
relationship with the female supervisor comes to a conclusion:

> Well there's this woman who was assigned to help him track down Russell
> Crowe's character . . . there's attraction [between Washington and the woman]
> . . . but Denzel Washington was a convict for killing someone . . . *in cold blood*!
> No two ways about it. Caught on film. But in that last scene they're not together.
> The woman's standing there holding her daughter, whom Denzel *saved*! He
> saved her daughter! He came through in a pinch. But she's not hugging him.
> They're way apart, all alone. That particular scene stands out in my head as one
> particular fish that's swimming against the stream.

In essence, Patrick explains that he admires this film because it does not
hedge its messages, it does not try to water down its implications with a pat
Hollywood ending. He agrees that the film uses the convicted Washington
character as a metaphor for strong masculinity. His criminality represents
the innate male impulses and potential for violence. Washington is in prison
for the very crimes he was accused of committing; he went berserk and
killed a suspect in cold blood during an investigation. He was not framed or
wrongfully imprisoned. Testosterone-driven male impulses for violence are
antithetical to civilized society and, in turn, the Washington character is its
metaphorical representative. However, the film's ending is surprisingly stark
when it comes to resolving the issue, earning Patrick's respect. It offers no
reconciliation between the feminine, here the representative of civilized order
through the supervisor assigned (by a female police commissioner) to watch
over Washington, and the masculine extreme. The two do not embrace, do
not kiss, there is no hint that they will be lovers or go on and make a new life
together. There is no hint that anything resembling the patriarchal order and

its extension through the nuclear family will reassert itself after the credits roll. Since the woman already has a daughter she has done just fine in raising, she doesn't need Washington to have any influence on her future, much less an ultra-(violent)-male like this ex-convict.

When I ask Patrick if he feels the imprisoned male character is symbolizing the male under attack, he quickly replies in the affirmative:

> Oh, I believe it is [the prisoner a symbol for the besieged modern male]. When they're going to make a movie, they want to make a character whom you automatically find interesting and you identify with. It can't *be* you because that wouldn't be incredibly interesting, but it has to have aspects of you. And outsiders are exactly what white American males feel like today.

When I asked whether the crux of the masculinity crisis in the action film was an issue with Patrick, he very much agreed that in many of the most popular action films of the past three decades at least, persecuted masculinity, masculinity on the fringe, masculinity that has been barred from influencing its future through a family, is a quiet, yet constant, theme. When I asked him to react to the idea that since the 1960s, there has been an inordinate number of action heroes living on the fringe, burnouts and mavericks who find their skills for violence and combat—the traditional domain of the male—unappreciated by society until a crisis presents itself that can only be solved by physical action, he immediately agrees with this and draws a connection to one of the seminal 1980s action films. In his words:

> That's pretty accurate. *Die Hard* is exactly what you're describing. The guy's divorcing, having trouble with the kids, commuting to his wife [to Los Angeles from New York], and then this terrorist act comes along and he is the only one that can do anything to save them.

Patrick's reading of *Die Hard* is quite astute in tying it to the masculinity crisis. But this same masculinity crisis subtext is what made the film controversial among some critics upon its release. The most scathing analysis of the film came from Yacowar in the film journal *Jump Cut*, arguing that *Die Hard* "has a deeper appeal in its political assumptions which speak to the sexist who craves to have his obsolete delusions reaffirmed."[6] Popular critics soon followed suit in putting *Die Hard* into a sociopolitical context as the film's blockbuster popularity made it a standard setter for action films in terms of narrative speed, big-budget stunts, and plot structure. (It defined the "location specific" action subgenre; a type of film confined to a specific area taken over by a gang of criminals, where only one man, accidentally trapped during the takeover, has a chance of defeating the enemy. Other films of this type are

Under Siege 1 and 2 [1992, 1995], *The Taking of Beverly Hills* [1991], *Speed 1 and 2* [1994, 1997], *Toy Soldiers* [1991], *Passenger 57* [1992], and *Sudden Death* [1995].) The film was characterized as advancing an anti-feminist parable slickly disguised by the shootouts and explosions, but the unanimous argument was assuming that the end of the film—where the Willis character and his wife are about to be driven away from the razed office building—promised a return to the patriarchy for the family unit, to be headed once more by hero and super male Willis.

Once more invoking Desser's argument that "genres are said to be popular precisely because they answer, within structured fantasy, social, historical, psychological, or cultural issues within the culture that produces and consumes them,"[7] the form of the *Die Hard* sequels again reflect social reality in terms of males' self-image of persecution, just as the original uses its disrespected outsider hero to dramatize the masculinity crisis. In simple terms, the sequels prove the critics wrong. How intentionally this was done we can only guess. A film that makes as much money as *Die Hard* did will not be influenced by what popular critics like Roger Ebert, or the *New York Times*, or *Newsweek* think of its sociopolitical implications, much less critical deconstructive analysis in obscure academic journals. However, the direction the sequels take are worth noting here. In the first sequel, as Willis and his family once again fall victim to a terrorist invasion at Dulles International Airport, we find out that the wife was not the one to change her career, but that Willis was. She still lives in Los Angeles, still works for the same corporation, and Willis was the one who followed her and got a job as an L.A. cop. Thus, as the film answers, within its structured fantasy, the issues of the culture producing it, it does so by reflecting the social currents of the time. The film, essentially, cannot afford to show an unambiguous reassertion of the patriarchy, cannot take the wife back to New York and take away her high-powered career, because the film would stand a tremendous chance of failing very badly. It would lose any hope of attracting a female audience and men would find it irrelevant and unrealistic.

Then, the second sequel takes away Willis's power in his family once more. Here, he is again on the verge of losing his wife, recovering from an alcoholic binge as the film opens and a terrorist threat faces New York. Exactly what happened to the family between *Die Hard 2* and *Die Hard with a Vengeance* is not clear, except that some sort of a conflict broke out between Willis and his wife and Willis is getting the short end of the stick. He is suddenly back on the New York police force, but we are not told exactly where his wife is. She, most likely, is still in Los Angeles working for the corporation. They could very well be divorced. Only the end of the film suggests that they might have been on a trial separation. However, as Willis's sidekick (Samuel L.

Jackson) gives him a quarter to "call your wife and beg her to forgive you," it is made obvious that the argument that tore them apart was either entirely Willis's fault, or he just has to swallow his pride, take the blame, and beg for forgiveness. After all, if she has a powerful career at a major corporation, she hardly needs to compromise. As we have seen in the first entry in the series, she can do more than get by on her own. Then, in the third sequel, *Live Free of Die Hard* (2007), the audience realizes that Willis's begging for forgiveness did not work after all. He is divorced and alone, needing to contend this time with a handful of a daughter in college, a headstrong girl who resents his meddling in her private life.

Ultimately, Patrick concurs that the action film today grounds its relevance for men in narratives about unappreciated action heroes who are not even needed by their own families anymore, unappreciated to a point, perhaps, and under attack often. This, in turn, Patrick believes is a reflection of sentiments toward men he sees in the culture, sentiments held by many women and figures in the feminist movement.

The following is a transcript of his explanation, quoted as accurately as possible to catch its halting manner. His approach to a more sensitive topic, loaded with volatile political implications, is one that has him grasping for the right words:

Guys that I work with, whatever their age, they all have kind of the similar attitude, and when they're younger, it's . . . most of the guys I work with are out of college, so they're not that young, but they tend to be more and more opinionated . . . but a lot of people . . . I do think that . . . well to their credit, they [women] are being proactive and there are a lot of powerful women out there, but they almost . . . try to make the . . . the masculine experience? Do you want to get an Oprah word in there? . . . they're trying to marginalize it and diminutize it.

But, ultimately, he explains, and many social commentators, sociologists, and anthropologists observing today's state affairs concur, that the social tides have turned in such a direction because men are not actively addressing and responding to their own crisis. Men do not become activists, they do not address their situation. Patrick, likewise, explains that he feels that men usually do not address matters of gender. He explains that he actually sees the "battle of the sexes," or the battle for women's equality, as "pretty much done." However, he feels the social dialogue about gender today is being dominated exclusively by extreme viewpoints, "militants on both sides," except that he believes women are allowed to be more militant than men, radical feminism has more of a voice in the culture and the media than those who disagree with it.

Patrick's viewpoint about gender relations, feminism, and masculinity identity crisis, in fact, has him straddling a precarious middle ground between his analysis of the action genre's statements about male insecurity, his beliefs that strong masculinity indeed needs to be tempered—as is evidenced in how he judges the good and bad action films—and personal observations about feminism and gender discourses. To illustrate that he means what he says about not having problems with feminism and women in power, he wants to point to both his wife and his jujitsu instructor. His wife has a career as an executive in the corporate world. His instructor, he explains, is a "no-nonsense woman," one of the top-ranked female practitioners of the art in the country. He explains that he admires the way this woman wants to become the second female professor in jujitsu in the United States. A professor is someone who has attained a fifth-degree black belt, and so far there is only one female professor. However, he can also add opinions about feminism that outside of our discussion would incite a riot:

> Me, I'm all for women's equality and empowerment. But they should stop whining about it and do it. It's similar to some unpopular social theories I've had. I mean, my ancestors: potato famine. That's all I have to say. They came over, they weren't allowed to grow the food that would keep them alive, so they came over. Poor as hell. They made their own way. Granted they had a couple of things going for them. They were white. But they might as well have been Chinese or black because they [Americans] didn't want anything to do with them as soon as they heard that brogue. And they made their way. And for all the strong Irish men, there were twice as many strong Irish women. They didn't need to whine about it, they just did it. And there are a lot of powerful women out there that are just doing it. They're making their own way. Now they're swimming upstream in a lot of cases . . . but it's not the 50s anymore.

Patrick's sentiments are strongly echoed by Peter, a twenty-three-year-old graduate student who feels the genre is speaking to the same feelings of persecution many men have in the culture today. Peter is actually an interviewee whom, upon first impression, could be described as a simple, but complicated individual. His answers are clearly spoken, to the point, and he told me upon being asked to partake in the interview that he most often does not look too closely at the deeper meanings of action films. As our discussion unfolded, however, he proved to be a much more thoughtful viewer than most. When it came to many of my gender-related questions, he proved to have strong feelings about the media and gender issues, feminism, and the representation of men in popular culture.

An especially interesting thing about Peter and our meeting place was the way it quickly identified an artistic interest he has. Questioning him about it revealed a very important moral and philosophical bent he was coming from, one that was reflected in his film preferences. Talking to Peter in his home, I was taken by his decorations and artwork. It ranged from paintings and decorated plates to statuettes of wolves. He, in fact, was wearing a T-shirt with a wolf on it. When discussing action heroes either falling into team player or loner categories, I asked him what he thought of the proverbial "lone wolf" and the association of wolves with loners. I quoted a comment I remembered Sylvester Stallone making at one time about reincarnation. Stallone said that he believed he had lived past lives and at one point he lived as a wolf. He said that he believed this wolf influence was why he naturally gravitated toward creating loner and outsider characters. When I mentioned this to Peter, however, it became the only part of the discussion when he became defensive. His tone of voice sounded agitated and his manner of speech was curt, more to the point. He quickly told me that such a comment just illustrated Stallone's ignorance. Wolves, Peter explained, are very social animals, they live and hunt in packs and are very family-oriented animals. Next to humans, Peter believes, only wolves are so devoted to the family unit and their offspring. He explained that he was always interested in the Native American idea of a spiritual connection to an animal and he felt such a connection to the wolf because of its social and family orientation. As it will shortly become evident, family values are very important to Peter and they shape his opinions of films and media messages.

But one of the reasons he likes the action film, he explains, is because he agrees with the metaphorical statements the films are making about the culture and the postfeminist environment trying to marginalize men. He, in fact, says that he feels the social marginalization of men is a very real issue because he otherwise holds what he feels to be progressive views about women and their depictions in the media. If he has been pushed to the point of believing a crisis exists, it indeed must. For example, he explains that he would give an overall mixed review to the *James Bond* series mainly because of their dealings with women. He explains that he can give me one of the very few impressions of the series I will ever hear coming from someone who does not think Sean Connery was the best Bond. As he makes a joke about how angry many Bond fans would be at him, he explains that he did not like the sort of macho belligerence that seemed to underlie Connery's performance. He explains that there is a "sexism" in his manner, his approach to the films, which he finds distasteful. Instead, he explains that he became more of a fan of Bond with the Pierce Brosnan films:

> The Bond role is becoming where . . . where the female is less and less of a blonde bimbo and more of another agent and another powerful figure, so I think that's pretty cool, actually.

Asking him if he feels the empowerment of the "Bond girl" is an improvement in the series, he replies:

> I like it better. It was just really annoying with some of the early Bonds. A lot because Sean Connery was completely over the top. I actually liked some of the more recent ones rather than. . . . I think it's a lot less of just a completely sexist thing. Which you run into a lot with action films, which is something that usually doesn't bother me all that much, but with Sean Connery it was so over the top and it was so obvious that the women were there just for looks and [for Bond] to use them and all.

In fact, talking to Peter about what makes a good action film and action hero in terms of masculine characterizations quickly yielded opinions that were remarkably similar to Patrick's comments. His opinion is that the action film primarily tries to represent and negotiate the contested meanings of masculinity today. Or the good action films, in his view, are the ones that are able to face the fact that the social definitions of masculinity are being contested and they reflect this in their storylines.

> I don't think the ideal male is a stereotypical macho man anymore. You don't meet that type of a man anymore on the street like you used to. There are people who are extremely sexist, but they are more and more rare. I think that the movie follows society and basically it's showing . . . by seeing the changes in the movies over time, if you do a close study, you tend to see differences what the society is doing . . . because movies are reacting . . . I mean it's a business and they're selling what society is craving and so you can see how society's changed over that time period.

I was immediately excited by his comments here about the media mirroring society because Peter had quickly proven to be much more thoughtful about the media and film messages than he originally suggested. As he had immediately addressed one of the fundamental debates of mass media studies, I wanted to hear him elaborate more about the media's reflection versus its shaping of culture in terms of masculinity.

> Yes, it very much reflects. . . . So if you say Hollywood tried to shape society and put out all of these hugely masculine, more like the original Bond films, and the women are nothing, they have nothing, Hollywood would lose so much money and the film would bomb. Because Hollywood can't change society. Society knows what it wants, so it would say we don't like those movies. Because that's no longer acceptable in society. I think Hollywood gets charged mostly because they're always on the edge of what society is moving to. And it has to be because otherwise it wouldn't make any money. It's always gotta be on that front-leading edge, just like any other business.

Just as he concedes in his last three sentences that Hollywood can also work at pushing boundaries of acceptability and being proactive in crafting messages, he also mentions that, to a degree, the typical action film may still be presenting role models or versions of a strong male that its audiences should be living up to:

> Sure, if we were still in the '60s, when I believe all these types of action films started. You [still] definitely have films that are just . . . like your Rambos, all that kind of stuff where it was all male, masculine, to fight, try and succeed, to be number one, and I would definitely agree that was all very testosterone driven. I don't think it's all it had to offer, but that was definitely a part of it.

He does keep pointing back to the Bond films, though, as the perfect example of both changing social attitudes toward gender roles and female empowerment, as well as the generic action film's negotiation of gender roles, rather than as a purely role-model vehicle.

> As we can see by the more recent Bonds, especially the last three, the women are now very strong figures. So in many of the scenes, the women can now kick Bond's ass. . . . But I would tend to say that the analyst [of the action film asking if the genre is talking about masculinity] is still right in one sense, in the way they're still defining what men should be and what men can be and all that because that's where men are today. But you no longer see the pure male testosterone-driven fighting. You really don't see that as much, and if you do, they don't make as much money because they're focusing toward that one audience, whereas the newer Bonds, they're focusing more toward [both] the men and women and everybody's enjoying them. [Women as strong heroes in the Bond films are] not just there yet, but they're right *there*, [in the middle of the action] and they have something to offer. So that's what a lot of women feel like today. That they're in a man's world and they're fighting to become a part of it.

Since he had brought the Bond films up when I asked him to tell me about some of his all-time favorite action films and he very enthusiastically started explaining why he finds the perceived sexism of the films objectionable, I was not expecting him to be as equally critical of what he sees as the persecution of males in society and their depiction in certain types of television programs and films. "I would definitely say that the attack is going on," he quickly and emphatically agrees with the thesis that men are in a decline in society. He explains that his views have been shaped by the school he has been studying in, as an undergraduate and graduate student, and especially by the campus his fiancée is affiliated with. As one of the several campuses of the university Peter attends is a women's college that has, at one point, been annexed by the main university, he feels that the ultra-feminist administration there has given him a glimpse of feminism that leads him to believe feminist ideology is trying to achieve more than equality. He feels this is actually a society-wide phenomenon and only the films of the action genre are able to address this.

> I think with this college . . . the women there—not necessarily the students there, but the people running it—if you read or hear what is written as far as how certain dorms are run and what the RAs have to read to the students, everything is based around a supposed feminist ideal of equality, but it isn't equality that they want. I've come very much to realize that they want to rule. . . . I am very much for equality. That bothers me not at all. I believe people should be equal. But they're not fighting for equality. They're fighting to rule.

Although using his school as the example of what he considers a radical anti-masculine movement, he does think this movement is society-wide and its effects make men feel as if they were under attack. The action film, he reiterates, is the one genre that is able to speak to this, that is, able to present marginalized men like the heroes of *Die Hard* or *Lethal Weapon*, where the male who has been discarded to the fringes of society, to near obsolescence, is able to prove himself. In his words:

> I think that comes out more in the action roles because in many ways guys will be able to associate with that. That their masculinity is still needed because men have been extremely dominated recently. Anywhere you go, men are afraid of being considered sexist. It's fear. And that fear has controlled us. Because every woman who yells out "rape," men are fearful of it. Because all of a sudden you're guilty before you're being considered. And someone can make that accusation and destroy you even though you've never seen them before and even if you're proven not guilty, it will still have destroyed you. I think that's very much changing the role of the action figure because men are afraid. But on the other hand they need to feel like masculinity is needed in one way or another and Hollywood is reacting to that.

But, throughout, Peter insists on straddling between extreme positions. When commenting on whether fighting and violence can be seen as an actual metaphor for masculinity, he says:

> Personally, I think that what has heretofore been called masculinity, with all the fighting and aggression, has nothing to do with masculinity. I think it has to do with power and control and you can very much see that in women as well as men. Historically, you have the Amazons and everyone else.

Peter's feelings about a mirror-media reflecting social concerns continue into his views of men and families, and again how a male-oriented genre like action/adventure functions to negotiate tensions men are under in today's world. When I ask him to comment on the issues of action heroes being separated from families, children, and girlfriends/spouses, he quickly agrees that this is a dramatization of a family unit crisis he has been interested in and worried about. His overall impression, he explains, is that in a world where feminism has been striving to erase all gender-based spheres of function and influence, women are encouraged to be active in as many places as possible, be that the home or in the workforce. But such is not the case for men. He explains:

> I think men have a problem because they have always been out of the house working . . . but they had a very strong effect on their children. They [the children] saw what we were doing. They saw our love and our work and our effect on them. Because we were the ones bringing home the bacon, so to speak. Whereas women had that close bond with the kids and raised them. Now women are performing both roles simultaneously, so men are asking what are we needed for? Because they don't have the role with the kids and they don't feel comfortable [in such a role exclusively] because no one's made it so they can be.

However, as with the previous issues discussed, Peter also does not completely concede to a socially constructed gender-role viewpoint entirely. He explains at length that there is, in his opinion, a serious social problem taking shape with too many children being raised in single parent households and households where both parents are working full time and unable to be with their small children, and too many women are giving up the child caretaker function. "And most people would jump up and down and call me sexist and everything else, but I don't think so," he explains. He says that while he feels it is for the better of small children as a whole if at least one parent is able to stay with them all day long, be that a man or a woman (he says he knows a family where the husband is a stock analyst and works from his home with his computers and phones while his wife works in an office), the child-rearing function is something women naturally find more satisfying than men. "Studies have shown this," he says, and adds that he believes most of the gender conflicts and acrimony today come from a wing of the feminist movement that he finds disingenuous when advocating equality. "I think the feminists have extremely weakened their cause because if they were fighting for equality, they would have no problems with women choosing to stay at home and raise kids." Again, with this argument he points to his and his fiancée's experiences with gender politics at the school they attend. He explains that his fiancée has decided that once they have children, she wants to be at home with them full time and that she feels that staying at home and raising children should be considered as much of a career as someone who is holding down a money-earning job. However, due to the ideological climate dominating the campus with which she is affiliated, Peter explains, she feels she is constantly pressured into justifying her viewpoints and the lifestyle choice she has already planned for the time she has children. Peter feels such a climate at the school is founded on hypocrisy, and it is much more widespread in the culture than at just one campus of that particular school. Of course, this is all subjective experience and viewpoint coming from Peter's testimony, but it colors his experience of the media. His sentiments, in turn, are what help shape his experience of the action genre. Ultimately, he feels society is such that men are left displaced, whether that is in the home or in the workplace. He concurs that the familyless, rejected heroes of the action film are the men who are dumped by wives and girlfriends and who, in turn, are frowned upon and marginalized for being too tough and aggressive in their lines of work, and they serve as a perfect metaphorical illustration for a man who is no longer wanted in the workforce or is often forced out of the family unit by independent women who do not want a husband, but want children.

> But I would definitely think that society is reacting through Hollywood to the changing of male roles and how they're basically up in the air. It will be very interesting to see how they change over the next ten years or so.

Testimonials from Patrick, Sam, and Peter are important because they are all articulate, they tell a concise story of their views of how the contemporary male experience intersects with the thematic and philosophical concerns of the action genre, and they make arguments the other interviewees either quietly agree with or strongly disagree with.

As demonstrated in the previous chapter, disclosure about emotional issues, matters of identity, and especially vulnerability and weakness, are often difficult for the male interviewees. The disorganization and general lack of direction spoken of in terms of an organized men's movement may be rooted in this general problem. The way many of the interviewees, unlike Patrick, Sam, and Peter, dodge the issues demonstrates the problem. Those interviewees demonstrate the fear some men hold that they cannot talk about their problems because politically correct conventional wisdom today states they should have nothing to complain about.

As detailed in the previous chapter, one of the male interviewees who began the interview with a great deal of enthusiasm, then quickly withdrew and tried to avoid voicing his personal opinions by hiding behind what others "would say," is Schwarzenegger fan Anthony. Just as much as he is prone to quote critics and explain what is generally believed about certain films by the critical community at large, when speaking to him about masculinity, I once more had to get past his oft-repeated comment-opening phrases that were variations on his most colorful phrase: "Let me try and think as to how the Ivory Tower egghead crowd would think." What the egghead crowd would think, according to Anthony, however, is wrong-headed, distorted opinion that equates masculinity with testosterone-driven, irrational aggression:

> They say that it's basically anger, aggression, strength, brutality that is the best and ultimate solution to a problem or to get what you want out of things, rather than intelligence or logic or reasoning. Compromise is kind of what they're thinking [is a better way than the masculine solution]. Because if it's masculinity [what the films are about], well, masculinity is sort of the thread that weaves together the film, which is sometimes a take-off of the real world, which is why wars occur, then look at what you get. Brutality, destruction, blah, blah, blah and there's probably a better way of going about it.

Anthony's explanation refers to how the elitist academic would sum up strong masculinity and its place in the world. For a man, says the academic, according to Anthony's understanding, aggression and the use of force are the first and main solutions to problems, rather than compromise and negotiation. Since it is violence that functions as the "thread that weaves together the [action] film," used as a reflection of the violence of the real world—the wars, the killings, the crime—then action films seem to be celebrating the male penchant to destroy, to commit war, rather than attempting to solve problems through nonviolent means. However, this is not Anthony's view of the action film, not the reason he likes it, but this is how he sees the elitist academic critic seeing the action film.

Anthony claims a thorough understanding of the Ivory Tower eggheads because he has a good friend whom he describes as a "feminist" college professor. This person is actually one of his former professors, someone he is still friends with, and someone he says he likes having amicable debates with. Thus, he explains that he can talk to the misconceptions the academic elites have about men, masculinity, and the male image in the media. The action film's depiction of men, which he admits to agreeing with after considerable prodding, in a metaphorical way represents an ideal. But once more, his own views are eventually gleaned only after we get past his overview of why the elites do not like those metaphorical views of masculinity.

> I think it paints a picture of a character who can get things done. Who's decisive, who's courageous, and who's willing to step up and do what it takes to get something done. Which is probably something you should have more of in the real world.

Overall, when talking about what *he* sees in the action film, Anthony explains that he sees some very positive and pro-social messages. Just as in the previous chapter, where he talked about Schwarzenegger's and Eastwood's moral and ethical fortitude, their strength of characters, the action heroes in his opinion represent values the world needs more of. Unfortunately, Anthony feels the world is not wise enough to realize this.

When I attempt to gauge Anthony's feelings about whether this wrong-headedness in society, this misconception by the cultural elites, is putting undue, unfair pressure on men, whether it is creating a crisis, Anthony becomes strikingly inarticulate. As talkative, as glib, and cocky as he started the interview, when I asked his opinions about the concept of a masculinity crisis, he becomes just as silent, ill at ease, and awkward. However, eventually I realized that Anthony's words about the misguided Ivory Tower eggheads are testimony enough about his belief in the crisis. Male characteristics, according to his words, are being demonized and unfairly reframed by the cultural dialogue on gender to denote destructiveness.

However, Anthony's overwhelming personality trait appears to be his dreaded apprehension of admitting to having a problem, much less having a weakness. On the one hand, he freely voices derogatory epithets at academics and cultural critics, very fond of the term "egghead," and he complains about the gross ignorance of these same academics. Yet, on the other hand, he is painfully reluctant to say there is a gender crisis created by the wrong-headedness he complains about. When I try to press him to respond in any way, with any reaction that comes to mind, to the concept of the crisis, he insists on using the word "challenge" instead. The term "challenge," of course, would present an interesting conundrum to this study, because the word has more positive connotations. A "challenge" can often be referred to in terms of a positive opportunity one is given to change in some way. In Anthony's case, however, I sense no positive meaning attached to the word. Or, at least his mockery of academics and feminists hints at no positive aspects he would attribute to men being "challenged" to change or redefine their masculinity. "Challenge," however, does not suggest that Anthony feels like he is in a threatened position, that he has a problem he worries about. By redefining the concept as a "challenge" instead of a "crisis," he does not place himself in a position of weakness.

When I try to discuss the matters of the action films' statements about the family, reproduction, and children, Anthony again remains curt, circumspect, and fond of repeating the word "challenge" over and over again until it seems to lose its weight, until it seems nothing more than a shield behind which he wants to hide, much like the phrases about what the "critics would say." Very importantly, he does not want to comment on how a "challenge" is different from a "crisis." When I try to reference the romantic relationship he is in and whether he has given thought to how a marriage might unfold in this world where so many wrong-headed intellectuals, cultural elites, and feminists are working to "challenge" people into reevaluating and reshaping basic relationships, he is again vague to a point of not wanting to answer my question. He finally agrees that "one" (like himself) will need to approach marriage as a new institution today due to the power of women. However, he refuses to say one way or another if he feels pressured by this, if films are talking to this issue, or if there are any specific things films should say about the issue.

Louis is yet another interviewee who becomes contradictory a number of times when I ask him what the action films are saying about masculinity and what they should be saying. Louis's contradictions, I believe, are rooted in reasons more complex than Anthony's aversion to appearing vulnerable. Louis negotiates many, but not all, of his media message interpretations with ideological and political viewpoints. For example, Louis is generally averse to what he sees as an irrational fixation the culture seems to have with how remote media personalities might or might not be treated as role models. He does not like the entire concept of the media role model, and he finds the idea absurd that so many are fixated on how young people's behavior should be affected by remote role models rather than role models in the family. Although he feels that films can portray proper and improper modes of behavior, even forms of masculinity, he does not want to concede that films have the power to control lives. As evidenced in the earlier chapter, Louis very highly values individuality and is averse to bureaucracies and institutions of power due to his upbringing and life in a communist country. He explained that because of the communist social controls, he had become a fan of action films and westerns. Louis, in turn, is highly individualistic and prizes self-reliance and personal responsibility. He highly prizes individualistic, Eastwood-like behavior in men in real life, people who make and live by their own rules and personal codes of honor. He feels uncomfortable with the concepts of media role models and crises because, presumably, they contradict his values of people being free to make up their own minds and form their own beliefs, much as he chose to believe in individuality despite what communism wanted to teach him. Likewise, he becomes reluctant and vague when talking about the issue of the families of action heroes. As much as he likes Charles Bronson for his teaming with Jill Ireland in so many films, Louis remains noncommittal and undecided as to whether the films reflect, shape, or forecast anything about the continued roles of action heroes in their families.

On the issue of the strong male image, Louis again appears sometimes of two minds, until he leads me to believe that his ideals of masculine strength lie mainly in individualistic masculinity. As he is not a particular fan of the muscular action hero movement and cares for neither Stallone nor Schwarzenegger, his major preference, he eventually explains, is for characters who are strong in character and commitment to individualistic codes of honor.

A number of interviewees choose to talk about the depictions of masculinity, the plight of strong males, and the families of action heroes in how the cops and commandos on the screen need to reflect the lives of real men in such professions. Getting them to consider the issue metaphorically, especially what the films might be saying to or about *all* men, not just those who are in police work, turned out to be a tricky endeavor. It becomes easy to stand behind real statistics and figures, just as Anthony stands behind the film critics and what he knows about what academics "would" say, rather than open up and talk about their feelings and opinions about a controversial and personal matter that might involve revealing and admitting to vulnerability.

When it comes to cop characters, the family lends itself easily to the plot, as the heroes, despite their violent professions, nevertheless live and function in everyday American society. Soldiers, or spies, mercenaries, military characters, or those in exotic government positions are more easily removable from the everyday realm of domesticity, and the films can avoid commenting about familial relationships. The broken relationship and divorce rate, however, is very high among action/adventure cops, and several interviewees will quickly fixate on quoting real statistics. An interesting reaction to this comes from Harry, an accountant and former Chicago Board of Trade professional.

Harry explains that such plot devices must be in those films if they hope to achieve a level of reality. The fact of the matter is, he explains, that men in police work have one of the highest rates of divorce in the country. He should know, he says, because his father was a cop and he grew up around the male police culture. Although his own parents were not divorced, Harry says that films trying to authenticate the police experience need to deal with the high rates of broken relationships. He explains that one needs to understand what goes on in the family of a real life cop, what the ultrahard masculinity a cop needs to display on the job will do when it, inevitably, gets transferred to the domestic environment, and what a film dealing with cops needs to be able to capture. Recalling his own background, he says:

> If you look at that type of a lifestyle, the guy being a cop, I grew up with that, my father was a Chicago cop. And they get this hardness about them . . . that they don't know how to relate to other people. They don't know how to communicate with other people. What they see day in and day out, they can only relate to the people they work with. So when it comes to their family lives, they don't know how to divide the job from their families. It all blends together for them. So they often get divorced because . . . they have to live with this hard, tough person who brings his job home. So yeah, that aspect of the movies is true. I know a lot of Chicago cops and a good majority of them end up being divorced.

Edward, who used to be a police officer, talks about a similar domestic problem cops have. However, as will be apparent when we discuss the male fans' critiques of machismo, Edward's take on the issue of the male identity crisis and its relationship to the family in the genre is quite different.

Harry, however, needs more prompting until he can go beyond analyzing the ways in which the action films are reflections of authentic details and how they are speaking metaphorically about masculinity in general. The more I try to discuss with him how a critic could possibly analyze the symbolic meaning of the action film and ask him to agree or disagree, it starts to look as if Harry might definitely be turning to the action film to confirm his very traditional, if not outright reactionary, views about gender and male and female abilities. He is not as self-aware, however, as Peter is. He is not as mindful of how his viewpoints might be controversial and how he must negotiate his values and worldviews with a larger world that would loudly condemn his statements as being sexist. He does not seem to be as anxious about "radical" feminism usurping his status in the world or harming the family unit as Peter is. Harry feels that the action film depicts a state of the world that is realistic and true to life when placing men in more powerful positions because that is where they are naturally, biologically destined to be. As he argues about the roles of men and women in society:

> There are so many jobs out there that men do that women can't do. Like I don't see a woman building a house. I don't see a woman doing heavy labor . . . [fighting] a war: they're not going to. Women just don't have the instincts that it takes to kill. Just like this show I was talking about [Men Are from Mars, Women Are from Venus]. Women can't do that. . . . There are so many things in society that men do that women can't. It would fall apart [if they did]. I mean I worked in industries, on the trading floor of the Board of Trade, and it's tough work, very high stress and you have to be a special type of woman to succeed there because it's a man's world down there and women can't do it. They break down too easy.

At forty-four, Harry can recall a lot of the earlier action films, some of the classic stars like John Wayne in his later years and Clint Eastwood in the beginning of his career. Incidentally, Harry is a very big fan of both actors and does not discriminate between them—or just does not seem to prefer one to the other—as Louis does. He does not pay attention to the change in acting styles or generational attitudes differing among the two actors. He does take note of the fact that Wayne was more likely to be playing very positive and uncomplicated heroes most of the time, whereas Eastwood might, on occasion, be playing characters of deeper ambiguity and residing within a moral gray zone. However, this still does not make a great impression on him. Quite predictably, Harry likes both actors because he perceives the strength and command in the roles they "always" play. Much like Louis, Harry is not open to any alternate readings I suggest "some critics might see" in Eastwood's work. He likes the way Eastwood "takes control of the whole movie" he appears in and says he likes the fact that Wayne is "always" a "dominating character" in his films. "Everybody looks up to him," Harry explain, and he likes "just the way he can take control."

In fact, Harry is the one action fan who seems to like every major male action star I can bring to mind. He likes Eastwood as much as he likes Schwarzenegger or Stallone or any of the actors portraying James Bond. Harry also likes Steven Seagal a lot. Interestingly, Harry does not train in the martial arts. As mentioned previously, it is quite remarkable how all the martial artists I interviewed disliked Seagal. They all said the same thing about him; Seagal is not appealing because he is too indestructible, he dominates everything and everyone in all his films. To David, the ninjutsu and jujitsu practitioner, this makes Seagal look more like a bully than a hero. This overwhelming strength, of course, is precisely why Harry likes Seagal so much. Harry even emphasizes that he will always watch a new Seagal movie.

As I argued in the previous chapter, with this method of data gathering and analysis there are moments where the researcher needs to record and observe the interviewees' comments at face value. Harry for example, explains that he likes action films, is a big fan of the *James Bond* series—most of which he owns on DVD or VHS tapes—and is an avid fan of John Wayne's and Clint Eastwood's action films, westerns, and war films. The details of these films that he focuses on when I asked him to explain why he likes films centered around masculine power. He likes Wayne because he is always so strong in all his films, everybody looks up to him, and he is in complete control of everyone and everything around him throughout the whole story. Harry also likes Eastwood because of his ability to "dominate" and "control" all of his films, and he likes the fact that in most of Eastwood's films there invariably comes a time when Eastwood has a showdown with a superior. Harry explains that this is exciting in a film and that it helps bolster the strength an Eastwood character exudes. This way, the Eastwood character has even more power than the mere mortal male who could never afford to be rebellious around a superior in his job. To Harry, these films are confirming his views about gender roles, yet it is striking that Harry is not aware how controversial his views are today. When I mention this to him in the course of our discussion, he either half-heartedly confirms it or does his best to evade the issue. Yet, again, someone who has worked in such positions as the Board of Trade and still functions in an organizational, white-collar setting as accounting, must be aware that many of the things he told me—with my encouragement, having explained to him that his identity is protected and that he needn't worry about voicing unpopular or controversial ideas—would be incendiary if voiced anywhere in a public forum. The working-class background Harry comes from and the very tough masculinity he describes manifested in street cops like his father certainly point to the roots of his sentiments about gender roles. Yet it is curious that he states as a fact that women cannot do many stressful jobs that men do, even after his work among the managerial, white-collar sectors of society that are both well integrated with women who would quickly condemn his viewpoints. If he very strongly disagrees with such political correctness, he is determined to hide it during this discussion, because he remains nonchalant about my repeated suggestions that there are "analysts" and "cultural critics" who would feel very differently from him. Much like Louis, in fact, Harry appears determined to negate the masculinity crisis issue and family crisis issue of the action film by insisting it is a nonissue today.

In fact, a surprising thing I noticed was how reluctant the older male interviewees were—those over forty years old—to take a committed stand on the masculinity crisis issue. When I bring the issue up with each one, they agree that the action narratives are talking to this social phenomenon, yet talking about it is not comfortable for any of these interviewees. As I worked to keep the discussion focused on the issue of the crisis, they all eventually told half-hearted, roundabout tales of how they had seen their work environments change, how child-rearing has changed, and how they had seen viewpoints of the nuclear family altering over time, yet all were reluctant to make strong comments on the issue.

One notable exception, however, is forty-three-year-old Dirk, who tells a complex story of how cultural definitions of masculinity are changing, how they *should* be changing, yet how critical he is of the treatment of men in a lot of media representations. It is especially interesting to listen to Dirk explain how James Bond, his favorite action character in both literature and on film, is the sort of man he would neither want to be like nor want to know in real life. "It is difficult to imagine how someone who behaved like Bond could sustain any meaningful relationship today or even any friendships," he explains. The sort of behavior he sees on the screen, he says, is an interesting fantasy and escapism from reality, a fantasy of omnipotent masculinity that is interesting to see and a fantasy he wants to see sustained throughout the *Bond* series.

In fact, when I ask Dirk to talk about what he does not like to see in a *Bond* film, or in any action film, he talks about the film denying him the opportunity to suspend his disbelief. The masculine power on screen has to be evident and should never disappear into a cardboard, one-dimensional character that gets overwhelmed by special effects. He explains that he does not like the *Bond* movies where the hero is a "one-dimensional mannequin" and has no personality. That was one of the main reasons he disliked the Roger Moore films, along with the way the Moore films treated Bond like a sight-gag. "The Roger Moore Bond films are just stupid," he says. "I like the *Bond* films as action films, but the Roger Moore films are comedies." He quickly points to *Octopussy* (1983) and a scene that especially offended him. Here, Bond is chased through a jungle and at one point he swings from one tree to the next on a vine. This in itself looks ridiculous, Dirk explains, but then they have to take the comedy even further by adding the Tarzan yell in the background. He explains that too much comedy, too much self-aware humor, ruins an action film for him. For example, Dirk says that he likes some of the *Lethal Weapon* films, especially the first one, but felt that the increasing humor in all the subsequent installments hurt the series. He especially disliked the last entry and he was very much annoyed by the addition of the Chris Rock character.

He also recalls first seeing a *Bond* film with Sean Connery when he was a boy and finding Connery's portrayal of the character very appealing. Connery as Bond seemed to embody everything a man should be: the toughness, the danger, the charisma. In fact, Dirk explains, the major problem he has with Roger Moore is that the toughness is not there anymore. His most colorful quote of the interview, in fact, is his comparison of the two actors on the most basic level. "The difference between Sean Connery and Roger Moore is that if Sean Connery told you he would kick your butt, you'd run away. But if Roger Moore said that, you would laugh at him."

Nevertheless, Dirk is repeatedly willing to add that as much as the strong, physical man of action and danger on the screen is appealing, that type of masculinity is an anachronism in real life. Such a man is appealing from the safe distance of the movie screen because he is unrealistic in real life, and perhaps he *should* be unrealistic in real life, Dirk says. He adds that he is of the generation where his father was very much "a man's man" and endorsed and reinforced that image of hard, macho masculinity. Yet Dirk insists that any well-adjusted male needs to see the shifting cultural currents and the altering definitions of masculinity. He explains that he understands the attack many men may feel they are under and that the action film is, in fact, a metaphor for this crisis. The outsider, marginalized hero of the action film, it is fair to say, according to Dirk, is a representative of classical masculinity. However, this classical male is a representative whose resentment he does not feel sympathy for if those men are not willing to accept reality and change with the times. One of the most surprising opinions Dirk voices refers to the generic resentful soldier of the *Rambo* mold, or of the Connery character's mold in *The Presidio*. As a veteran, he says he has seen such sentiments in real life, yet an intelligent man, an intelligent soldier even, needs to adjust with the times. "One of the sayings they have in the army," he explains, "is that the U.S. army has never fought a war it hasn't been punished for." Thus, he can understand the post-Vietnam anger, he claims, so that the *Rambo* and *Presidio* sentiments are understandable, but he also thinks that it is unrealistic for soldiers to expect more than that.

Nevertheless, Dirk is also pointedly critical of a lot of male characterizations in the media and the confrontational stance of feminism toward the cultural construction of masculinity. Much as Peter argues that the culture no longer allows for any exclusively male territories, Dirk says that he feels the media, outside of the action genre, often specifically mock men no matter how they try to define their masculinity. In Dirk's viewpoint, it is frustrating to realize that men can no longer define masculinity in *any* way without being mocked for it. He, in fact, explains that he is a fan of John Woo's films and their stories of codes of honor and ritualistic bonds of conduct between men because such films treat the subject with seriousness. He adds, however, that as much as feminism has, in the past, advocated a reconceptualization of masculinity from a stoic model to something more "sensitive" and emotional, men are still criticized when they do show their emotions. Or more precisely, in Dirk's opinion, men are *mocked* when they show emotion. He feels men are put in a no-win situation when it comes to the definition of their gender identity because "men are a joke if they show their feelings and they're a joke if they don't show their feelings."

Generally, for most of the younger male interviewees, from both the eighteen- to twenty-five-year-old group and the twenty-six- to thirty-year-olds, discussing the issue of action films and the male identity crisis does not always come easily. In fact, it required quite an effort to get the information from the interviewees, to get them to react to theory and analysis without putting words in their mouths. Putting words in their mouths, however, was never a real problem because there were a number of interviewees who strongly disagreed with the concept of the masculinity crisis. For others, however, they generally explained that they were *hoping* it is only a small minority of the feminist movement, a wing of the movement usually vocal on college campuses but not representative of the greater population, that is critical of male power or that wants to negate the legitimacy of the nuclear family in favor of a new, matriarchal model.

As the analysis and the debate over masculine messages, issues, and imagery continues, and will continue, no doubt, for a long time into the future and beyond this study, a fascinating perspective about politically incorrect, provocative, and offensive messages is offered by Dwayne, one of the youngest members of the subject pool. Dwayne, twenty-one, is not only an action fan, but he is a passionate follower of professional wrestling and has part-time jobs working for various amateur wrestling organizations. He explains that parallels can be drawn between the usual wrestling "storylines" and the way the violent, male-oriented narratives of the action film mirror the real life concerns of men.

In the case of wrestling, he explains that the storylines are broad, exaggerated representations of current social concerns and the "plot" unfolding in the ring shows a wrestler dealing with the problem the way everybody in the audience wishes they sometimes could. One hypothetical example he offers of how such a storyline would be written, even in one of the provincial amateur organizations he is involved in, involves a representation of the typical business-world conflict:

> Now you have one wrestler who hates his boss. And now he will actually do what everyone dreams of doing, which is kicking him and dropping him to the floor. None of us could ever do that, but this wrestler would confront the boss and, you know, beat the tar out of him. And that's something that people who don't like their bosses would love to do.

Dwayne referred to a favorite World Wrestling Entertainment storyline as another typical plot used because of its social relevance in dealing with domestic discord. The root of the discord he describes can actually be tied to interpersonal gender conflicts stemming from economic power in the hands of the wife in a relationship and the way this power upsets the expectations of a man who has looked forward to the privileges of the traditional patriarchal family unit. The storyline had a rank-and-file wrestler "marrying" WWE owner Vince McMahon's daughter. In the course of the relationship, the wrestler becomes disenchanted with his wife's power and the economic inequity tilting in her favor. In turn, the wife also realized the advantages of the old saw that says women always marry up and became dissatisfied with a husband who is her inferior in finances and social status. As the demographics of the professional wrestling fan base also tilt toward young males, the storyline is resolved by granting the wrestler a status of moral superiority, even though his family disintegrates and he winds up on the losing end. Basically, Vince McMahon has a cadre of wrestlers, *at his daughter's request*, go forth and break up the union by beating up the husband and ordering a divorce.

The action film, Dwayne explains, also represents real-world problems "times ten." The typical action plot, as he has come to expect, can be taken from most news headlines. He says that if someone wants to understand this, they should imagine some crime-related news story, like a carjacking, then imagine an action film about a city-wide gang of carjackers that is involved with a terrorist plot to plant bombs and take over an entire city. The plot, thematic, and philosophical concerns of the action film need to have relevance in people's lives, just like the wrestling storylines do. Furthermore, he explains that even the most controversial turns taken by stories in both wrestling and the action film need to be understood in terms of what social conditions are making them attractive to audiences.

In our discussion of rogue, outsider, marginalized heroes of action films who antagonize authority and like to flaunt conventions, Dwayne and I compare the action movie to a highly acclaimed documentary on wrestling, *Hitman Hart: Wrestling with Shadows* (1999) and its discussion of the rise of the most obnoxious heels as the new crowd favorites. In fact, Dwayne says that if he would be writing storylines for a wrestling organization, he would keep in mind that the worst villains are actually the biggest crowd favorites. Those who are loud, obnoxious, sleazy, and sexist will get the best reactions from the crowds. This is a major point of the documentary, with its focus, wrestler Brett "The Hitman" Hart, explaining how he is troubled by the fact that the audiences like the most evil characters today. As he is quoted in the documentary: "Something was happening to the fans. All the characters they were supposed to hate they were cheering for." He recalls a storyline he was involved with where he is being beaten by Stone Cold Steve Austin, one of the most evil characters in the WWF (before the World Wrestling Federation became World Wrestling Entertainment) at that point, yet the fans are cheering for Austin. "And here I am," Hart says, "being beaten on by this horrible bad guy, he's trying to smash my knee, trying to end my career, and they're cheering for him. So I'm thinking, just a little while ago I used to be your hero, and now you're cheering for this bad guy. What a cold blooded bunch of people you are. . . . And the fact is that I don't see the audience's point of view." But the audience's point of view, which I discuss with Dwayne, is hinted at by one of the fans interviewed earlier in the documentary. Here, a man says that he enjoys wrestling, with all its violence and sometimes offensive images and storylines, "because it's just fun. And there are not a lot of things in life that are fun anymore."

Dwayne agrees with this and therein, he says, lies the reason for the popularity of that evil and, in a way, the popularity of antiheroes, or male action heroes that feel slighted and resentful and angry, even though politically correct conventional wisdom says that they have no right to be angry. Because of the prevailing, censorious politically correct rules of propriety that overwhelm every sector of life today, there is an attractive rebel appeal in somebody doing something that is so obviously offensive or improper. Thus, the louder society and intellectuals and feminists will condemn macho men who like to brawl, drive their cars fast, drink beer, leer at pornography and strip shows, the more of a rebel appeal it will have.

SUMMARY

When I ask each of my male interviewees if they think the action films are right, that masculinity is losing its relevance in the world, the majority say that they *hope* not. The action film gives many of its fans a shape for their anxieties about life as a man today and a vision of a shape of things they hope will not come in the near future.

For the male high users of the action film, the narratives deal with the definitions, limitations, and possibilities of masculinity. Just as Peter's testimony suggests, the definitions in the era of the new millennium are up for contention, being shaped and reshaped by society, men themselves, and their relationships with women and their families. All of the interviewees agree that masculinity, at some level, even if not overtly and completely, is tied to strength and power. How much power men actually have, what they can apply their strength to and how the rest of the world regards them for it are at the heart of the action/adventure narratives.

Peter put it succinctly in making the very strong statement that an out-and-out endorsement of machismo, an advertisement of male power, control, and domination, is something that is no longer feasible in entertainment. Certainly as films need to attract the largest audiences possible to recoup their ever-increasing production budgets and star salaries, they need to attract a female audience as well as a male audience. For this reason, in the era of postfeminism, political correctness, and "girl power," stories of the unreconstructed, domineering macho man will rarely, if ever again, be seen in a mainstream film. Of course, there will always exist a segment of the male population who would be interested in such unreconstructed macho, as Harry's testimony demonstrates, but they are definitely a minority.

However, this is not the entire story of the men who watch and interpret action films. There are viewers who are not just analytical, but very critical.

NOTES

1. Richard Schickel, *Clint Eastwood* (New York: Alfred A. Knopf, 1996), 230.

2. Samuel Wilson Fussell, *Muscle: Confessions of an Unlikely Bodybuilder* (New York: Avon Books, 1991).

3. Schickel, *Clint Eastwood*, 344.

4. Yvonne Tasker, *Spectacular Bodies: Gender, Genre and the Action Cinema* (New York: Routledge, 1993).

5. Robert Warshow, "Movie Chronicle: The Westerner," in *Film Theory and Criticism*, eds. Gerald Mast, Marshall Cohen, and Leo Braudy (New York: Oxford University Press, 1992), 454.

6. Maurice Yacowar, "The White Man's Mythic Invincibility," *Jump Cut* 34 (1989): 2–4.

7. David Desser, "The Martial Arts Film in the 1990s," in *Film Genre 2000: New Critical Essays*, ed. Winston Wheeler Dixon (Albany: State University of New York Press, 2000), 103.

7

The Opposition: Men with a Challenge—
Managing a Well-Deserved "Crisis"

We love to see action heroes that are vulnerable, that are sensitive, that are family people, that are accessible.

—Steven Seagal[1]

Dwayne is a good segue to this chapter, because as I attempt to discuss the issues of a male identity crisis, he also insists on referring to current gender relations as a "challenge," rather than a "crisis," for men. Just as most of the women interviewed will explain in the next chapter, there are several male interviewees who have strong opinions about why a masculinity crisis is deserved by men. The majority of the interviewees, even if they do not agree with the thesis of the crisis, do not deny that the messages are in the film. All but two men, nineteen-year-old Richard and twenty-one-year-old Tim, agree that messages about men losing power, respect, and losing status are definitely in the films, even if they personally feel that the crisis is something men *need* to go through.

One of the strongest voices here is Edward, the former police officer, who explains that machismo is something that men need to be forced to abandon. Edward, of course, is interesting because he is forty-seven years old. Many of the younger interviewees who do not resent the crisis, the men in their late teens or early twenties, I was actually not as surprised by as I was by Edward's statements. The younger ones are educated and socialized, have taken their first important steps toward developing serious romantic relationships and are moving toward marriage and the consideration of having children, on college campuses that are the flashpoints of gender politics and often the homes of more radical wings of feminism, as is evidenced in Peter's testimony.

Edward explains that when he compares the masculinity of old films and the masculinity of newer ones, he actually sees qualities in the older films that men need to start emulating in order to have better relationships with women and families. The masculinity he recalls from old films, the westerns, for example, are *not* ones he sees as advocating insensitive, uncommunicative, and tough machismo. As Edward sees it, it is actually the newer films that present a model of masculinity that, if emulated, would do nothing but alienate men from the greater society, especially women. "Some of the [films] I was impressed with," he says, "were the ones where a person could be masculine but at the same time he could be sensitive and understanding, even humble." The newer films, he says, are showing a version of masculinity that celebrates toughness and macho for its own sake. The most important and noteworthy thing about Edward's opinion, though, is that he does not trace such behavior back to the 1950s John Wayne school of masculinity. Edward, in fact, is a Wayne fan, and he begins the interview by explaining how his taste in action films was shaped by the earliest films he remembers from his childhood: westerns and war films. As he explains:

> I think in a great deal of [modern] movies, like the Sylvester Stallone-type movies, too many people are hung up on being a tough guy. You know, and that's not important to me and I don't think that makes that good of a movie. . . . Current films are more about characters going off and taking out forty people with a machine gun.

This, however, is a sharp contrast to the films of Edward's youth:

> I mean, even going back to something like *Sergeant York* with Gary Cooper, he was a hero but he couldn't even believe that he was a hero. He was very humble, but when the guys in his unit were getting killed, he would rise to the occasion and he did what he had to do.

When I want to discuss the issue of the action heroes and broken families, men deprived of their children, he again agrees that if a hard, macho man is barred from his children and a woman wants nothing to do with him, he, most likely, deserves it. But once again, he argues that the masculinity and manly codes of honor and conduct glorified in the westerns of his youth would not be putting a man at odds with women and offspring. If masculinity is under attack, Edward explains, it is because men cannot be as adaptive and mature as men of old.

> I think it [masculinity] has been [under attack] for a while. Sure, especially since in traditional masculinity, the man was the bread-winner. The woman stayed at

home. And we know that doesn't happen very often. The roles have changed dramatically. But I don't know if people have grasped that, if they adjusted to it a lot.

Since Edward indicated that he likes a number of Arnold Schwarzenegger's films, I also wanted to discuss the odd phenomenon of how dangerous it is to be related to Schwarzenegger in most of his films. Often he is losing his family, sometimes violently, or an ex-wife is keeping him from seeing his kids. Edward agrees with this, but he disagrees that this is representative of any unfair treatment men are getting in the real world. In fact, he states that "I have a different take on what those films" mean. His take is that if men are barred from their families, it is well deserved and they are wrong for not wanting to change with the times. As he explains:

It's a comment that the man may need to pay more attention to his family. That he needs to be more sensitive, 'cause he's gonna loose it. Because even on the end of that one movie, someone tells him that he can make up with his daughter and he ended up making up with her. . . . So I think those movies are sending out a message that the role of the man has changed quite a bit and he has to be more attentive to his family situation and, to use a trendy phrase, he needs to be more in touch with his feminine side.

Ultimately, the most interesting comment from Edward on the nature of masculinity, the changing image and role of men, suggests something of a self-destruction program in masculinity itself. It certainly helps explain why men are not as active in managing their image and social roles as feminist women are, and why they are not responding to their social condition even if they feel they are in a state of "crisis." As Edward says, "I think the *image* of the traditional man is under attack, but I think if someone is a man, they won't feel threatened." Traditional masculinity is stoic, is able to endure and work through hardship, it does not express itself too freely, much as traditional men are supposed to be the "strong, silent types." By the same token then, real men are not supposed to complain about being under attack, about being relegated to obsolescence, about being derided and stigmatized by feminism. In short, they should take it like a man.

Interviewing David, the physicist and martial artist, on the issue of the action film's masculinity provided one of the most interesting experiences during the completion of this project. As thoughtful as David can be about the entertainment he consumes, even entertainment he says he approaches for strictly lightweight diversions, his forceful renegotiation of the text of the action film is remarkable. Even as I present statements to him about what the "critics" or "analysts" might be saying about masculinity, David refuses to acknowledge the possibility of alternate interpretations. David does not believe that films are talking to disenfranchised men through messages of solidarity. He puts little stock in the idea of the masculinity crisis. Whatever crisis men may say they feel, David is willing to accept in terms of a justifiable change in the social landscape where men are losing inordinate economic power and privileges they may have unfairly gained in the past.

Being acquainted with David before this study, I was aware of his moderately liberal social and political viewpoints, his convictions based on his commitment to his ideals of fairness. As he repeatedly mentions that he sees the crisis thesis coming from a male worry about losing unfairly gained ground, I can see the comments being consistent with his political convictions. As David is African American, his commentary about rectifying past injustice and ill-gotten gains by one sector of society once again make me conjecture about how personal experiences and past political ideals are influencing his opposition to the idea of the masculinity crisis. However, as David himself, at one point, suggested that I read an *Atlantic* magazine article by Christina Hoff-Sommers about schools disadvantaging male students—an article he *agreed with*—I had entered the interview expecting more of a mixed set of opinions coming from him than his unequivocal opposition to the crisis and decline argument.

Even getting David to reflect on the crisis theory presented a challenge, because he appeared so unable to frame the action films he knew so well with the tenets of the theory I quoted to him. In a reading that cannot entirely be defined as oppositional, David refuses to grant credence to the idea that the films are speaking to disenfranchised men in a tone of comradeship. He does pay attention to narratives of downtrodden and marginalized heroes, yet negotiates the text according to his empowerment doctrine of the martial arts.

When David says that he indeed sees the action film speaking to issues of masculinity, he explains that the stories are examinations of the concepts of how males interact in high-stress, dangerous professions and exclusively male social circles. He sees the films as ruminations on the nature of heroism, an examination of codes of honor and codes of conduct of men in martial professions like the military and police work. In his words, the action films are about:

> Masculinity and violence and the appropriateness of violence and when people are forced into violence. Do you have an ordinary person who's thrust into a violent situation or if you have a trained professional who has certain obligations, like defending the innocents, taking it upon himself to save a town.

David does admit that most of the modern, post-1960s action heroes will generally be found on the fringes of society and will not be as pure as the western and war heroes of the 1950s, but he reads the phenomenon in terms of the maturation of American society. He says, "I think this is maybe a reflection of society's idea of masculinity, but sort of tied into this is the idea of our nation growing up in that people have always done certain things, violence has always been around people's behavior." In other words, David feels the use of the marginalized male action hero represents the culture "growing up" and realizes that it does not take perfect people to rise to the occasion and do heroic things. He explains this in the following passage:

> Maybe the hero isn't the best person, maybe he isn't Galahad coming in on his white horse. He might be marginalized or whatever, but when called upon, he will do what needs to be done and even if they don't fit in, they have some connections to society by doing what needs to be done.

Then, in terms of the action film making a statement about the ideals of masculinity, he adds:

> Movies reflect our changing ideals of masculinity. In *Gladiator* and *The Patriot*, they both lose sons and to us they have the ability to show emotions, to cry. To us it is okay to see a Russell Crowe type of action hero being emotional and crying. . . . I think the films are speaking to a more complex view of men than what was previously shown. . . . This is showing that you don't have to be a choirboy to do this, or even a father figure to do this, but it lies within the reach of ordinary people to do what is required. . . . You can have someone who may not be the best person, but still have it in them to be heroic.

Testimony to this effect is forthcoming throughout our discussion of masculinity, and David keeps insisting that the action film's messages, in his eyes, are a reassurance to men that they do not have to be as perfect as the traditional, old-fashioned media depictions of masculinity suggested a hero needs to be, or a "real man" needs to be.

David does not believe in the crisis because he explains that he does not see it in his own life or in his profession. In physics, he says, men are not outnumbered and it does not look like their power base is being threatened. "Sadly, I'm in a field where there are very few women. They are facing a lot of obstacles and for various reasons they are unable to continue."

David's most interesting opinion of the modern action film is that rather than bemoaning the fact that traditional masculinity is no longer respected, he sees these films as offering a greater range of opportunities, templates men can use to define their gender identities and define what it means to be a hero. He explains that the current social changes are more of a "healthy thing" than a crisis:

> Men have a greater chance of exploring themselves than in earlier times. In terms of some schooling [affirming the Hoff-Sommers work he recommended],

there may be some difficulty, but then disabilities don't translate well into future life disabilities . . . [this is] a question of panic by those who might be in power of sharing that power what might be unrightfully theirs, than a question of actually winning or losing.

These sentiments, especially the commentary that the action film's metaphysical core is more about exploring morals and values are echoed by Rom, a twenty-eight-year-old computer consultant, an immigrant originally from India. As our discussion centers on defining action heroes, defining the values of the action film, and how heroism is enacted, Rom keeps insisting that such definitions can easily be applied to women. He argues that as far as he sees, the generic male action hero is someone with such universal characteristics, someone a woman should be able to identify with just as well as a man, that he cannot see the films are representations of a condition that is unique only to men.

This viewpoint, in turn, is taken by Richard, a interviewee who can often be quite critical of the action film and who can take very strong positions on the violence of the genre, going as far as supporting government censorship. Richard, too, feels that the genre is about universal qualities of heroism, not the representation of a uniquely male experience. Richard, nineteen, is also a very idealistic young man who quickly and forcefully disagrees with some of the sociological and evolutionary underpinnings I paraphrase concerning theories of mate selection and reproduction. He, in essence, disagrees that neither male qualities of dominance nor eminence have anything to do with the chances of a man successfully mating. Thus, he again discounts that such concerns are a part of the family-deprived hero plot lines. For most men and women, Richard believes, morality and character are the most important factors in choosing a mate, not income or social status. He explains that this is how he will go about his own spouse selection one day. Thus, we can hypothesize that his own value systems are coloring his own reading of what statements the genre makes about family. Instead of seeing the crisis, he sees a moral undertone to the films, just as David does.

One of the most interesting individuals who forcefully disagrees with the crisis theory, yet describes himself as an action fan through and through, is Ray. As discussed earlier, Ray's immigrant background makes him gravitate toward the outsider heroes, the rogues and rebels. Ray, however, also does not subscribe to the crisis, and this, most obviously, has to stem from his family background and upbringing. Just as all but one of the female interviewees claimed to have felt their media habits were shaped by the men in their lives, Ray explains that the biggest influence in his life was his mother. Ray's mother raised him by herself and he neither knew his father nor ever had a stepfather or any permanent male figure in his life. Not only was a woman the major influence in Ray's upbringing, but a mother with whom he always had a very good relationship and whom he admires for being able to raise him by herself. Ray says that he feels no identity crisis in his life, feels no crisis of masculinity in the world at large, and, in turn, does not believe the action films are speaking to any such crises. In fact, Ray explains that he likes the kinds of action films that have very strong and capable female characters. He also likes films where female action heroines carry the entire picture.

His words and sentiments I found quite reminiscent of comments James Cameron has made about his upbringing. Although not raised by a single mother, Cameron had repeatedly said that he likes to put very strong women in his films because they remind him of how strong and decisive his own mother was.

MEN TO BOYS: THE DECLINE OF ACTION HEROES, MACHISMO, AND THE SEXIEST MEN ALIVE

To what degree the action film will continue as a vehicle for the examination of masculinity was suddenly brought into question for me during my discussion with Sam and his reflections on the original rebel male action heroes of the 1960s. Sam, as mentioned before, is a film buff and he prefers older films to newer ones, and he believes the action heroes of a generation ago can be taken more seriously. Overall, he is one of the best interviewees because his testimony does not reflect only his subjective tastes and impression. Rather, he often ruminates on the state of the film industry, which he likes observing, and has reflections about the culture and its relationship to the entertainment media that would fit in well among discussions in any graduate media course. He believes that as an artistic vehicle for the examination of masculinity, through the examination for how shifting cultural values are impacting masculinity and how the restructuring of society in terms of economics and gender politics may be creating a masculine identity crisis, many current action films are no longer used to their full potential. The two main reasons for this, Sam feels, lie in the approach the film industry takes to filmmaking today and the overall quality of the male action heroes.

Sam, just as much as the overwhelming majority of the interviewees, if not more so, argues that technology in films is replacing thought, especially about complex and controversial subjects. Technology is causing the problem, he explains, coupled, actually, with marketing. He says that as a fan of the filmic art form, something that interests him so much that he has devoted time to classes in a local college for his personal enrichment, he is upset at seeing story, theme, and meaningful character development disappearing from mainstream Hollywood films.

To see films dealing with issues of masculinity, dealing with the topic in a thoughtful manner where a definite statement can be found, Sam feels that one is better off looking at older films. As previously discussed, he feels *A Clockwork Orange* or *The Dirty Dozen* does a much better job of conveying statements about the changing roles of men and the outsider status of traditional, strong masculinity. He says that one of the best old films he can think of as a demonstration of the concept of the displaced masculine, macho man and his conflict with civilized society is *The Seven Samurai* (1954). If one understands Japan's rigid class system and social structure, he explains, one can see the severity of the problem of a romance between a man from the samurai class, a class that has become obsolete at the time the story is supposed to portray, and a girl from the farmer class in the village he comes to protect. He is too violent, too much of a warrior, and essentially he is too much of a man to be accepted by the villagers as the mate for one of their women. In these films, he explains, the message is not derailed by the pyrotechnics and the special effects. He feels that the *Terminator* films are trying to make interesting statements about masculinity, but James Cameron is not quite able to pull it off:

> I think James Cameron *is* trying to say some things about masculinity and there is an unusual kind of father figure element and how to grow up and be a man and men's roles. But I don't think it was fleshed out really as well as it could have been.

Plus, on top of the technology-choked films, Sam explains that he is frustrated by the overbearing nature of today's film-marketing efforts. He feels that every year, the marketing campaigns that lead up to the summer blockbuster season are a tiresome affair, with so much advertising and merchandising bombarding the potential moviegoers that they may eventually be repelled by the films instead of being attracted to them. He says that that is what happens to him every year. He explains that once a film is hyped to the level of each of the new *Star Wars* films in the early 2000s, or every new *Star Trek* or *Transformers* or their various mega-budget kindred, he begins to wonder if there is a lot of hype to try to cover up a bad film. If a film is good and its producers have confidence in their product, Sam argues, why can't they trust it to stand on its own merits and attract an audience through word of mouth? He, in turn, after going and watching any one of these "movie events," feels the exact sort of letdown that he feared. Today's films, he argues, are too timid to make statements about anything, let alone powerful statements about something as potentially controversial as masculinity and gender politics. Older films, however, have made very clear and well-articulated statements, he says.

Sam also makes the fascinating comment that he does not feel that most of today's action stars are really capable of presenting an argument *about* or *for* strong masculinity because none of them are really decent representatives of strong, confident, macho masculinity. There are a few exceptions, he says, and he repeatedly uses Harrison Ford as an example. However, he would not even turn to either Arnold Schwarzenegger or Sylvester Stallone as a demonstration of what a strong male should look and act like. Then, when it comes to actors like Tom Cruise or Keanu Reeves or Ben Affleck or twotime "Sexiest Man Alive," Brad Pitt, it looks like strong, classical masculinity might already be gone from the movie screens. Sam, although only twenty-seven, says something that each of the older male interviewees confirmed; that the new generation of action stars are boys, rather than men. Even though Cruise was forty-six, at the time this project was undertaken, and Pitt was forty-five, there is still a boyishness about them, whereas Sam's favorite actors are "men."

Elaborating the point, Sam says that his favorite action heroes are Toshiro Mifune, the Japanese actor seen in a number of Akira Kurosawa's most famous films, as well as Lee Marvin, Steve McQueen, James Coburn, James Garner, and Clint Eastwood. These actors were "tough guys, old school kind of, didn't have to have the muscles, more of the look." Sam especially loves Clint Eastwood's spaghetti westerns, which he owns on DVD and "I watch those religiously." In these actors and the characters they play, first of all, he explains that he sees a sense of style, a sense of "coolness," that none of today's younger stars have. "Coolness" is a masculine trait for Sam. "Coolness" he immediately associates with men and it denotes machismo, a natural, unfaked toughness and charisma. As he explains:

> Especially Steve McQueen. McQueen had a power or he . . . let's put it this way, when these guys come on screen, they look like they're going to explode any second. You know they're not, but it's as if they've got . . . you know, I could tap into it if I want to . . . but it's like I don't have to.

However, for Sam, "coolness" does *not* deal with being uncommunicative and stoic. He defines it more as a type of strength, physicality, ferocity that one can believe an actor on screen really has and is not faking. As a matter of fact, at one point he explains that one of the big differences between older and newer action heroes is how the old ones could rely on their wits and quick repartee to get out of certain dangerous situations, not necessarily just their fists and brawn. But, comparing two generations further, he adds:

> But you look at Keanu Reeves and you look at Tom Cruise, and quite frankly, Steve McQueen is gonna kick both their asses. There isn't the machismo [in the

young actors]. You just take a look at *Bullitt*, I mean that guy is just nuts to look
at. He's gonna get his man. Whereas I take a look at Tom Cruise and I'm just
like . . . I'm not buying it.

Sam, essentially, argues that for a true masculine action star, as far as he is
concerned, there should be a blending of the role and the actor. He does not like
to see behind the stage and know how these action stars are really unlike the
characters they play on screen. He likes Harrison Ford, for example, because
he used to have a strenuous, manual laborer job before becoming a star. Ford's
biography usually includes how he had a job as a carpenter, something he had
actually considered abandoning acting for when his big break seemed to elude
him, just before he was offered the *Star Wars* role. Sam also tells of how much
he was excited by stories of Ford working on his time off in a helicopter-flying
river patrol environmental program. At one time, in fact, Ford made headlines
for rescuing a number of people from a boating accident. Such stories perfectly
fuse the on-screen hero and the real-life man. The on-screen macho, coupled
with the real-life tough guy behavior—much more, in Sam's eyes, than being
temperamental or fighting with paparazzi, ala Sean Penn—creates the sort of
charisma that is at the core of classical masculinity:

> I guess it's the old saying "women want to be with him, men want to *be* him."
> You look at the action stars like a Schwarzenegger or a Sylvester Stallone, even
> a Keanu Reeves and these modern guys, and no, no I don't [want to be them].
> You go to Ben Affleck and one of these guys, and they're trying to mold that
> image more, but again they fail. And I guess it's because there isn't that tough-
> ness to back it up. These old guys . . . they could back it up. When they weren't
> making movies, they were out racing cars, they were out livin' it up. . . . They
> walked the walk, they talked the talk. Same with Clint Eastwood.

It is interesting to note, however, that one classic action hero Sam dislikes very
much—actually "hate" is the term he uses—is John Wayne. Despite the fact that
conventional wisdom and film punditry points to Wayne as the main embodiment of classical Hollywood machismo, Sam does not like his conservative,
insider, pro-status-quo persona. For Sam, the edgy, rebel image of a McQueen or
Eastwood seem more masculine. Although Sam concedes that from everything
he knows about John Wayne, his persona, politics, and opinions, his view of the
actor might have been colored, and he is not judging his films fairly. He says that
the basic Wayne image as a status quo-champion is very dislikable.

> [I see Wayne as] the loud American. . . . I'm nauseated by him. Except I love
> him in *The Searchers*. He's basically nuts in that. He's so driven, he's so ob-
> sessed. Not like in all his other movies: "let's get the commies," with the flag
> flapping in the background.

Sam's sentiments are shared, again, to a certain extent by the older interviewees, men who remember Steve McQueen's or James Coburn's or Lee Marvin's movies when they ran in the theaters. Louis, for example, agrees with the idea that today's young action actors are really overgrown, immature boys. Of course, this irritates him because the immaturity does not allow for the stoic self-control he prizes so highly.

An interesting addition to Sam's viewpoint that strong masculinity might already be completely gone from the genre is his opinion that even the musclemen, the Stallones and Van Diesels, are not genuinely masculine either. When the physique becomes conspicuously exaggerated, when the muscularity is unusually large, when it comes in bodybuilder proportions, the characters the actor might play start turning into a cartoon he can no longer relate to. The over-the-top exaggerations bring attention to the very artifice of the masculine image on screen. As Sam sees it, the more the parts are exaggerated, the larger the muscles are pumped, the smaller and the more fake the sum total of the masculine image becomes. He sums this up in rather interesting terms:

> You look at Schwarzenegger like a cartoon character, or most of those films [as such]. . . . It's so over the top, it's so blatant. That he's got a gun that should be strapped on like an attack helicopter. It gets to the point where . . . like we mentioned before, if the advertising is that big, you smell something strange with the movie.

SUMMARY

Overall, this chapter is an interesting contrast when it comes to men's definitions of masculinity. The interviewees speaking here put the emphasis of the separation of "masculinity" from the ideas of overwhelming strength, power, and conspicuous posturing. As Edward explains, there is no need to be a "tough guy" all the time to be a man. For those men who are skeptical of the crisis concept, masculinity need not be defined as the "stronger sex."

NOTE

1. Marshall Julius, *Action!: The Action Movie A–Z* (Bloomington: Indiana University Press, 1996), 184.

8

What Women Want: Women Talk about Modern Masculinity in the Action Film

Don't call me 'babe'!

—Pamela Anderson, *Barb Wire*

In her studies of female spouse selection, anthropologist Heather Remoff argues that women will tend to pick those men as husbands who appear to have the potential to make good fathers.[1] However, she adds that a woman will pick the father material even if she believes she will never want to have children. This is an interesting premise and something I was reminded of throughout the data gathering from the female interviewees. Talking to the women revealed a preference for decidedly more social action heroes and plots than what the men were looking for.

As the previous chapters have demonstrated, male action/adventure fans believe that many films deal with the male anxiety of losing control and influence over their families because the cultural tides are turning against traditional masculinity and the patriarchal nuclear family unit. From the male perspective, the families of the action film are contested ground, and men have to prove in ever more epic ways why they are worthy of being kept around by a wife or a girlfriend. This need to prove themselves worthy goes hand in hand with needing to prove they still have a place at all in the civilized world. By throwing themselves in harm's way, the action heroes prove that when motivated by a personal moral code, the capacity to inflict violence redeems masculinity in the civilized world. Even those men who do not entirely believe that there is an assault on masculinity in the real world do concede that the films explore the message. However, some men will go as far as interpreting the action narrative as a warning for men. These fans believe that action films are an omen of a coming state of disenfranchisement unless they learn to change their rigid, patriarchal, ultra-masculine selves. Rather than standing as a requiem for macho, some viewers interpret the film as a warning of the loneliness, marginalization, and loss of power men are sure to face unless they learn to change their ways and accept the fact that women will have equal control of the world.

This is close to the interpretation that many female viewers take away from the action/adventure experience. Although male viewers often focus on the problematic relationship between action heroes and society, women are interested in the way their favorite action heroes are able to act as well-integrated protectors of society, can work well within a unit of heroes focused on a mission, or how action heroes fight evil to protect their families.

Heterosexual women, however, also get an extra amount of pleasure from the action film that men do not.

PLEASURES FOR THE FEMININE GAZE

One basic-level appeal of the action adventure film for a female audience is often talked about with a smirk. It is true that many women will admit to liking the genre because of the attractive male stars. Very fit men, especially in films where the fetishizing gaze of the camera is set upon their muscular bodies, are an attraction for a lot of female viewers. Even in Janice Radway's study of romance novels, she states that one appeal of the books' male characters is on the level of "masturbatory titillation," although all of her subjects eventually argue that a truly good male character must have such ephemeral qualities as "tenderness," "intelligence," "sensitivity," and the ability to recognize how he cannot bear to live life without the heroine.[2]

Frank testimony comes from twenty-seven-year-old Ruby who explains that first and foremost, a good action hero needs to a have a powerful, muscular build. She enjoys watching such men because they are attractive. She prefers the muscular, well-exercised physique on a man, and an action hero should be a man at his best. During my interview with Ruby, I also had my books about Jackie Chan, Sylvester Stallone, and Arnold Schwarzenegger on hand, as I did during my interview with Jeff, along with still photos from a *James Bond* film and *Armageddon*. Ruby, in turn, would repeatedly indicate that if she had a choice in watching any of those films based on the still photos, she would be interested in seeing the Stallone and Schwarzenegger vehicles. Stills from *Rambo II* and photos of Schwarzenegger performing bodybuilding competition poses were rated as the most interesting and attractive by Ruby. When I showed her photos of Jackie Chan, especially a shirtless "beefcake" publicity still from early in Chan's career, she explains that the pose had no effect on her because Chan's build is too slight and skinny. She quickly points to his chest and explains that for Chan to improve, he needs to build up his pectorals more. This criticism, however, is appended by Ruby's explanation that she is generally a fan of Chan's films because she has respect for his physical prowess in performing all of his own stunts. However, to get her full devotion, action heroes have to meet her strict standards of attractiveness.

Stephanie speaks to the same effect, explaining that other than not being the average female who would probably prefer a romantic drama or relationship film, she likes the heroes of an action film to be more rugged and macho than sensitive and emotional. She is especially a fan of *Cobra*, one of Stallone's films that had him being accused of going to the well at the height of his career, creating an urban Rambo clone who is one of his most taciturn, abrasive, and uncommunicative characters. Stephanie, however, says that she might turn to different films for different reasons. But the action film is part and parcel of its strong and rugged macho men. However, we do have to keep in mind that she admits that the action film is her first choice of entertainment and she is turning to its pleasures more than the pleasures of other genres. Stallone fan Helen says:

> I guess I would have to say that as a woman, I very much enjoy seeing the big-muscled tight bodies on the screen and I would beam with pride to walk alongside him. The same way the men drool over Pamela Anderson. But I don't think I have ever seen Steven Seagal in that light [sexually attractive], yet he is an action hero. . . . I sometimes display Rambo wallpaper on my computer and the reaction I get from men is more of a roll of the eyes and "you have to be kidding, that's not real."

Helen's "Rambo IV" treatment, of course, has her heroine, Christine, becoming romantically involved with Rambo as she puts herself in the world of the fictional character and fulfills her fantasies in the Rambo fantasy world.

Her comment about doing something that men have always done, openly leering and commenting on the bodies of attractive women, is echoed in Cindy's interview. As will be fully demonstrated in the next chapter when Cindy speaks about politics and social institutions, she is one of the most outspoken and angriest interviewees when it comes to voicing social critique. She argues that the action film gives women the same sort of opportunity to gaze at the idealized bodies of the opposite sex that men have so often done when the media objectifies women. For her, this has the significance of a social statement, doing something that society has not condoned for women as much as it has for men. When talking of her attraction to Wesley Snipes's films, of whom she is a big fan, she adds that the viewing experience includes the attraction to Snipes's muscular body.

The issue of the pleasure of the gaze upon the male physique, however, ventures into the territory of how masculinity might be constructed and the pressures it exerts upon men in comments made by Diana. Diana's words, which I would later quote to the other interviewees to see if they agreed, prompted a mainly tacit approval of her sentiments, even though it begins negating some of the titillating pleasure of the genre. Diana comments that she worries very much about the impact the idealized male bodies in the action films might have on young boys. In her own words:

> What the runway is for a woman, or *Cosmo* magazine or whatever, the action adventure film is for the man. . . . Men are definitely suffering, just as the women suffer. It's just that men just don't talk about it. The women will talk about their thighs, their hair, whatever's bad about their body image. The men don't talk about it with their friends. They don't talk about it with their wives. . . . They just go and mope about it silently or do something about it, but don't say this is why they're doing it.

Diana, however, adds that the pressure might not be as bad today, where the hypermuscularity of Stallone and Schwarzenegger has been replaced by the more wiry and supple, more "realistic," physiques of Brad Pitt or Ben Affleck. But she does argue that the films' definition of proper masculine behavior, as she interprets it, is harming young men by expecting a standard that is not emotionally healthy. Aside from the fit bodies, she explains that many action films' insistence on stoicism and the repression of feelings is creating more of that male "suffering."

Although Diana would not comment about how much discussion she has about this topic with her husband, our forty-four-year-old interviewee Harry, who works out regularly, she does make highly qualified statements about her pregnancy at the time of the interview and how it is shaping her media opinions. The qualification of the statements is through her commitment to parental responsibility. As strongly as she criticizes aspects of the genre, she insists that she believes it is the parent's responsibility to raise the children and instill them with values, worldviews, and a level of self-esteem that should protect them from media images.

The strongest protest I get, however, when quoting Diana comes from Selina, a twenty-year-old undergraduate. She feels the pressures any men might feel from the fit bodies on the action/adventure screen are nothing compared to what women feel:

> No way! No way! Not at all. Girls are totally different. Girls in everyday life just have to look a certain way. For men . . . they would like you if you're fat . . . or they don't say I gotta look like Arnold, or okay, they might and they would want

to go to the gym and bulk up. I think it's much easier for them because society accepts them more than a bigger woman who doesn't look a certain way . . . a man can look any way and women will flock.

Even as I mention the rise in the number of men getting cosmetic surgery, she still does not agree that men are under pressure similar to what women face at the hands of the media.

Selina's protest, however, quite interestingly, came soon after I asked her about masculine messages in the action film and she replied with the following comment:

The one message they are trying to send out is one of overt masculinity because they have to act a certain way; don't open your mouth too much, be a loner type, but be sexy at the same time. But you know, like what should I really be? Like you have to be big and strong, yet cold, yet desirable and a whole bunch of stuff overall.

But Selina's very strong disagreement about male pressures, it seems, is set off only when I tried to make a comparison to female body image problems. I did not bring up the issue of masculinity within the framework of pressure, but merely asked her what statements, if any, the films might be making about masculinity. At that point, she replied with an anecdote about a cousin she has, a very young boy, who likes to watch action films and likes to imitate characters he sees, acting big and tough. At that point, she talked about the dominant male standard of behavior being one of tough, quiet stoicism. When I asked her, after this comment, if this is in any way comparable to female body image pressures, as Diana claimed, she delivered a very vehement repudiation of the runway/*Cosmo* magazine/action film comparison. As if attempting to monopolize pressure, she quickly delivered her reply about society and women not caring what a man might look like.

Ultimately, despite the visual, titillating pleasure offered by the sight of strong male physiques, other than Ruby, none of the women indicated preferring the exaggerated bodybuilder physique. They chose instead the more "realistic" fitness of Mel Gibson or Tom Cruise, while at the same time acknowledging that they can understand male body image problems.

CHARACTER MATTERS

The strength and appeal of the action hero for women, ultimately, is not in the purely physical realm alone. The words of these interviewees help recall Radway's descriptions of how female romance readers are looking not so much for the mechanical, physical aspects of sex in their novels, but more of a concentration on the psychic, emotional states of the characters during the act. As she quotes a romance publishing house's editor:

> [S]ex in romances must be sensual, breathy—enough to make the pulse race, but not rough-guy, explicit, constantly brutal . . . the predominant flavor must be an understanding of female *emotions*: hesitancy, doubt, anger, confusion, loss of control, exhilaration, etc.[3]

Similarly, women are especially concerned with the strength of character of an action hero, his commitment to a cause or commitment to protecting or rescuing people he cares about, rather than his brute physical strength and proficiency in delivering creative violence.

Even Stephanie, a fan of the rugged and muscular macho heroes, an avid fan of *Cobra*, explains that one of the appeals of the Stallone character in that film is his dedication to a mission, no matter what the personal costs. The greatest personal cost for the protagonist, in fact, is not even the physical danger but the social and professional isolation it puts him in. The character is almost the very embodiment of Connery's "ugly dog" thesis from *The Presidio*. He is a cop so far on the edge in the tactics he uses that he is almost a political liability for any of the police brass if they need to call on his special unit's assistance in solving ultra-violent serial killings. Likewise, he is shown living a near-monastic personal life, alone in his beach-side loft that he turned into a private crime lab. When he does get romantic with a woman he is protecting from a gang of fascist psychopaths, he explains that any woman would be "pretty crazy" to want to get involved with him. Stephanie, however, explains that the character is not just on the fringe of the system, a sulking, simmering, marginalized zealot, but someone who seems proud of his outcast status. His main strength is that of his character and commitment to a mission, which gives him a status of moral superiority over the compromising, morally bankrupt members of the police establishment.

Selina paints a picture of the ideal man by describing the George Clooney character from the three *Ocean's* films:

> He was a good guy that loved his wife. He was a good guy! You know, he did some bad things. He was a thief. He was skilled in whatever he did [thievery]. But he was also, well, he also didn't have a bad body, but he got along with everybody. He stuck out to the end.

In fact, Selina explains that Clooney was much preferable and overall much more attractive than Brad Pitt in the same films, simply because the character traits of a man elevate him much higher than simple physical attributes. As far as Selina is concerned, the Clooney/Pitt comparison proved that "you might not look the best, but as long as you act correctly to whom you're supposed to [you are the perfect man]."

The George Clooney example from the *Ocean's* films is significant because Selina touches upon an issue that is key in all of the female interviewees' testimonies. In the first film, the Clooney character's plot to rob casinos is motivated by his resentment over having lost his wife, and mainly because he lost her to a casino owner. In the case of this film, the setup of the crime spree is done in standard "caper" film conventions. A likable group of criminals embark on a justifiable mission to heist a valuable prize, the mission becoming more of a large puzzle to solve—having to overcome impenetrable vaults, elude security systems, meet difficult deadlines as they work their way though a daunting maze to reach the money/the diamonds/the priceless art treasure—than a reprehensible and antisocial act of criminality. Essentially, no one in the "caper" movie is supposed to get hurt as a result of the criminal protagonists' actions, and on some level they may even be justified in what they do. But the protagonists of the "caper" are professionals, they stick together in a well-functioning unit, a microcosm of efficient social order. The "caper" film, as is the case of the *Ocean's* series, is often light and comedic in tone. Caroll describes this class of films often overlapping with the action/adventure genres:

> [C]aper films represent persons involved in perpetrating crimes that we do not customarily consider to be upstanding ethically. However, the characters in such fictions are standardly possessed of certain striking virtues such that, in the absence of emphasis of countervailing virtues in their opposite number, or possibly given the emphasis on the outright vice of their opponents, we are encouraged to ally ourselves morally with the caper. The virtues in question here—such as strength, fortitude, ingenuity, bravery, competence, beauty, generosity, and so on—are more often than not Grecian, rather than Christian. And it is because the characters exhibit these virtues—it is because we perceive (and are led to perceive) these characters as virtuous—that we cast our moral allegiance with them.[4]

For Selina, Clooney's justification lies in his mission to get back at the man who took his wife. It is, essentially, in a very ominously justified, mildly warped way, a mission for the family. Family-oriented action heroes, as will be discussed very shortly in full, have a very strong attraction for these women. But something else that is important for Selina in the *Ocean's* films is the group orientation of the hero, the fact that he is a team player, someone who fits into an organized social structure and can act toward—preferably as the leader—the achievement of a common goal.

REAL MEN BOND: WOMEN'S VIEWS OF
THE ACTION HERO AND THE COHESIVE SOCIAL UNIT

Unlike men, the female interviewees are very seldom drawn toward the rugged, gruff loner. The anti-social tough guy on the fringes, the hero who cannot communicate, cannot get along with authority figures, spouses, lovers, and partners is not attractive for most of the female viewers among this subject pool. The fact that so many of the classic action heroes function exactly as such helps bolster the thesis that the golden age of the action genre, giving rise to Eastwood, Schwarzenegger, Stallone, Chuck Norris, and many of their imitators, created male stars who were more of the male's ideal than the female's. The generic action film, where a hero agreed to a mission only upon the stipulations that he gets to use his own weapons, his own truck, and his own tactics and does not need to work with a partner, was certainly successful for a time, but successful with a male audience. As the female members of my subject pool explain, a woman's action hero has to be comfortable within a group, his anti-social urges must be contained, and he must not be intimidated by civilized society in which women are making gains in positions of power and influence.

Listening to women talk about loner heroes and team players, parallels to anthropological work on exclusively male social structures and the process of male bonding become remarkably uncanny. In fact, a sort of demographic shift that occurs in the audience base of the action films, from the "women's ideals" of the 1940s, 1950s, and early 1960s to action heroes of the Schwarzenegger and Stallone eras, also marks a stronger appearance of the marginalized, aggressively anti-social loner, the tough guy of the fringe bitterly carrying a chip on his shoulder for having lost ground. When the male group does show up in the film, however, when teams of action heroes prepare to carry out a mission, when the headlining action star is a charismatic leader of men, or two charismatic male stars do a buddy picture, women once again seem to be interested.

Even among the female Stallone fans in the subject pool, fans of a star who has often been averse to partnerships on screen, all rate his buddy action comedy *Tango and Cash* (1990) quite highly. In fact, to footnote Stallone's aversion to bonding on-screen and add weight to how much he was able to still attract women to his *Rambo* films through his emotional accessibility, willingness to suffer, and his glistening, pumped muscularity, Marc Shapiro's 2000 biography of James Cameron and its details of the genesis of *Rambo II* provides an interesting anecdote. As Cameron wrote the first draft of the screenplay, the film was going to be a buddy film. Rambo would have been teamed with a young partner to rescue the POWs. Stallone, though, quickly took issue with the title character not doing the mission alone and rewrote the script. However, generally, in the eyes of the female viewer, a man who can bond with a unit of other men, or better yet, lead them, is one of the most attractive possible incarnations of masculinity possible.

Since Shapiro's book, however, an interesting postscript can be added to Rambo's work with partners. In the latest chapter in the series, Rambo works to free the captured missionaries from a Burmese prison with the aid of a team of mercenaries. The inclusion of the mercenaries, according to various interviews Stallone had given about the project, was inspired in some part by the post–September 11 and Iraq War cultural atmosphere and in part by Stallone's advanced years. Although still remarkably muscular, having filmed *Rambo* right after *Rocky Balboa*, Stallone acknowledged some of the critics' and fans' skepticism of how plausible a story can be where a sixty-two-year-old man is single-handedly wiping out armies the way he had done two decades ago. But a more pointed concern for Stallone, according to his DVD commentary for the film and various television and print-media interviews, was the depiction of realistic military operations in a time when wars are being fought in Iraq and Afghanistan. It would be disrespectful to the real soldiers, he said, to show one man single-handedly destroying armies of enemies when in the real world thousands have so far died in battles against the Taliban and in the ongoing efforts to pacify Iraq. Although he had never addressed the issue, critics of his back-to-Vietnam-themed *Rambo II* raised the same objection about the story of one lone soldier taking on and destroying and entire Vietnamese army while thousands had fought and died attempting the same thing and failing in the real world.

As Lionel Tiger prefaces the 1984 edition of his book on male bonding, *Men in Groups*, the male-male social group is something that has long received "treatment . . . in films and advertising. For what it is worth, it has become a truism in Hollywood that 'buddy movies' will sell—films centering on the experience of males getting on with or without each other and finally about their affection for each other without this becoming even implicitly erotic."[5]

The earliest and best examples of the attractiveness of the male bonding films were many of the 1940s war films with John Wayne, as well as Wayne's teaming with director Howard Hawks for several westerns. While Hawks has a legacy as one of the most versatile of Hollywood directors, making classics in genres as diverse as film noir, the screwball comedy, science fiction, and the war film, he also made several of Wayne's most memorable westerns, like *Red River* (1948), *Rio Bravo* (1959) (and *Rio Bravo*'s near-identical remakes), *El Dorado* (1967), and *Rio Lobo* (1970). The dynamics of the all-male team had, in fact, been a career-long interest of Hawks. His male bonding stories usually centered a story on a team of professionals forming a tight-knit relationship in their pursuit of a dangerous profession. Skill is always an important issue in the Hawks films, with the men of the group concerned with how good each man is in performing his duties, whether that be sharp-shooting and quick-drawing, driving, or fighting.

The Wayne persona was built in great part out of the conventions of stories that examined the male bond, and Wayne, in turn, always had a sizable female fan base. The Wayne character, when found within a group, as mentioned in the previous chapters, was the leader and he would strive to integrate new, boyish members into the cohesive unit, to teach them to "be men." He was very much a father figure to his young charges and the all-male team building, the rearing of boys into men, especially in the war films, was for the greater good of society as a whole.

The issue of the emotions of the Wayne characters, as we are seeing from these testimonials that female audiences prize heroes who are more expressive of their feelings, should also be touched upon briefly here. As Wayne always had a good number of female fans, it is an issue worth taking a closer look at because it is something that has long been muddled by revisionist and ill-informed critics. The templates for the discussion of "harmful" and "enlightened" masculine images always have a dichotomy of current, "sensitive" male actors who are not afraid to be weak and cry if need be, and the classical models of hard, silent, stoic masculinity from the "old days," embodied by Wayne. As Emanuel Levy's analysis of the various components of the Wayne masculine image points out, even in the actor's most rousing and rugged war films, his characters are shown to often wear their machismo as an armor, as a guise covering up a gentler, more sensitive core. As Levy writes:

> In most of his war movies, Wayne's roughness is more of a façade. In *Flying Leathernecks*, Wayne is frustrated when he does not get mail from his family and he is the one to write a letter of condolence to the victims' families. His leaders are by no means insensitive, especially when it comes to respect for soldiers who have died in duty. In *They Were Expendable*, he states firmly, "a serviceman is supposed to have a funeral — that's a tribute to the way he's spent his life. Escort, firing squad, wrapped in the flag he served under and died for." Wayne even recites poetry — awkwardly — in honor of one of the casualties who "was always quotin' verse."[6]

Such films should be seen in a context they have been removed from for a long time, yet one that is now easily comparable to today's media "reacting to the events of 9/11." Those war movies were products of their time, they were crafted to glorify the war effort, "support the troops" and build the country's morale after it had entered World War II in the aftermath of an attack on America.

Where women begin disconnecting from action stories, however, would be with the introduction of the quasi-sociopathic loners, society's cynical throw-aways who fight as a result of provocation and personal insult, or to settle scores against a feminized "system" that no longer honors them. The thugs of *The Dirty Dozen*, for example, the anti-heroes, the outsiders and angry, marginalized men who have no appeal for a female audience, as part of their anger can often be seen as a metaphorical protest against a feminized society. As Tiger's male-bonding theory presents, the organization of men in gender-exclusive groups is for the ultimate advantage of a larger society, a system "characterized by the genetic advantage of those males who could dominate, who were willing and able to bond to dominate and hunt, and who could none the less maintain affectionate if undemocratic relationships with females and young,"[7] and not merely the aggrandizement of the individual. Actors like Mel Gibson, Tom Cruise (both former Sexiest Man Alive honorees), or Harrison Ford, who can play the leaders of men (as Ford played the ultimate American leader, no less than the president of the United States in *Air Force One* [1997]), are the female interviewees' top choices as action heroes.

Although many of the female interviewees do voice a considerable level of pessimism about real social institutions, as will be discussed in greater detail in the following chapter, they see a good action hero as one who fights to im-prove the world. They see a good action film as one with hope and outlook.

When Kelly talks about a good action hero, she explains that he can have a "dangerous" edge, that he can have a dark side, but only as far as having the capacity to get violent when an overwhelmingly bad situation requires it. These are the qualities she sees in her favorite literary action hero. Kelly claims that she is an "obsessive compulsive Clive Cussler fan," and she was excited when one of her favorite novels, *Sahara*, was being adapted to film by Cussler himself. She says that she will usually feel "totally engulfed" in the books because of their visual style, because she can clearly see all the action sequences. She also says that she is inspired by Cussler to pursue a career as a novelist one day. The books, centered around heroic underwater explorer Dirk Pitt, are very much filmic in their plots, action sequences and pacing, but with a wholesome hero who works with a team on missions to stop various larger-than-life villains.

In a 1998 compendium of Cussler's Dirk Pitt books, the character is de-scribed in a capsule summary on the first page as:

The consummate man of action who lives by the moment and for the moment . . . without regret. A graduate of the Air Force Academy, son of a United States senator, and special projects director for the U.S. National Underwater and Marine Agency (NUMA), he is cool, courageous, and resourceful—a man of complete honor at all times and of absolute ruthlessness whenever necessary.

With a taste for fast cars, beautiful women, and tequila on the rocks with lime, he lives as passionately as he works. Pitt answers to no one but Admiral James Sandecker, the wily commander of NUMA, and trusts no one but the shrewd, street-smart Al Giordino, a friend since childhood and his partner in undersea adventures for twenty years.

Although the Pitt character often lives by his wits and butts heads with government bureaucrats, his connection to the establishment is secure. Much like James Bond, he works for a government agency, gets along at least with his immediate supervisor, and is a team leader in the marine agency that employs him.

The Pitt character, as he was conceived and his adventures executed, is very much rooted in films from the John Wayne and Gary Cooper era. Cussler himself has repeatedly stated that he had Errol Flynn in mind when describing Pitt's looks, especially Flynn's mischievous, bad-boy smirk. In each of the Pitt books, on numerous occasions, Pitt is described as flashing a "devilish smile." With a "ruthless" edge, Pitt is nevertheless a man for the people, a champion for a society that may often be flawed, but one well worth fighting for. As Cussler explained during an interview I once conducted with him, "Dirk Pitt is all there for the American flag, mothers and apple pie. When he subdues the villain, he shakes hands with the girl, kisses his horse and rides off into the sunset. He's like John Wayne, Gary Cooper."[8]

A combination of these characteristics, Cussler explains, is behind the sizable female fan base he enjoys:

Fifty percent of my readership are women and I've gotten letters from women saying things like "I'd dump my husband for Dirk Pitt." . . . Some women still want a hero on a horse to come and sweep them off their feet and carry them away. Some women still fantasize about that. If you want the women, you have to have the romance. "You and me and the bay at Monterey."[9]

When Kelly describes her attraction to Pitt, she says:

In a film I like the murkiness of a shady character. I think it gives a character . . . but there is always something very appealing to the Boy Scout. Dirk Pitt is evil in his own little ways. There's darkness underneath. Like in his past is where he has his dark side. But I like his chivalry. There's something very satisfying in the chivalry. It's very appealing. But he's not just clean all the time. He's allowed to be both. Because I think too clean is just nauseating. Too bad doesn't give you a wholesome feeling.

When I talked to Diana and asked to discuss the issue of the loner hero and the team player, the leader figure, she quickly went from a general, hypothetical explanation of how fascinating a predicament it is when a man is forced to solve a problem completely alone to an overall preference for the action hero who works in a team. Imagining someone suddenly victimized, thrown into a situation where everyone is against him or her, Diana says, is a very powerful and interesting concept. Indeed, the theme of the wrongly accused, victimized outsider has been one of Alfred Hitchcock's oft-recurring themes. Diana says that it was exactly this wrongly persecuted-man theme that made her such a big fan of *The Fugitive* (1993). However, she says that she is uncomfortable with someone who is loner by choice. Someone who is so angry and alienated as to choose to live apart from organized society, to reject all of its conventions, she does not find as interesting a character as one who chooses to work in a cohesive team to achieve some sort of a positive goal.

This, in fact, is representative of what all of the women say about the action heroes. Some, like Stallone-fans Kathleen, Stephanie, Jane, and Helen, tell of their enjoyment of films where the hero is very much a loner, at odds with society and fighting to live an individualistic existence on his own terms. The concept is interesting to them, and it has a lot of dramatic potential. They, just like Diana, especially like the films where the hero is forced outside of the system, where he becomes a wrongly hunted man and he has to fight to save his life and prove his innocence. However, even they enjoy films where the team of men is a well-functioning, cohesive unit seeking to fulfill a righteous common goal.

ACTION HEROES, WOMEN, AND FAMILIES

A very important aspect of the action film for any of these interviewees, naturally, is the hero's relationship to women. All of these women explain that they like to see stories where there is a mutually active and respectful partnership between the action hero and a woman in his life. As seen in the previous chapter, in Peter's testimony about the *James Bond* films improving when the "Bond girls" are more of a partner for the hero, even men will often prefer such a union between the sexes. *James Bond* enthusiast Dirk also adds:

> I don't know about you, but for a long time I've been annoyed when the hero is fighting for his life and the woman is there and she's just shrinking against the wall. That's just stupid. I mean, step in, don't be such a wuss! Just because I like guys to behave like action heroes doesn't mean I want women to be useless.

Helen's "Rambo IV" story demonstrates the ideal action story for her, one she takes the initiative in creating when she, in essence, usurps the power of the creators over the Rambo world, asserts her own power as the fan, and rewrites the narrative according to her own value system. The reason, she says, is because the story needs to reflect current social realities:

[The hero's role is] no longer to protect the little woman because sometimes the little woman can not only protect herself but the man too, and most men have not learned to handle this. The woman is finally stepping out to say, "hey, anything you can do, I can do."

The important feature of her Rambo story is its resolution of the hostage crisis when Christine goes to the Middle East and rescues Rambo, then the two of them fight side by side to get all the hostages home. This, she says, is something she would like to see in action films because it reflects the sensibilities of the times and the preferences of modern women. Too much of what she still sees, however, is offensive and frustrating for her:

I really hate it when the first thing the woman does when she opens the door to see the bad guy is scream. Put a sock in it! I learned early on in school that no man was going to protect me, nor should he. First thing my father taught me, "if you are going to hit a boy in self-defense, don't do it with an open hand. Close that fist and make it count." And I did. I have never started a fight but I have never backed down from one. I don't walk behind a man and I don't want to walk in front of him. I walk beside him. And no, I don't think I am equal to him. There are a lot of things a man does that I believe a woman shouldn't. Not because she can't but she is not built to do it. I think a woman can be soft and sexy and *kick butt* too. I really hate seeing these little blond pieces of fluff. I guess you . . . have to read my Rambo to see my alter ego.

These sentiments about willingness are typical of the female interviewees. While they are drawn to characters that are willing to fight for the family, fight to protect children and women, the *willingness* is the important factor. The will for the battle is what defines the hero's heroism and gives him that attractive aura as a champion of the family unit, the ideal mate who best protects his offspring. What the women don't like, however, is the stories' suggestion that they are universally weaker and in *need* of protection.

As Kathleen explains:

I think it's in a man's nature to want to be the provider, the protector, the leader. There's nothing wrong with that, just as there's nothing wrong with a woman wanting to be comforted, the mother, the nurturer, the homemaker. There's also nothing wrong with a man who wants to express his feelings and weaknesses, or a woman who proves herself to be just as strong and capable as a man. I think that sometimes political correctness goes too far and strangles these ideas, deeming them as old fashioned.

Kelly also points to the treatment of women in the Dirk Pitt novels as an important attraction for her. "I like the way he does not forget his female characters," she says, "and they do play strong roles, he has strong female characters." She explains that she likes the fact that a recurring love interest for Pitt is Congresswoman Loren Smith, a person who loves Pitt, yet is not obsessively clinging to him. She loves him, but she does not need him.

Cussler has remarked that he always liked the way readers have reacted to those characters and claims that the best comment he has ever gotten about the books came from a woman journalist who said, "Loren Smith is the woman we all want to be, and Dirk Pitt is the man we all want."[10] Although Pitt and Loren Smith become lovers in one of the books, their relationship is not exclusive and Pitt usually beds women all over the world on all of his adventures. Cussler, however, says that "Pitt's women are never harsh, stupid bimbos. They've all made it in the world and carry their own weight."[11]

Nevertheless, Cussler also adds that he feels there needs to be a limit to the toughness of a female character in an action story. Some of my interviewees would agree with this sentiment, while others disagree strongly. During my interview with Cussler, he explained:

> My female characters are still women. You can't have a woman beating up a man. I mean, a 120-pound woman is not going to beat up a man, even if she knows judo. All he has to do is tackle her. You start getting out of the mold when they're wielding ninja swords and beating up 200-pound men. I don't think they fly.

Interestingly, the very large female fan base that reads Cussler's books seems to be satisfied with such gender differentiation. It is also interesting that Kelly herself is satisfied with books that create female characters that are such a mix of old-fashioned and feminist tendencies. I say this because Kelly is interested in just such physical pastimes that Cussler describes as ill-fitting for women. Kelly is on the rugby team of her college—explaining that getting on the field and hitting people can have a very satisfying, stress-release function—she likes racing cars she restores with her father and brother, she is considering studying boxing, and has, at one point, considered joining the Reserve Officers Training Corp.

Kelly also realizes that her persona represents the threat many men feel as their exclusive arenas are disappearing. She plays rugby, she races, she wants to box, all things that at one time were the reserved domains of men. However, she also believes that men need not feel threatened by this. She makes one of the most interesting comments of all the interviewees when she says:

> Women aren't the submissive types anymore. We can do anything men can do. We have limitations, but we can accomplish anything. *Anyone* can. Men can do anything women can, except child birth. I think it's a double-sided coin. If men could see that they can do anything we can do, they would realize we could do anything they can do and not feel threatened.

Action stories, generally, need to treat women as equals to attract a female audience and carefully tread that middle line in creating female characters that are neither too tough nor so weak as to *need* a man's protection. The action hero's willingness to give protection, to risk his life to help a woman, is a very attractive package for female viewers. Bodyguard and protector movies, in fact, have often been very successful. Kevin Costner's *The Bodyguard* (1991) may have been his last unqualified blockbuster hit. But here he protects an intensely willful and independent woman. Similarly, during his 1990s drought of blockbuster films, Sylvester Stallone scored a very big hit with *The Specialist* in 1994, pleasing female audiences with his role as a mercenary protecting icy, headstrong Sharon Stone from gangsters and baring his physique in an explicit sex scene.

The preference to see this respect from a man has even inspired some interesting interpretations of the text from Diana. She explains that she is a fan of the *James Bond* films because she sees Bond as a character who treats women with the respect afforded one's equals. As she explains, Bond "will respect a woman and act upon her ideas as if she is an equal. They are always very agreeable to do whatever he wants in the passion sense. [He] treats them as equals, chases after them, [making for] an interesting dynamic balance."

When I ask her if she can truly see Bond as the sort of character who is capable of maintaining a relationship with a woman—outside of *On Her Majesty's Secret Service* (1969), where he gets married briefly, then made a widower by an assassin—she cannot completely commit to a prediction one way or another. However, she does insist that Bond is committed to treating the women in his life as equals.

However, by the same token, the other female interviewees, aside from Connie, are not Bond fans. Connie likes Bond because, she explains, she is a fan of spy films in general. She likes the travelogue aspects of the film. She explains that she likes films that take her to interesting and exotic parts of the world, showing her new things she has never seen or thought existed before.

The most pointedly negative reaction to Bond, however, comes from Kathleen. She says that Bond has always made her "uncomfortable." The smoothness, the slickness of the character, the way in which he is presented as a completely irresistible man, a man no woman can ever reject, bothers her. Kathleen explains that a hero who will woo a woman, who will work to earn her, will fight for her, who will impress her, and essentially be her "hero" is somehow more attractive than someone who is a hypnotic female magnet. She also adds that when it comes to the action, she does not feel Bond is rugged enough. He does not get "down and dirty" in the course of completing his missions, does not feel as much pain and shed as much blood, does not suffer for his victories, as much as Rambo does. Although she is quite right in pointing out that Bond is always more of a cerebral hero than most of his American counterparts, often relying on subterfuge, trickery, wits, charisma, and technology rather than his muscles to get himself out of a dangerous bind, I point out that Bond has varied in levels of toughness throughout his incarnations over forty years. Although Roger Moore has been the least physical of the Bonds, Sean Connery is generally regarded by fans as the best Bond because of his overt machismo and toughness. Other Bonds like Pierce Brosnan, Timothy Dalton, and George Lazenby reside somewhere in the middle of the Connery/Moore spectrum. Daniel Craig, the latest Bond, is the most prominent throwback to the toughness of Sean Connery. Craig is also the most muscular of all the Bonds so far. Kathleen agrees that Connery is tough enough in the role and that she generally likes Connery's movies, but it is not the actor she has a problem with but the character. She apparently seems to be bothered by the idea of a hero who can take away a woman's choice in selecting him for a mate or even a temporary lover.

Other than demanding respect from a perfect action hero, the female interviewees like to evaluate him in terms of a romantic or life partner. Helen, for example, compares her favorite classic action hero, John Wayne, to the type of ragged-edge burnout Mel Gibson plays in the first *Lethal Weapon* film in terms of how they fare as possible mates:

> I have to agree that Wayne's characters were, for the most part, more wholesome a hero. If you compare him, for instance, to Mel Gibson in *Lethal Weapon*. If you strip away how he takes down the bad guys and just concentrate on the hero, he really doesn't look that appealing. He was a drunk, a womanizer, he smoked like a chimney, not exactly the take home to meet the family type. And that seemed to be the type of action figure that came forth [today]. I personally think they go too far with profanity. I think the F . . . word could be deleted entirely. And I am not a prude. I have worked years with truck drivers and cement finishers. They don't come any nastier. Wayne, on the other hand, rarely smoked, couldn't be classified as a drunk and was usually well groomed and well mannered around the women. Even his living quarters were usually neat and clean.

Emanuel Levy agrees with this analysis, writing:

A consistent trait of Wayne's sex image was his tenderness with women. His gentle courtship had none of the compulsive womanizing of the male chauvinist. He was deeply emotional, which he expressed eloquently with his eyes and his voice.[12]

Comparing him to James Bond, Joan Mellen writes, "Bond's crude sexual exhibitionism shows the need endlessly to prove a capacity the more secure Wayne always took for granted with neither self-doubt nor anxiety. Because his very reflexes guide him in how to be a man, he requires neither intellect nor the brutalization of women to prove himself."[13] Molly Haskell writes of Wayne, that when a loner, "If he thought he was better off on his own, it was not from the narcissism of the compulsive lover, but because he hadn't yet come to understand what he would come to understand: that men and women could be not only lovers but friends."[14]

Such sentiments, then again, harken back to the self-analysis offered by Clive Cussler about his ever-enduring Dirk Pitt and his "obsessive compulsive" fan, Kelly, and the importance of chivalry in the hero. The ideal action hero for women is a gentleman, lusty enough at the right moments, even vulnerable, but overall a gentleman without psychoses or any festering inner rage and resentment.

Even more pointedly, when it comes to the male-female relationships in the action film, all the interviewees, but for Stephanie, indicated that the films are the most interesting when the hero needs to protect the family.

When Lonni, a John Woo fan, talks about one of her favorite Woo films, *Face/Off*, she explains that the film is given an extra element of interest, just an extra subplot of a troubled family, that makes the entire film memorable, rather than letting it blend into a line of more run-of-the-mill action films. As she explains:

More films now have men that are three dimensional characters than like the Arnold Schwarzenegger movies a while ago. Like, okay, go rescue these people, end of story, but there's no real feeling about it. As in like the John Travolta film, *Face/Off*. He has this mission to save these people, but there's a whole story behind it about this family and there's dysfunction and he had this whole tragedy with his younger son.

Face/Off indeed is an interesting film to bring up, because the family lives of both the hero and villain determine their behaviors throughout the film. What first appears to be a primary plot, a canister of nerve gas set to explode somewhere in Los Angeles and wipe out masses of innocents, soon enough turns into a Hitchcockian "mcguffin," melting into the background while the two main characters and their relationships with families quickly drive the film.

The fantastic plot of *Face/Off* is essentially driven by the concept of how polar opposite models of masculinity have different impacts on the family. One model is the sensitive and well-meaning professional, the other the high-testosterone, dangerous, volatile tough guy. The story involves driven, yet decent and sensitive, FBI agent Travolta undergoing surgery and getting master criminal Nicolas Cage's face grafted onto his skull in order to infiltrate Cage's gang and find out where the nerve gas is hidden. At the same time, due to a more fantastic turn of events, Cage winds up with a graft of Travolta's face and likewise assumes his opponent's identity. The most important parts of the film, however, deal with the two men needing to fool each other's wives. At the same time, they actually end up helping their respective family units. The FBI agent in Cage's guise tells Cage's wife that indeed she needs to get away from a life of crime and raise their son in a safe environment with a future. By the same token, the new man in Travolta's house winds up saving a marriage that has been deteriorating since the death of their son. The super criminal, it turns out, is able to bring the dwindling passion back to the bedroom, his aggressive sexuality reigniting the wife's commitment to the union. The new Travolta, then, is also able to help the old Travolta's daughter through a crisis she has with an obsessive, abusive boyfriend. In a moment of concerned paternal advice, the criminal gives the daughter a switchblade and explains that the next moment the boy won't take "no" for an answer, she needs to stab him in just the right place in the inner thigh and twist the blade to cause the proper amount of damage to the arteries.

Face/Off is very much *The Enemy Within* retold through the conventions of the action/adventure film. The central point of view through which the radical opposite constructs of masculinity are seen, however, is not the man himself trying to negotiate a middle ground between his two halves but the family unit. The film asks how much of a man, or what model of masculinity, is proper for the survival of the family. Much like *Star Trek*, the film concludes that a man needs to be a balance of both tough guy and sensitive modern man. In the beginning of the film, both the macho man's and the sensitive man's families are in a crisis, and only through the influence of each man's opposite do the families survive. Or rather, the FBI agent's family survives completely intact, because the sensitive Travolta eventually gets his old face back and goes home as good as new, while Cage gets killed. Although Cage's wife dies, his son, however, survives and gets adopted by Travolta's family where the boy will have the proper environment to grow and mature as healthy, pro-social male.

It is notable that Lonni also tells how she is a very big fan on *Gone in 60 Seconds* (2000), a caper/action film with Nicolas Cage. This is a film Lonni owns on DVD and has seen at least five times. Why does she like it so much? She explains that the family aspects of the plot appeal to her the most, the way the Cage character risks his life to steal fifty cars in one night to save his brother from an organized crime ring. She also says that she is very close to her brothers and defending one of them was the only time in her life when she got violent. She adds that she is not an aggressive and violent person, and indeed, she does not seem to be when one meets her and talks with her. Rather small and slight in build, Lonni is also soft-spoken, thoughtful, and polite. However, she does tell of the one incident in her life when a younger brother was being pushed around in school and she got into a fight with his assailant.

The final unanimous point for the female interviewees is the issue of the masculinity crisis. On the one hand, they can all conceive of it in theory, they understand the abstraction of men feeling displaced and frustrated by the social changes of the past thirty or so years. On the other hand, none of them think it constitutes a real crisis or that men are actually losing their hold on power in society.

As Helen says:

> I suppose to look at action heroes through men's eyes you could agree with the critics that this is the trend of the action films and the sequels are not kind to the hero. And I would probably agree that from the men's point of view they are feeling that they are losing power, influence and *some* respect. . . . Men don't understand this and they don't like it.

The woman's approach to the masculinity crisis is to claim the "crisis" is a concept exaggerating female gains in society to a level of a threat. None of the interviewees claim that they approach gender relations with any sort of an agenda to radically alter society in a way to tilt the balance of power in favor of women. They all state, in fairly similar terms to Helen's statements about wanting to walk neither in front of nor behind a man, that their main concern is that men and women function on an equal level.

As these women watch and enjoy the action film, they explain that they tacitly accept the fact that the narratives could indeed be speaking to male resentments, insecurities, and fears. However, in a technically oppositional approach to the text, they ignore these statements and enjoy the films on a generalized, universal level. They all explain that feelings of persecution and victimization are universal. Whether or not a man watching the action film will interpret the texts as speaking specifically, or even in thinly veiled metaphors, to their life experiences, these women claim that they, too, can watch the film and relate to the put-upon protagonists on a general level. As Diana told of her enjoyment of *The Fugitive*, or Helen or Kathleen talked about Stallone's films as a personally motivating, or Amy said that she is inspired by Stallone's achievements as an artist, narratives of struggle, power, and victimization can be removed from their gendered context and applied to the universal struggles of life.

VICTIMS

Another important wrinkle needs to be added to these interviews when it comes to analyzing how these women see themselves. Both Jane, a graduate student, and Cindy, a college senior with no immediate plans other than starting a career (undecided at the time of the interview) after graduation, explicitly call themselves feminists. Cindy, however, calls herself a feminist reluctantly. Each of the other women either have career plans, even if undecided during the interview as they were in college, or had been in the workforce for years, or they were balancing college with a career they were planning on staying with after completing their bachelor's degrees. Stephanie, for example, works for a mortgage company and plans on continuing work there after completing her bachelor's because she feels the company offers very lucrative avenues for advancement. Stephanie, however, also has a very strong reaction to my question about how media images influence or put pressure, including body image pressure, on people: "Oh, I'm just sick of that. I think people should just start living their own lives and take responsibility for themselves. I'm tired of hearing all these complaints about how people feel pressured by the media and pressured to look a certain way. That's just ridiculous." Of course, her reaction is very negative as read on the page, but listening to her in person offers an extra edge of anger and condescension coloring her tone. Now if one were to discuss the matter in person with Stephanie, their reaction might be twofold. First, some might say that Stephanie can afford to be dismissive of the body image argument because she is, to put it in scholarly terms, very much an image of "hegemonic femininity." It would not be much of a risk to assume that most people, men and women alike, would agree on calling Stephanie very attractive. In turn, their reaction would be to claim that Stephanie might not be so responsive to the pressure argument since she has the looks most women feel unfairly pressured to achieve. But with this fact about Stephanie's appearance out of the way, her words and tone are again very important. They are words repeated by others. She, essentially, resents the argument that the power of the media is stronger than the cognitive powers and will of individuals. At one point, for example, Cindy says that she calls herself a feminist, but "it's not because I'm so oppressed and everything." At one point, Lonni recites a long complaint about there not being enough films with female heroes, then quickly qualifies everything she said by stating "but I'm not really a feminist," because, again, she does not feel victimized. Both imply that they understand feminism to be going hand in hand with victimization and powerlessness. Interestingly, this is similar to the men's reluctance to talk about the "crisis" because they do not like putting themselves in the position of being a victim.

A similar disagreement, although less vehement in tone, comes from Jane, likewise skeptical of too much power afforded the media. Although Jane does qualify her dismissal of the unrealistic-standards pressure argument, whether that is pressure on men or women, by saying that she does not discount that *some* people, *sometime* might put enough stock in media messages as to try and model their behavior and appearance accordingly, she is ultimately skeptical. Jane, of course, works in academic circles where the unrealistic pressures of the media issue is in greater vogue and much a subject of discussion while Stephanie, Cindy, and Lonni do not. But all of these women are hostile to the idea on the grounds that it paints them as a victim who cannot decide the course of her own life without taking direction from the media.

Cindy, the most liberal and often angriest member of the female subject pool, says about the idea that media messages influence behavior, whether toward violence or body image expectations or feelings of crisis and persecution (this must be imagined as being recited in an exasperated tone of someone being forced to reply to an issue they find ridiculous):

> You know, I think that's the problem with the world today: that everybody constantly has to blame somebody. That's all we do. Blame, blame, blame. Blame the media, blame your family, blame the government, constantly blaming someone instead of just taking responsibility for your life.

SUMMARY

When women watch the action adventure film, they enjoy it on many of the same levels as men do. For women, however, the added pleasure of gazing at the objectified male body exists in this genre, despite the power of the character on screen. These interviewees also have the tendency to think of the male characters in terms of the ideal mate. Thus, the more sociable action heroes, the family-minded heroes are preferred. The stories of confrontation, danger, struggle, and power can be enjoyed on a universal level. But the stories of the male protagonists can also be seen as representations of ideal or problematic masculinity. Watching a film about someone fleeing wrongful persecution, victimization by crime, threatened by war and global instability, or being repressed by bureaucratic power is something people relate to regardless of gender. Their rejection of the masculinity crisis and negotiated meaning of feminism, however, shows even women's weariness of gender combat.

NOTES

1. Heather T. Remoff, *Sexual Choice: A Woman's Decision: Why and How Women Choose the Men They Do as Sexual Partners* (New York: Dutton, 1984).

2. Janice Radway, *Reading the Romance: Women, Patriarchy, and Popular Literature* (Chapel Hill: University of North Carolina Press, 1991).

3. Radway, *Reading the Romance*, 141.

4. Noel Caroll, "The Paradox of Suspense," in *Suspense: Conceptualizations, Theoretical Analyses, and Empirical Explorations*, eds. Peter Vorderer, Hans J. Wulff, and Mike Friedrichsen (Mahwah, NJ: Lawrence Erlbaum, 1996), 79.

5. Lionel Tiger, *Men in Groups* (New York: Marion Boyars Publishers, 1984), 15.

6. Emanuel Levy, *John Wayne: Prophet of the American Way of Life* (Metuchen, NJ: Scarecrow Press, 1988), 27–28.

7. Tiger, *Men in Groups*, 52.

8. Interview with Clive Cussler, March 28, 2001.

9. Interview with Clive Cussler.

10. Clive Cussler and Craig Dirgo, *Clive Cussler and Dirk Pitt Revealed* (New York: Pocket Books, 1998), 77.

11. Cussler and Dirgo, *Clive Cussler and Dirk Pitt Revealed*, 77.

12. Levy, *John Wayne*, 157.

13. Joan Mellen, *Big Bad Wolves: Masculinity in the American Film* (New York: Pantheon, 1997), 264.

14. Molly Haskel, *From Reverence to Rape* (New York: Holt, Rinehart and Winston, 1974), 506.

9

Bloody Fun: The Appeal of Watching Violence

The system stinks.

—Clint Eastwood, *Dirty Harry*

One of the surprising findings of this study is the fact that so many interviewees talked about being disturbed by depictions of violence in entertainment. A number of them discussed worrying about the influences violence might have on young children. One might expect that every man and woman who is a devotee of action films would not subscribe to the ideas of media violence being a menace to society. However, this is not the case. In fact, many of the action fans explain that they like action because, other than the narratives fulfilling their needs for speedy, excitatory sensations, they find certain depictions of violence very disturbing. The action genre, on the other hand, they say, provides acceptable visions of violence. However, the action/adventure film, as explained in the beginning of this book, is controversial, mainly, because of its violence. Studying the action genre's role in the lives of its most avid fans would be incomplete without discussing the issue of violence and what it means to them. The replies the interviewees gave tie the issue of violence to values, morality, and the state of social and governmental institutions, all of which are colored by gendered interpretations.

In recent research on audiences and violent entertainment, an argument has been made by the cultural studies school that studying violence should be motivated by a need to understand its utility in the lives of fans.[1] I therefore asked all of the interviewees what the appeal of violence in action movies is and what they found enjoyable about seeing destruction.

Steve, and avid *Bond* fan, presented the idea of the genre being overwhelmingly about violence. Steve was the second person I interviewed, so his comment was well timed. I could repeat it to each of the other interviewees to see if they agreed. Steve said that "the action film is 90 percent violence." My interviewees, except for Richard, agreed that this is pretty much true. However, the interviewees also argued that violence was a narrative and symbolic tool in the genre, a metaphorical device leading toward the examination of a social or philosophical concern.

As presented in Chapter 5, the genre itself is seen by many of its fans as an art form negotiating various value systems and worldviews. Some explain that the genre tells morality tales about helping others, or overcoming insurmountable odds, or belief in one's self. None of the interviewees said that watching violence in itself is pleasurable or exciting. Seeing an act of violence in itself, something getting annihilated, someone getting hurt, does not create the pleasure of the film. When discussing the issue of violence, the interviewees, except Richard and Edward, explain that the acts of violence are metaphorical. The metaphors resolve conflicts of gender and issues of power discussed in the previous chapters. Violence can also be the symbolic tool for discussing issues of contention, conflicts of power between individuals and modern governmental and social institutions. Men's and women's views of these institutions often differ and sometimes unexpectedly so.

For all the interviewees, except Cindy, Jane, and Selina, who are also avid fans of horror, violence is acceptable mainly in its stylized action/adventure manifestation. As discussed earlier, what helps set the action genre apart from many other genres where violence is performed is the stylized manner of execution. A lot of the action genre's violence looks decidedly unrealistic. Once again, as discussed before, there is little doubt in the minds of these viewers of action/adventure at least, that one man, armed with only a single machine gun, going up against an army of fifty evildoers, would stand very little chance of success. In turn, action films generally do not let their screens overflow with as much blood or depict as much suffering as a horror film or a war film would. This, however, does vary on occasion. The *Rambo* films, for instance, as hyperbolic and outlandish as they could get, show a fair amount of realistic bodily damage and graphic torture. Although the *Rambo* films were not as wrenching in their violence as *Saving Private Ryan* or *Blackhawk Down*, the brutality of their torture sequences, especially the electroshock and maiming sequence of the second film and the annihilation of the Burmese village in the fourth, was a long way off from the antiseptic, computer-generated mayhem of the *Mission: Impossible* films. For the majority of the participants in this study, graphic gore and bodily damage are unacceptable.

Interestingly enough, horror fans Cindy, Jane, and Selina are the three interviewees who do not have problems with gratuitous bodily damage, and they dispel the stereotype of squeamish females. As stated in Chapter 8, for Cindy the violence is enjoyable because it creates a feeling of pleasurable suspense, tension, and excitement. She has no problems with violence no matter how graphic it gets. Jane, similarly, explains that she used to watch the most graphic horror films as long as she can remember, since she was a small child, watching them at slumber parties or movie parties where she and her friends would rent a batch of the most gory films and view them back to back through the night. Selina, however, explains that for her there is a marked difference between the violence of the horror film and the violence of the action film. As she tries to grasp the correct terminology to describe this difference, she settles on describing the horror as having "evil" violence. She illustrates the point by referring to the gratuitous carnage perpetrated in horror films like the Freddy (*Nightmare on Elm Street*), Jason (*Friday the 13th*), *Child's Play*, and *Scream* movies. Selina classifies the violence committed by the killers of these films, pretty much the stars of the films because Freddy, Jason, and masked slasher of the *Scream* films are the most important recurring characters in the series, as being evil. This "evil violence," although having an appeal with the suspense and tension it creates, is still not as enjoyable as the violence of the action genre. The violence of the action genre is a metaphorical means to an end that will help solve the philosophical challenge each film presents. The violence in the action films is a symbolic struggle, a noble, righteous anger focused at injustice.

Although outside the scope of this study, we can hypothesize about horror's appeal to a female audience in light of Clover's work on gender and horror. Her focus on a tradition of low-budget horror films from the 1960s and onward identifies entertainment that functions to challenge hegemonic authority. She explains that such films comprise "a marginal genre that appeals to marginal people (not, by and large, middle-aged, middle-class whites) who may not have quite the same investment in the status quo."[2] This school of horror, the horror the women in my subject pool grew up on, is a departure from what Stephen King has identified as traditional horror, a genre "as conservative as an Illinois Republican in a three piece pinstripe suit."[3] The modern slasher horror is a departure from the old school of vampires and zombies who *must* be destroyed to reestablish the status quo, the classical style that sets up the monster as the "other," "the outsider" who had to be killed. As Clover argues, the modern, low-budget slasher horror often deals with morality tales about assaults on women and their mission of revenge.

Peter puts the symbolic function of the action genre in one of the most succinct summaries when he says "it's not about the violence. The violence stands to represent the drive, the motivation of characters. It's this intense drive to achieve something."

The violence of the action films for all of the interviewees needs to be un-derlined by a purpose and needs to have a moral grounding. To these active viewers, the violence of the action/adventure is not, critics to the contrary, "senseless" violence. As David very pointedly explained, for him there are films of either "mindless" or "mindful" violence. When the films are mindful, when they address such philosophical issues as the nature of violence, corrup-tion in society, or the codes of honor and conduct of warriors, they have been successfully executed and enjoyable to watch. In fact, David's sensitivity to violence is evidenced by his dislike for horror. On the one hand, he explains, he finds most horror films and slasher films to be silly and not very scary. Lis-tening to some of the horror he references, I begin to realize that he is mainly aware of some of the cheaper efforts in horror, the teen-sex and gore horror found in the *Nightmare on Elm Street* or *Friday the 13th* school of horror filmmaking, rather than some of the "classics" of that genre like *The Shining* (1980), or *Psycho* (1960), the first *Halloween* (1980), or *The Exorcist* (1973). I did not press him on this issue, but his explanation of why he does not like the "horror genre" and his approach to violence is interesting. He explains that when he thinks of horror, he recalls an incident in his past when, through a school exchange program in the seventh grade, he traveled to Japan and was taken on a field trip to the Peace Museum in Hiroshima. Some of the exhibits he saw were quite unsettling, he explains:

> I remember a few things that stuck with me. I was, I remember seeing this wax sculpture of a mother and her children where the wax was melting off of them and there was another case of a shadow being burned into the ground where someone had been vaporized. And I remember leaving feeling a little bit ashamed to be a human being because we've done such horrible things . . . Sort of compared to that, most of the horror films, etc. seem sort of cartoonish after that.

As for the role of violent films in helping people deal with the ugliness and violence of the real world, he adds:

> But I think that what the movies do is they might help people who might not be exposed to such things on a regular basis to have a buffering, or what to do when they do see it. . . . I think some people get some vicarious pleasure out of it . . . if they've been through September 11 and they see an action film or a war film, they might go and think that this is a symbolic representation that America might still be strong.

But, on the other hand, David explains that ultimately, the action films, or films in general, should still be responding to September 11 and the conflicts in Iraq and Afghanistan with more of a mindful approach than simple jingoistic going-in-to-get-the-terrorist films. Once again, if the violence has an acceptable moral and thematic grounding, the films are more satisfying to watch.

Overall, the violence of the action film, for these interviewees, works if it is used as an entertainment vehicle with a moral grounding, if the violence functions according to an ethical set of standards. In turn, the moral grounding these interviewees refer to is the use of violence by heroes to accomplish a mission, to vanquish an evil in a way so the greater social order benefits. Neal Gabler's 2002 *New York Times* piece summed up the appeal of superheroes well. He analyzed superhero stories and came to a conclusion similar to what the people in this study believe; that the success of the superhero is not simply that he has powers ordinary people do not, but that when the superhero is applying his skills, when he is getting violent with an enemy, the whole of society benefits from it.[4]

Looking at how men and women see the current social order, the status of institutions, such as the government, the courts, the police forces, and business, and how violent stories are used to examine them, an interesting and unexpected picture begins to form. As Helen's earlier comments criticizing the justice system and the prison system attest, she has a set of beliefs she prescribes to, then unwinds by watching the action genre because it offers a symbolic solution to that problem. The problem itself, recalling Helen's statements, especially about not being a lot of justice these days, is quite bleak.

Similarly, when I asked Louis if he felt governmental, business, or criminal justice institutions were generally corrupt today, his first reaction was nonverbal. He looked at me as if I had asked him which direction the sun rises and sets. He was actually frustrated by my explanation that many other interviewees did not feel the system was in as bad a shape as action films like *Dirty Harry*, or its various imitations of rogue cop films, seem to be portraying. In his words, "Anyone who doesn't think the system is extremely corrupt and ineffective is living in a fantasy world. They need to open their eyes and look around them, and look at what is happening in this world every day. They need to grow up and live in the real world." He explained that he watches the action film for a similar cathartic release of frustrations and because the action films offer the type of unambiguous victory of good and destruction of evil and corruption he would like to see in the real world.

Louis's level of cynicism about the system, governmental, and social institutions, though, sets him apart from many of the male respondents. As a whole, the male viewers do not seem to want to verbalize opinions about the country's governing and financial institutions being as corrupt as what the action genre seems to suggest. This, however, is not to suggest that they do not harbor such feelings. Commentary from the men generally comes in the form of explaining that the action film needs to create certain narrative devices that increase the tension, complications that put the hero in as much peril as possible. This can be effectively achieved, they say, if the hero is not only fighting the villains, but also finds himself betrayed by his own superiors and misunderstood by the people he is trying to help.

However, as mentioned, two interviewees take very strong exception to the aggression of the genre, both the actual depictions of violence, as well as the cynicism and pessimism toward social institutions: Richard, a nineteen-year-old undergraduate and aspiring actor, and Edward, the former police officer. Both are avid viewers of action, but only because they are able to ignore what they deem to be offensive worldviews and faulty moral underpinnings of the genre. Although both interviewees indicate they enjoy action films—Edward explaining that he grew up on westerns and war films, Richard recalling "older" action films like the *Indiana Jones* films—both believe in "media effects," especially the harmful effects of violence. However, both men are particularly offended by themes that suggest the system is so faulty as to require vigilantism to achieve justice.

Richard begins talking about why the action film, despite the fact that many very successful representatives of the genre go against his sensibilities, reflects his life experiences by trying to explain—at first vaguely—that action heroes are so universal that many people can in some way relate to them. Since this is so vague, so inarticulate an answer that I need to insist that he elaborate even further, he becomes harder to pin down for a specific answer. As he is an artist himself and has some technical knowledge of the acting craft, he often can—and does—easily fall back onto a general analysis and critique of the genre as a whole. As I try to press him to explain if he sees parallels between his own experiences as a college student and aspiring actor, he initially evades a direct comparison. Eventually, he explains that in most action films, good action films, the focus is always on overcoming great obstacles and rising to a seemingly insurmountable challenge. In his own life, he compares this to his acting and auditioning endeavors. He explains that the process is a constant competition, one where he is always measuring himself against professionals already in the field and all the scores of other people who are competing for roles he is trying out for. In his own words: "You look at TV and commercials and the actors there and you realize that I could do that even better. So it's that obstacle you are trying to overcome going for the roles." On a smaller scale, on the immediate, every day level, he explains that he sees the usual college routine as presenting a series of challenges he can compare to an action hero's road of trials. He explains that presently he had a series of conflicts with his roommate that reminded him of the frustrations of an action hero. The typical stress factors of life, in his opinion, are frustrating enough for most people to see parallels between their existence and that of action heroes, even if they do not find themselves in mortal danger.

Richard's oppositional stance to action films, however, involves their violence. Although this was an issue I wanted to end the interview with, as it is the most controversial aspect of the genre and the aspect I was concerned would make the interviewees the most defensive, Richard immediately brought it into the open in the beginning of our talk. When I asked him which action films he remembers disliking, he quickly told me that he does not like films with a lot of graphic violence. Although he mentioned bad acting as the main reason he would be turned off from an action film, he also does not like gratuitous violence. In fact, he later explains that to him, "action/adventure" does not need to involve violence. A film can "just have adventure," he says, "and it doesn't mean it has to be violent." Although for a moment I thought he might be referring to films where there is no confrontation between people but more of a dangerous challenge posed for the characters, films in the vein of *The Perfect Storm* (2000) or *Vertical Limit* (2001), or various disaster films with characters pitted against nature, Richard explained that even the *Indiana Jones* films are not violent for him. Films that Richard has an objection to are the ones with cynical and aggressive worldviews. Discussing action films' statements about the government, law enforcement, and the justice system, he agrees that many films are unduly pessimistic and nihilistic. He does not agree with this sort of nihilism, and he believes that films with such bleak storylines are hurting society.

Richard, in fact, very well illustrates the tenets of the third-person effect theory[5] and the phenomenon of attributing greater media effects on others than on himself.[6] Although he readily offers a critique of the action film's bleak outlook on the system, he does not indicate that he makes viewing decisions based on such themes. He explains that he is able to ignore themes and messages he personally disagrees with to be able to enjoy other aspects of the film, namely the excitement of the fast narratives and stories of main characters facing daunting challenges. At the same time, he does explain that he is, in principle, opposed to some themes and generally worried about the effects of the violence on young people.

Edward's approach to action films are similar, his opinions are also well in line with the third-person effect. His most striking argument against media violence comes in his recollections of his time as a police officer. He recalls times in the holding cells of the Chicago police when large groups of gang members were arrested and they signaled their defiance by reciting violent, anti-police rap lyrics. He explains that he was shocked to realize how popular the 1983 Al Pacino film *Scarface* was among gang members and drug dealers.

A favorite mantra of many of the young hoodlums he saw arrested was that of the Pacino character from the film, "the world is yours."

Edward's opinion of the genre and the obligations of filmmakers to society, similar to Louis's views, is that they should show the ideal. However, instead of viewing and reconceptualizing films like the *Dirty Harry* series or the *Death Wish* films, as Louis does, Edward readily claims that he finds both films offensive and dangerous. What becomes very incongruous in the interview, however, is his claims that he watched all the installments of both series. Just like Richard, Edward favors government intervention in the matter, feeling that the federal government should regulate the media. At this point, I slightly changed the terminology in my questioning, using the word "censorship," as that term is usually loaded with heavy, negative connotations, and advocates of government intervention in the media often moderate their stance if this term is applied. This is not the case with Edward, or Richard for that matter. He is not fazed by my use of the term.

> BD: Today we can hear politicians of virtually all political leanings say that something needs to be done about media violence. Do you agree with this?
>
> Edward: Yes, I do. I think there is no doubt that government needs to do something today. I believe a clear link can be drawn between violence in films and crime and the government needs to do something.
>
> BD: But you don't feel uncomfortable with the government censoring art and expression?
>
> Edward: No, I don't think there is a danger of that.

By this, he means that he does not feel the freedoms of artists will truly be impinged upon. In a near exact replay of the interview with Richard, I also presented the argument to Edward that his watching and spending his money on action films could actually be contributing to more of that media violence he is afraid of and wants controlled. Like Richard, Edward argues that the films he watches are not the problem. He explains that he likes to watch only a certain type of action film, the ones where the action and situations are plausible. Just as he commented previously, there are ones he considers to be so extreme as to be "an insult to [his] intelligence." The films he does not like are those with stunts and special effects so over the top as to make the films unrealistic and insulting. These films, coincidentally, the ones that have dangerous levels of violence.

Unlike Richard who explains that he can tune out the unwanted and offensive messages of the action film, Edward sees himself as a selective and responsible action viewer. Mainly, he tries to identify the action films that are unacceptably violent or where the action heroes do not possess the character traits he admires, and he stays away from those films.

A number of the younger female interviewees approach the genre of the action film as a barometer of disturbing social trends, as well as a reflection of personal experiences and identity. However, these same females also voice some of the most cynical comments about the state of the system and government and social institutions. This is actually very surprising, given the preference the women showed for a more social hero, as discussed in Chapter 8.

Perhaps the least cynical of the lot is Diana, the thirty-three-year-old expectant mother. Having been impressed by other interviewees' cynicism, I quoted something to Diana I heard remarked somewhere in a news program. I had a vague recollection of someone saying that "the only honest and honorable politicians are the ones that haven't been caught yet." While this remark is certainly very pessimistic, it did strike me as closely resembling the sentiments of a lot of key action films. So I asked Diana if she thought this is true, and if she thinks the action films dramatize such cynicism. Her replies were (a qualified) "no" and "yes," respectively. She qualified the first answer by adding that she "doesn't *want* to believe" that the only honest politicians are the ones that are secretly getting away with their lies and crimes. But she added that, indeed, the action genre often does exploit such pessimism and paranoia about institutions.

Cindy, a twenty-three-year-old undergraduate, voiced the most pessimistic and negative comments about the status quo of social and governmental institutions. She is an interesting interviewee because of her very animated and opinionated stream-of-consciousness replies to my questions. She explains that she is drawn to the action genre in particular, and violent films in general, because they offer the most realistic rendering of the world and of human nature. There has to be reality to a film she will give her time and money to, and she explains that generally films that leave behind all semblance of reality are the ones she cannot pay attention to. Often, without my prompting, she veers onto films she disliked, was angered by, or bored by to the point of falling asleep to better illustrate why she likes what she does. She often ventures onto the topic of science fiction and explains that such films, in comparison to action, present such a naïve and foolishly optimistic view of life and the world that she cannot bear to pay attention to them. On the one hand, with science fiction, the films offer scenarios she finds too fantastic to be able to relate to. She explains that thinking about contact with aliens and otherworldly, fantastic situations is something she has no patience for. However, the *implications* of such scenarios are equally frustrating for her, being unable to see a hopeful outcome to contact with "little green men." In her words: "If there are little green men out there, they're probably nice peaceful little people. And if we find them, we'll probably fuck them up the way we fucked up our own people." On this topic, she quickly references the first *X-Files* film (1998), explaining how she "had to" rent it with a boyfriend but hated the entire film.

Cindy's comments about archetypal action characters are the most interesting, as she says that she always likes the villains the most. As that aspect of film viewing has been given treatment by research before, namely Fiske and his observation of homeless men watching *Die Hard* and rooting for the terrorists,[7] identification with the villain is mainly tied to feelings of disaffection and alienation. This, in large part, could be responsible for the general darkening of the action heroes in the post-Vietnam and post-Watergate eras, where male heroes, aside from the state of gender conflict, seem almost to have one foot in villainy and disrepute while the other one is in the world of the system, status quo, and the protection of an ungrateful society that does not value their efforts. Cindy herself very readily admits to feelings of disaffection, claiming so many things about the political process, the government, and politicians have disgusted her that she hardly ever votes. However, although her critiques of the status of the country run very deep and often with anger, they are qualified by certain moments of idealism. Her views of generic villainy, furthermore, appear to be a continuation of her greater worldviews. As she initially remarks about the government:

> As long as government is not the most corrupt in the world, I have no problem with seeing them depicted the way they are . . . but I know as much as people might criticize the government, I do understand that it [the presidency] has to be a very tough job. . . . But as I've said time and time again and what I understand of history, we have the most corrupt government in the world, but it works. It gives women the right that they're not stuck at home taking care of the kids and popping out babies. I can go into politics or into law enforcement or I can, you know . . . I can, you know, say that Bush is an idiot without getting killed whereas in another country if I criticize the government, I can get shot. I'm not stuck in Iran having to be all covered from head to toe, except for my eyes. But it's because of our government that I have the right to do and say the things that I do, but they are also corrupt in the way they are and people don't want to accept that. They want to see that they're all good and they're all decent and they don't do under-the-table deals, and it bothers them to see movies that show them the way they are.

From these sentiments come Cindy's beliefs that imperfect, tainted heroes or villains are closer to the reality of human nature. Her first words on the subject of villains is a very enthusiastic "I love villains!" On the artistic level, she believes characters painted in morally ambiguous shades of gray make for a better artwork. As she explains:

> I think it's *so* unrealistic to put a character in a movie who's all good. That's not life. That's not what real people are like. Everybody has their dark side. I

think nuns can be some of the worst people in the world, they probably slept with a hundred guys and smoked pot and that's why they became nuns in the first place, to make up for it.

Of the nature of the villain, she explains that villains are usually the most interesting ones to watch on screen and a good villain is usually more multi-faceted than the hero, someone who is easier to identify with for her. Again in her own words:

> Devil: pure evil. Angels and God: pure good. And villains are right in the middle. They draw people to them, they have to seem charming and alluring and sensuous. Then the good guy: oh, this is so wrong and we have to do something about it and blah, blah, and he's so pissed off about it.

In direct contrast to interviewees like Louis, Edward, and Helen, perhaps hypothetically because of the generational difference, Cindy is bored with the absolutes of the genre, characters and situations she can accurately foresee. As she explains, she feels the film *Training Day* (2001) should also be classified as an action film and says that the most intriguing character is automatically the villain.

> With the good guy, you know how on the end of the day he will do the good thing, but with Denzel it's like, what's he gonna do next? You see him with his girlfriend and son and that's one side [of his personality]. You see him with three wise guys and that's another side. You see him fucking with Ethan Hawke's character and that's another side. . . . I hated Denzel, but he was more interesting than Ethan Hawke. Villains are so multi-dimensional. Psychotic and sociopathic and alluring. Like the first depiction of Dracula. He wasn't pure evil. He was charming and attractive and made his victims *want* to be taken. Very sensual and sexual and appealing.

Interestingly, with these quotes she also stumbles onto a bit of trivia about literary characters most often adapted to the screen. Of all the famous characters of literature, none have appeared on film as many times as Dracula, usually as an explicit symbol of dark, pent-up sexuality, of forbidden and dangerous pleasure. Literary criticism, in fact, has long cast *Dracula* as a Victorian morality tale of hegemonic masculinity striving to control and repress female sexuality symbolized by the alluring vampire.

Similarly, more of Cindy's testimony specifically reveals that her attraction to the villain is not purely an artistic desire to see more fully rounded, more complex and challenging characters. As her comments on masculinity and the concept of a crisis illustrate, the action narrative for her is a playing field of contested power. As is the case for all the women, not only does she show no regard for the issue of men feeling a loss of power, but she repeatedly becomes hostile to the opinion as I try to press the issue. In fact, she argues that critics who see the marginalized male character losing ground in the genre are misreading the narratives. The fact that men wind up winning the battles, defeating the villains, even coming back for more adventures in sequels, to Cindy, is ultimately ample proof that male power is well in control within the action film. The most interesting and suggestive aspect of Cindy's personality is that when I asked her who her favorite action actors are, she had a difficult time responding. She actually paused for a long time at that point, tried to search for an answer, but could not bring herself to commit to any actor as a favorite. She says that she likes the first *Die Hard* film and liked *Lethal Weapon*, but does not necessarily consider herself a Bruce Willis fan or a Mel Gibson fan. She usually likes the villains, she insists. One action actor she eventually remembers liking a lot, always making the effort to see his films, is Wesley Snipes. As Snipes is an African American, Cindy's allegiance to him is telling. She proclaims fandom of an actor whose race was, for a long time, a mark of action villainy, the race of drug dealers, gang members, and pimps. As if illustrating the key Newcomb and Alley thesis of entertainment demonizing the opposition to the status quo, Cindy finds an easier allegiance with the symbolic minority.[8] However, she enjoys seeing the villain endowed with the most power for the better part of the action narratives, the ones with the power to set events in motion to which the hero can only react. She explains that she likes the "attitude" of a good villain, the sarcasm he will be adept at cutting the hero with. "The villains are *always* sarcastic," she says, and "sarcasm is a great trait in a villain." Sarcasm is also defiance, mockery of dominant social mores as a villain hurls them at the hero, in a way a display of superior wit and intelligence. Cindy, in fact, says that the best villains, while technically insane, are superbly intelligent, yet underestimated by their opponents in the film. "The criminally insane," she explains, "are usually the most intelligent people in the world."

Ultimately, as a reflection of Cindy's beliefs and personality, her use of the action genre is a fascinating one. It is an almost exclusively oppositional use of the text, aligning her sympathies with characters designed to be the most antipathetic. However, her favorite characters also represent the most aggressive and destructive opposition to a system she finds "the most corrupt in the world," and, if not often, at least depending on various administrations in power, a system she sees as a threat to her rights and freedom of choices as a woman.

Erika and Selina, also undergraduate action-watchers, quickly take note and approve of the antagonistic stance the action films take to government and large bureaucratic institutions. When I ask them what they feel the messages of the action films are and what they enjoy about or agree with in the greater themes of their favorite films, they point out that the action film speaks to the corruption of the world. This is the reality of the world they see, although they both say that they *wish* the problem were not without real-life solutions. Similar to Helen's sentiments, they feel the action films are relevant today because they offer a symbolic solution to the problems of the world they feel they are faced with.

Although Erika is similar to Cindy in her preference for films grounded in reality and expresses a strong dislike for science fiction and fantasy, Selina explains that she likes certain subgenres of science fiction because they deal with the sort of social critique she sees in the anti-authoritarian action films. She used to be a big fan of the *X-Files*, and she likes UFO-themed television programs and movies and entertainment dealing with conspiracies and coverups.

She found the perfect combination of the two in the 1998 film *Enemy of the State* with Gene Hackman and Will Smith. She calls this film one of her action favorites, and while it does not include elements of the supernatural or fantastic, it has an *X-Files*-like plot of a government conspiracy and an innocent man nearly falling victim to a murderous coverup. The plot involves Will Smith accidentally receiving evidence of the National Security Agency assassinating a senator who would have introduced legislation curtailing government computer surveillance. Although the rest of the plot is a series of stunt and special-effect punctuated chases and confrontations between assassins and Smith, directed at an extremely kinetic pace by Tony Scott (*Top Gun* [1986], *Beverly Hills Cop II* [1987], *Crimson Tide* [1994]), the film very severely demonizes the government, depicting it almost as a large criminal organization with its armies of black-clad hit men. What was most interesting about the film was the way it set the entire National Security Agency against Smith, implicating the entire intelligence community in crimes, not only "rogue elements," as media criticism has often accused films of letting the status quo off the hook when it comes to wrong doing.[9] When I asked Selina if this aspect of the film made an impression on her, her response was enthusiastic and immediate. She claimed that the very parts of the plot where the intelligence community is accused of criminality made an impression on her and made her appreciate the film as much as she did. She explained that she is a fan of conspiracy theory entertainment because she believes that conspiracies are going on, that large-scale crimes are being committed by the government and businesses, and action films give form to all the wrongdoing she believes is going on in the country.

Selina's comments about race and the disaffected action film also brought an interesting wrinkle to the analysis of the genre. Selina is one of four African

American interviewees. David, Steve, and Charles are the other three. As all four talk about the social significance and implications of the genre, race is never something they bring up, admit to being a consideration when they turn to the genre, or admit to preferences for African American heroes. Their testimony, actually, is notably to the contrary.

When I first asked Selina how she felt about the predominantly white crop of action heroes, with only a relatively recent move into the American mainstream by Asians like Jet Li, Jackie Chan, and Chow Yun Fat, her response was neutral. Given the passion with which she would later speak about government conspiracies, her feelings about race and the action film are relatively low-key. Mentioning how black characters are most often seen in the low-level villainous roles of drug dealers, gang members, thugs, and "muscle" for white arch villains and crime king pins, if not secondary good guy roles of wrong-headed bureaucrats who yell at rebellious white heroes or sidekicks and buddies, I asked her about her approach of the genre as a fan. Here she appears detached from the issue. She explains that she looks at the problem in terms of how many African American actors are at least given the opportunity to appear on screen, even if it means taking the roles of secondary characters. "Yes, I understand it is a problem," she says, with a dispassionate tone and expression that make their impression when one sits face to face with Selina in the interview. "But at least I think about the actors being given an opportunity to work in these films." She talks about race only in a metaphorical analysis of the popularity of conspiracy theory stories. She explains that she felt the conspiracy theory became so popular over the past two decades because it was symbolic of more and more formerly marginalized groups finding a voice to challenge the dominant culture. "Well, you see that in the world today. You have a lot more people speaking up now. Like women, black people, the NAACP criticizing TV networks for not enough black people in shows, so you have this kind of criticism in the world today."

A similarly neutral, detached analysis came from David. When it comes to matters of race, he explains that he has come to accept that the depiction of black characters in film—or a lack thereof—is a reflection of today's cultural and social realities and something he needs to be able to detach himself from if he wants a chance to be entertained by film. As he explains:

> If you look overall, you don't see a large population of African American actors integrated into mainstream movies. You have some movies aimed at African American audiences and action is a part of it. You have something like *Boyz n the Hood* or that, what was that . . . film with a black samurai, *Ghost Dog*. But in general, how many Hollywood films can you think of where you have a meaningful interaction between black and white people? College is a bit of an artificial environment, but outside of it, there is very little meaningful interac-

tion between blacks and whites. They may work together, but they go home to different neighborhoods, they send their kids to different schools, they worship in different churches. . . . When you go to the movies, a number of [the movies] separate along racial lines. So if you do have a black character, they seem almost an aberration. Like say you look at the suspense film . . . say *Seven*, he is the only one there, but he is really just one character pasted onto a completely white world, with no family, no background. . . . Or *Along Came a Spider*, etc. Or when you have a film like the *Fellowship of the Ring*, there are no African Americans, or in *Harry Potter*. *Harry Potter* is more reasonable because it's in England. So this rings true across genres.

He, too, as most people, primarily goes to the movies for entertainment, so depictions of race ultimately need to be ignored and the film accepted for what it is. Overall, he explains, the depiction of black characters in action films is almost always, in every sense, limited, one dimensional and stereotyped. Aside from villainy, David explains that the depictions of all African Americans are a broad caricature as far as he sees it. However, in his own words:

I think that it's rare to just see a realistic portrayal of blacks in an action movie, but that just reflects Hollywood's disability in general. In this case, Hollywood is a reflection of society. But if I go to a movie and I'm going to watch something, like some action flick, I may notice these things, but if I want to have any chance of enjoying it, I have to look at the movie beyond those grounds.

These detached attitudes are seen in the testimonials from Charles and Steve as well. When Steve, an African American undergraduate student, talks about action films, especially the *James Bond* films he is an avid fan of, a similar distance from race can be observed. Steve voices social critique in terms of explaining the frustrations of life caused by an overly bureaucratized society and the pleasure offered by an action film where heroes are at odds with authority figures and are able to defy such authority with James Bond–like quick-witted, glib coolness, but he, essentially, has the same attitude toward the viewing experience as David and Selina do. He watches movies to be entertained, and he needs to keep that viewing experience entertaining by strategically paying attention to certain messages and images and ignoring others. His viewing behavior, just like David's and Richard's when choosing to ignore offensive pessimism, is a true oppositional use of the text. All of these interviewees acknowledge problematic ideological and thematic aspects in the preferred meanings of the text, yet they choose to read and enjoy a version of the films they have revised in their own minds. Steve is able to identify with the Bond character in terms of such universal qualities as his toughness, suaveness, sexual confidence, and power, ignoring the fact that the character is a different race, and that Steve's own race is very rarely seen in the Bond films.

Most often set in the real world, the action/adventure film can be seen as a more direct representation of life's most frustrating problems. The action film, in the majority of instances, save for times when crossed with genres like science fiction, does not hide behind aliens, monsters, and ghosts to deal with criminals, terrorists, and corrupt bureaucracies. If a genre stands as a symbolic solution to the world's problems, the action film's violent stories must represent stress factors that are the most pressing upon its viewers. As we talk to them, we can hear them reveal their concern over safety, crime, war, violence, power, and a social structure that can be unresponsive to people's needs. Listening to men and women talk about these issues reveals a fascinating picture of the ideals of manhood, heroism, and how ultimately men and women see the social problems of the action film resolved.

Listening to women talk about social systems whose problems the violent stories are attempting to solve symbolically, it is interesting to note a remarkable level of cynicism. Women who value social males, value men who can bond into groups to solve crises, are also the most cynical when it comes to today's social institutions. The bonds that exist today, their testimonials over the past chapters indicate, are flawed and need to be fixed. The system is fraught with corruption, inefficiency, and sexism. Social and governmental systems ignore or shelter wrongdoers and conspire to maintain positions of ill-gotten power and exclusive, discriminatory privileges. Such problems, the female viewers feel, need to be torn down and replaced with new, inclusive, pro-social alternatives. Men who work in teams, who fight for a common goal, can best accomplish this.

Male fans of the individualistic, unattached outsider do not, for the greater part, voice social critique as loudly as women. They see their favorite films speaking to an assault on their positions in society, but explain that they hope the crisis will not last. Whether this is another manifestation of a male reluctance to disclose is open to conjecture. However, as the testimonials in Chapter 6 demonstrate, stoicism, at least as evidenced here, is a male quality, no matter how much an interviewer will try and press his interviewees to be as frank as possible.

NOTES

1. For one of the best collections of British cultural studies research on media violence, the book *Ill Effects: The Media/Violence Debate*, eds. Martin Barker and Julian Petley (London: Routledge, 1998), should be looked at. It is a collection of excellent studies and essays by scholars including Barker and Petley, David Gauntlett, David

Buckingham, Patricia Holland, Sara Bragg, Sue Turnbull, Mark Kermode, Annette Hill, and Graham Murdock.

2. Carol J. Clover, *Men, Women, and Chain Saws: Gender in the Modern Horror Film* (Princeton, NJ: Princeton University Press, 1992), 231.

3. Stephen King, *Danse Macabre* (New York: Berkley Books, 1980), 152.

4. Neal Gabler, "Inside Every Superhero Lurks a Nerd." *New York Times*, May 12, 2002.

5. Notable third-person effect studies have been published in W. Phillips Davison, "The Third Person Effect in Communication," *Public Opinion Quarterly* 47 (1983): 1–15, and Douglas M. McLeod, Benjamin H. Detenber, and William P. Eveland, "Behind the Third Person Effect: Differentiating Perceptual Processes for Self and Other," *Journal of Communication* 51, no. 4 (2001): 678–695.

6. Richard M. Perloff, "Perceptions and Conceptions of Political Media Impact: The Third Person Effect and Beyond," in *The Psychology of Political Communication*, ed. Ann N. Crigler (Ann Arbor: University of Michigan Press, 1996), 177–197.

7. John Fiske and Robert Dawson, "Watching Homeless Men Watch *Die Hard*," in *The Audience and Its Landscape*, eds. James Hay, Lawrence Grossberg, and Ellen Wartella (Boulder, CO: Westview Press, 1996), 297–316.

8. Horace Newcomb and Robert S. Alley, *The Producer's Medium* (Oxford: Oxford University Press, 1983).

9. Todd Gitlin, *The Whole World Is Watching* (Berkeley: University of California Press, 1982).

10

Conclusion: I'll Be Back? The Future of Action and Masculinity in Popular Culture

If we stay the course, we are dead.

—Christian Bale, *Terminator Salvation*

One of the most thoughtful action/science fiction summer blockbusters of the past decade is Steven Spielberg's *Minority Report*. Going beyond the pyrotechnics and special effects that overwhelm most summer fare, the film repeatedly challenges its main characters with difficult moral choices. The story contemplates the existence of free will and wonders whether or not all of our actions might really be preordained by fate. It asks how one can do either the greater good or the lesser evil. Its ending is touched with just enough ambiguity to subtly undermine some of the customary Spielberg glow of optimism. Although the final shots of the film are literally bathed in a golden glow of a setting sun, perhaps some of the audience might wonder if the final dismantling of a questionable police agency is really for the benefit of freedom and justice.

The story deals with a crime-fighting organization so extreme that it pursues and arrests people before they commit crimes. Chief John Anderton (Tom Cruise), the program's most zealous advocate, its chief cop (who eventually falls victim to his own system), in turn, is a man slowly unraveling after losing his family. After his son is abducted due to a moment of negligence, after his wife leaves him, and between bouts of depression and drug use, he invests his energy in a quasi-fascistic police force.

The film is propelled by the classic action film themes: fears of societal disorder and violence, male fears of not being able to protect his family, losing families, being rejected by spouses, and betrayal by father figures. Anderton

suffers each of these predicaments and attempts to reestablish order in a chaotic world through his draconian law-enforcement organization. Lightening
the mood, however, is the balance achieved between extreme male propensities. Anderton wins at the end not by simply exacting revenge on the people
trying to set him up, by punishing the surrogate father who framed him, but
by reestablishing a relationship with his ex-wife and starting a new family.
The last shot is of Anderton standing side by side with his pregnant wife.

"Revenge may very well be the mainspring of American popular culture,"
writes Carol J. Clover,[1] and genres from horror to mysteries, suspense and
science fiction have always presented ever-more creative, terse, or gleeful
morality plays about evening the score, getting payback, or teaching lessons
to those who have trespassed against us. But no other genre is so perfectly
suited to show narratives about people venting their frustrations, getting even
with those who have overstepped their boundaries, than the action/adventure
genre. The genre is clearly about that thrill of the moment when you have
turned the tables, gotten an upper hand on your oppressors, then taken your
time and exacted well-deserved retribution. The action genre is comprised of
narratives about power, those who have been unjustly deprived of their share
getting the opportunity to return the compliment.

Stylistically, the action film is an art form about the moment of payback.
Violence rules these films and it always has. Filmmakers have always in-
vested these films with as much violence as they could get away with, given
social mores and governmental regulations.

As the testimonials of men and women have shown, the appeal of this
often-controversial genre is complex. The reasons these people make the action film their first choice of entertainment can be divided among numerous
personal and societal motivating factors. What they see in the action films
also varies, but does so according to these same social, personal, and gender-based filters that color their perception. The interviewees' words have
provided a glimpse of the gender-related messages they see in the films, the
value systems they see reflected, reinforced, or negotiated in the narratives.
The way viewers are socialized, the social forces they want to rebel against,
their generational backgrounds, their age, and their race have all played more
or less of a role in what viewers watch, how much they enjoy a film, and what
they get out of the viewing experience.

Speaking of lesser roles influencing media use and interpretation, Chapter
2 took note of the socioeconomic class of the interviewees for this study.
There were more men who described either their upbringing or current status as middle class than working class. Eighteen men fell in the category of
middle class, while only eleven were in the working class. Two interviewees,
Rom and Vipul, both originally from India, described themselves as being of

an upper-class background. Both of these men were equally unresponsive to the theory of a masculinity crisis. Rom especially insisted on seeing action heroes as universal characters, not speaking to specific male problems.

Of the women, however, the majority were of working-class background. Their families, where they were first socialized in the use of the action genre, were positioned within blue-collar, working-class segments of society. Only three women identified themselves as middle class and one woman, Connie, describes her family as upper middle class. The working-class women's enjoyment of action films is noteworthy. They defy traditional gendered media use expectations. Women are usually expected to be fans of melodramas and romantic films, not action/adventure. Staying within traditionally gendered behavior, however, would be expected of the lower classes. It recalls the body image and bodybuilding work by Klein that presented women of the upper classes, women coming from better educated circles, as being more apt to challenge traditional gender roles and gendered rules of behavior.[2]

However, another important factor in the case of all the interviewees is education. The majority of them either have a college education or they were in college at the time of the study. As seen in case of Louis, Sam, Kathleen, Vin, and other interviewees coming from working-class backgrounds, social mobility is either something they have achieved or something they are looking forward to achieving. Outlook and hope within the existing system might not engender overly strong criticism. But, then again, criticism can come in various forms. Louis, for example, is an immigrant success story. He came to the United States as an adult, started his life over and built a successful career in the medical profession. He could very well be an example of the patriotic, flag-waving immigrant stereotype. However, he is not, or at least not in an uncritical way. As quoted before, he feels anyone who does not think the government is corrupt and inefficient is living in a fantasy world. Talking about the courts and the justice system, he explains that he sees them as being inefficient and corrupt as well, tilting the scales in favor of criminals and allowing for an environment where power, social status, influence, and money corrupt justice. He is deeply suspicious of all social institutions, but not as suspicion manifested in the left-wing critical cultural commentators. Despite his hostility to the system, he presents himself as staunchly conservative.

The fact that the women were more hostile to and critical of social institutions could be linked to their class backgrounds, although I do not hasten to say this is the only factor in their pessimism. Their education, no doubt, is an important variable in influencing their worldviews, *especially* their pessimism. The majority of women in college are eventually exposed to various "women's studies" courses and programs that concentrate on how women have been historically disadvantaged and oppressed. When explaining that she has little sympathy for men's crises, Cindy points to one of her women's and minorities's classes that showed her how women are still being treated unfairly. She spoke of being outraged when a female guest in her class detailed experiences with sexual harassment, having been asked questions about her sex life on a job interview.

In the case of men, action/adventure is generally, stereotypically, regarded as lower-class entertainment. As the Chapter 3 overview of how cultural critics have long dismissed the genre demonstrated, the genre has long been regarded as shallow and thoughtless, a "pornography of violence" at worse, as the novelist Tom Wolfe once wrote.[3] Men of the higher classes are traditionally not expected to watch such gauche entertainment as stories of revenge, sex, and violence. Although none of the men claimed that they watched action films specifically to gain satisfaction from seeing corporate villains get killed and blue-collar heroes being glorified, the issue certainly warrants further exploration. For example, Fiske's analysis of homeless men watching *Die Hard* brought him to comment on how those in his study enjoyed seeing the yuppie captives being terrorized by the villains, then tuning out of the film once the villains were being beaten on the end of the film.[4] As King presents his textual analysis of cop action films, he strongly—and I believe correctly—argues for the class conflict elements in the stories.[5] However, I believe that the masculinity crisis encompasses all social classes. Patrick, a computer engineer with a master's degree, for example, spoke about the issue of family-deprived males and how he feels all men are under attack today. His wife has a lucrative executive position in the corporate world. Anthony is also a successful businessman, and he spoke about "challenges" and the ignorance of the egg-headed academic types.

Denby, quoted from *New York* magazine in Chapter 5, wrote that the modern American action film, at its apex in the 1980s, is a line of films even many of today's very young audiences still refer to as the best example of the genre, heavily preoccupied with payback, marked by that "lumped despair that goes beneath . . . politics."[6] There is a cultural crisis that most of the successful films from this era address, wrongs the action heroes seek to avenge. The crisis involves the role of men in society, in all sectors and socioeconomic classes. Coming from the mouths of some of the toughest action heroes like Clint Eastwood and Sylvester Stallone, there isn't much that is special about men anymore. There is little they have done in the past that women cannot do today. The men of the action films, spanning from the 1960s to the millennium, have come a long way from towering heroes in the John Wayne mold. And much of this road has been downhill. Both men and women talk about the crisis in the action film, the crisis of masculinity, as well as various other cultural crises and gender conflicts, even though some of the men only feel comfortable discussing the issue as a "challenge," not a crisis.

Men, just like the interviewees of this book, have always liked action. The industry has always known this, and they made films about males battling evil, fighting wars, and righting wrongs, just as they have tried to do in real life. Men have always gone to watch these films, in part to watch their exaggerated tales of heroism, in part to satisfy a need for high-speed, high-stimulation entertainment. Psychologists have documented media use by personalities who gravitate toward suspenseful entertainment to satisfy their needs for constant excitatory pleasures. Listening to the interviewees of this study talk about their need to see entertainment where "there is always something going on" helps support this picture of the high-stimulation seekers. But listening to both men and women talk about their histories with action raises new questions.

Since action films have always been the entertainment territory of men, finding very active female viewers devoted to the genre is surprising. I said as much to my female interviewees, except they all remarked that they are not like most women. Of course, everybody would, perhaps often, like to say that they are not like everyone else, that they are unique, they surpass the ordinary, and go against the grain on their own terms. But there is something indeed markedly unique about all of the high-viewing women. All but one of the interviewees mentions a very heavy male influence upon their viewing habits. Interestingly, most explain that this influence had begun in early childhood, growing up with brothers who liked the action and who made most of the viewing decisions in the household. Only one interviewee, Diana, spoke of being turned on to action at a later age, in her teenage years when she started dating. In her case, boyfriends made the viewing decisions and she then became hooked on action.

Of course, on the issue of women and social class, we could also hypothesize that girls in middle-class families are more sheltered from the rougher, courser aspects of life. Fighting and violence are not something "ladies" should be exposed to. Brothers, fathers, and even mothers might be more concerned in a middle-class environment with raising girls to be these gentle ladies, rather than letting them see violent sports and killing. Therefore, this sheltering atmosphere of the middle class might account for a dearth of female action fans in genteel suburbs.

These testimonies, of course, raise questions about the need for high stimulation. It suggests the stimulation need is something developed and cultivated by a certain type of media use. Zillmann has hypothesized about evolution-induced proclivities for needing constant, rapid stimulation.[7] Although he might not be incorrect, these findings could suggest future avenues for research. Despite the fact that these female interviewees claim they had come to like these films because they were constantly exposed to them, we do not know if the conditioning of high-stimulation entertainment is possible for everyone. Are there other women who grew up in similar households full of action-watching brothers and fathers but who did not become action fans? Is there a certain proclivity in some that can be developed into a habit, or can socialization strictly account for the taste in violent entertainment? Furthermore, we also know that not all men watch action. Are they averse to this type of film simply because of socialization or because of certain psychological predeterminants that keep them from wanting to engage in these chaotic narratives of danger and destruction?

Listening to the action fans talk, both men and women, and examining the text of the action films helped paint a multifaceted view of specific action styles and celebrities attracting fans with specific personalities. Active viewers of the genre can be observed according to the level of emotional disclosure they are comfortable with and the extent to which they can bear to deal with uncertainty, suspense, and weakness. As the interviews revealed, how emotional and how stoic certain action heroes are is a key issue for the fans. There are certain fans for whom the stoicism of action heroes is paramount. The action hero needs to be sufficiently larger than life and immune from such human shortcoming as fear and pain. Fans of Clint Eastwood and Arnold Schwarzenegger are especially concerned with this stoicism. Actors earn these viewers' favor by specializing in the type of hero that can literally stand in the middle of war zones without flinching, without succumbing to fear. As Louis puts it in no uncertain terms, his favorite heroes, characters played by Clint Eastwood and Charles Bronson, almost "look bored" in the middle of the mayhem.

As had been argued from a psychological perspective on the attractiveness of suspense, one of its main appeals as a form of entertainment is that suspense fulfills a need to control one's world, one's often uncontrollable circumstances. The feelings of suspense are created by out-of-control situations, then, as the plots are resolved, heroes reassert their control over the world. The best heroes tame the chaos of life. Videogaming by some could be indicative of this drive to control and helps account for the video game and action film connection that goes as far back as the 1980s. As Clint Eastwood had said, the people in a theater showing an action film might be sitting there in fear. They might be afraid of the uncontrollables in their own lives, the forces of fate, so they watch films that offer a fantasy respite from this fear.

In turn, it was revealing to listen to the interviewees talk about action actors in a way that erases the distinctions between the real person and the fictional character. Fans of various action actors talked about this. Not only the fans of

Eastwood and Schwarzenegger, but also fans of the more emotional Stallone connect the actor with the characters. Of course, actors and their publicity machines are aware of this preference in fans and they often shrewdly exploit it. Schwarzenegger's documented myth-making, for example, or Stallone's none-too-subtle comparisons of his own life to Rocky's struggles appeals to fans. Talking to an interviewee like Anthony reveals a need for reassurance that what unfolds on the screen is not an entirely fantastic construct. Similarly, listening to Stallone's fans talk about their fondness for the star yields more discussion of the real man and not just the screen characters. As far as they see it, especially as they begin talking about their admiration for Stallone's real life perseverance through professional struggle and personal hardships growing up, they can see the connection between the underdog characters in the films and the triumphant underdog in real life. This connection between artist and art, of course, is seen in other areas as well; authors of military thrillers tout their real military exploits and rap musicians shoot at each other to establish their dangerous street credentials. Despite the popularity of such "behind the scenes" programs as the *Access Hollywood* and *Entertainment Tonight*, shows that expose the constructs of entertainment, audiences of various media seem to want to know that the art they see is somehow real.

Preferences for these more or less emotional characters and action actors again seem to fall along gender lines. Although there are male fans of more emotionally expressive actors like Stallone, who specializes in characters who are not entirely stoic and invulnerable, women seem to prefer *all* of the emotionally accessible actors/characters over the cool Eastwood or self-mocking, robotic Schwarzenegger. As a matter of fact, among these women, there are no Eastwood or Schwarzenegger fans. Once more, this raises interesting points for discussion, hypothesis, and points toward further avenues of research. To what degree can we account for socialization in the emotional preferences of the female interviewees? This, of course, is a sensitive area because it brings various gender stereotypes to the surface, despite the fact that the women in this group are already defying many stereotypes by talking about their avid enjoyment of action and violence. Furthermore, as these women all explained that they did not like romantic melodramas, they nevertheless are drawn to actors like Stallone, Mel Gibson, and Harrison Ford, the most emotionally accessible and expressive of the genre's actors. If emotional expression is a result of social conditioning alone, these women would again not be leaning toward such actors exclusively. The male domination of their early entertainment use, one might reasonably hypothesize, might not have let a greater degree of need for emotional expression develop in these women.

When men talk about the masculinity crisis in films, they talk about what society expects of them and how it regards them once they have fulfilled their duties. The heroes of action films are warriors who are thrust into situations where they need to fight, yet they are punished for it in return. At the philosophical core of the *Spider-Man* films is the question of what would make someone fight for a society that does not appreciate him. Certain scenes have no less than biblical shadings as the villain of the first film, in a devilish, sneering mask, repeatedly tries to tempt the hero into renouncing his commitment to goodness. To stay a hero, the Green Goblin taunts Spider-Man, is to set himself up for persecution and suffering at the hands of the very people he tries to protect. This theme, however, is well established in comic books, with a strong tradition of the misunderstood hero fighting to save a world that views him as an outlaw menace. The men of action films are often cast aside as brutes, primitives, "Neanderthals," as Dirty Harry is regularly labeled in each episode of the series. Each *Dirty Harry* installment ends on a downbeat note, with Eastwood quietly disappearing into the distance. We, the audience, know he did right and fought for justice, but we also know he will never be rewarded for it. Listening to each of the interviewees halfheartedly admit that the action film pretty much says that men should be tough and that they do not necessarily feel that toughness is wrong reminds me of the Sean Connery speech from *The Presidio*. It speaks not only to soldiers within the context of one particular film, but also speaks to the general state of the "masculinity crisis." The world still expects men to solve problems, to solve crises, yet mocks them for it. It reminds me of Dirk's comments about the honor and male bonding of the Asian action films. In one breath, Dirk explains that the bitterness of *The Presidio* speech is not entirely justified, then tells how frustrating it is for men to change when they are taunted for whatever they try to change into. He likes the Asian action films because men display a greater range of emotions, yet he feels frustrated knowing that men are made into a joke if they become too emotional.

The male action viewers either worry about or are cautiously optimistic about the future. The future is, in fact, a major issue of the genre. The film storylines worry about the legacy of action heroes. If these characters are so maligned in their own time, what will be their legacy? If they have children, how much will they be able to influence them? This is an issue the action protagonists need to worry about because women have the power to keep them from their children. The future of the action hero's offspring is squarely in the hands of wives and girlfriends, and these women are often a step away from throwing the tough guys out of the house and keeping their children from them. The male viewers of the film either agree this worry is realistic, or they *hope* it is not a problem. The more optimistic interviewees tend to feel, as Tiger states, that "all they have to do is behave in a reasonably civil, even gentlemanly ways [and] everything will turn out peaceably and well."[8]

Although there are two divorced male interviewees among the men, neither of them is willing to comment on the issue. Edward, in fact, strongly argues that through the family-deprived action heroes, men are being given a justly deserved warning about the future.

Taking the male and female testimonials hand in hand, I believe these interviewees are watching a genre that deals with a real social problem and they are genuinely concerned with finding a future where the problem will have been solved in a mutually beneficial way. None of the men watch the films, I believe, because they view them as a cathartic backlash against the power of women. Even the most reactionary of the interviewees, Harry, appears to be strikingly untroubled by the power of women. He simply feels that women are incapable of holding on to stressful positions of power permanently and feels no great threat from women. Whether or not his calm is genuine, we cannot know for sure, and we are left to take his words at face value. Harry just feels, or *likes* to feel, that action films where men have absolute power are realistic. Men do, however, often see the films as giving a voice to their fears, but the films do it in a very stoic, nonchalant way. As a whole, the male interviewees also seem to be genuinely longing for a future where men and women can live as true equals, not one gender seeking to dominate the other, seeking retribution, seeking to avenge past injustice, to turn the tables, or make the other side suffer as it has suffered before. At this point, the media and the culture need to let this equilibrium develop.

The controversies regarding the violence of the action film, those ominous displays of aggression, anti-heroes who flaunt the social graces, can, I believe, be looked at as a warning, if not a suggestion, as to the future of cultural criticism. Some of what Dwayne told me about the social relevance of wrestling and what Sam said about the lack of real men in the action film has important implications. On the one hand, with the phenomenon of pretty boys taking over the roles of action heroes, the genre's future as a dangerous art form of rugged masculinity might be on shaky ground. Matt Damon and Ben Affleck, one suspects, could not raise the specter of domineering, dangerous masculinity. Russell Crowe, Hugh Jackman, and Vin Diesel perhaps, but many of the latest action actors seem too sensitive and nice for even the toughest feminists to worry about. Whether or not the true, classic tough guys will reappear in films wholesale is, at this point, open to conjecture.

The recent crop of sequels to old action films, from *Rambo* to *Indiana Jones* to *Die Hard*, is an interesting phenomenon. Was the resurrection of these franchises a part of the post–September 11, Afghanistan/Iraq era rediscovery of the hard-bodied fighting men? In 2001, Camille Paglia hypothesized that in the era of terrorism, when the New York City firefighters, Rudolph Giuliani, and the special forces in Afghanistan were becoming the new cultural icons, classical, strong masculinity would be rediscovered and embraced by Americans again.[9] For a while it certainly was, although by the waning days of the Bush presidency, macho masculinity had become a tainted commodity once more. George W. Bush and his policies that became so unpopular so quickly, had, in the collective imagination, morphed into a representation of the failures of old-fashioned, strong masculinity. In the span of a few years, traditional masculinity had become as tainted as it had in the aftermath of Vietnam. In fact, the 2008 presidential election was defined by many as a war of contrasting images of manhood. John McCain, who couldn't successfully escape the charge that he was merely a continuation of George W. Bush, was, in effect, painted as the embodiment of old-guard, Cold-War–era, aggressive manliness. He was, after all, even endorsed by Sylvester Stallone, just as Rambo's return to the screen included a plot of wrong-headed pacifists learning a lesson about the need for muscles and brute firepower. In contrast, the youthful Barack Obama was cast as the new vision of a modern, enlightened, diplomatic manhood. One of the bedrock foundations of the Obama campaign was a new foreign policy based on measured, cautious diplomacy and not the belligerent, macho aggressiveness of the Bush presidency. Moreover, even Obama's toughest challenge within the Democratic Party came from Hillary Clinton. So, again we are left to ponder the future direction of action cinema and where the resurrection of some of the hardest, most traditional images of cinematic manhood fit into the sociopolitical currents.

Perhaps the return of John Rambo, *Die Hard*'s John McClane, Indiana Jones, and a tougher, more ruthless James Bond are but coincidences. *Rambo*, after all, was very popular and successful, all the while the John McCain candidacy for president was sinking and Barack Obama enjoyed popularity unseen since Franklin D. Roosevelt.

Maybe a more plausible reason for the "reboot" of these classic franchises lies in simple name recognition. A general rule of thumb in filmmaking is that name recognition is the surest way to justify the high-risk investments many studio films require. From a favorite star to a well-known property, it is less of a risk to invest budgets well in excess of a hundred million dollars if the film offers something the audience is already familiar with. Everything from comic books to the *Lord of the Rings* trilogy and the *Harry Potter* novels to popular video games like *Resident Evil* and *Tomb Raider* have been adapted into films because of their "brand" name recognition. Thus, the mid- to late 2000s have seen an inordinate amount of remakes of old films and television series. Furthermore, as the people who were children in the 1970s and 1980s have taken over executive positions in Hollywood, their nostalgia for "classics" like *Rocky*, *Rambo*, *Die Hard*, *The Terminator*, and *Indiana Jones* must have been a major impetus for the resurrection of these franchises. It is noteworthy how even the toys this generation grew up playing with, like the Transformers and G.I. Joe, were given their own multimillion dollar film franchises too.

However, more aggressive forms of masculinity, more blatantly sexist and misogynist masculinity, can find other outlets in the media—if given the inspiration. For example, male violence running amok in professional wrestling rings has been worrying scholars and policymakers more than usual since the mid-1990s. Although hyperbolic, often very unrealistic and loaded with enough self-parody, professional wrestling, especially in the guise of World Wrestling Entertainment, the most successful of the wrestling organizations, has been operating at a level of mean-spirited sleaziness that has never been seen in action films. The lack of that moral undertone to violence all the action interviewees talked about has especially been the point of controversy in wrestling. Criticism charges that there is basically no moral subtext at all to current wrestling; there is no good and no evil, there is no universal, transcendent justice achieved through violence. In the documentary I discussed with Dwayne, *Hitman Hart: Wrestling with Shadows* (1998), Vince McMahon puts the issue in no uncertain terms when he says "we in the WWF think that you, the audience, are, quite frankly, tired of having your intelligence insulted. We also think that you are tired of the same old simplistic theory of good guys versus bad guys. Surely, the era of the superhero who urged you to say your prayers and take your vitamins is definitely passe."[10] The vulgarity and sexism of "stripper matches," "special event" mud-wrestling, "Thanksgiving special" gravy wrestling with women who look like silicone-inflated centerfolds cannot compare to even the most sexist Bond girl depictions in the early 1960s. As the documentary presents, however, there is an appeal in all of this for people who believe there is "not much in life that is just fun anymore," as one of the wrestling fans profiled explains. This, I believe, can tie back into the masculinity crisis.

There, indeed, is little fun in a cultural atmosphere where disagreeing parties seek to demonize one another instead of engaging in dialogue, sensible debate, or simply agree to disagree with one another's opinions, lifestyles, and tastes. Labeling the fans of action/adventure "drooling, hormone-addled adolescents" without seeking to understand what it is about the entertainment that might be important to them diminishes that "fun," and it helps build animosity, especially when so much of the condemnation is directed at men. Tying the viewing of a Sunday afternoon football game to spousal abuse likewise builds that animosity. Referring to masculinity as an epidemic that needs to be cured, and blaming swimsuit magazines for date rape and sexual harassment can likewise build resentment. Cultural critics bemoaning the coarsening of the culture over the past decade, the disappearance of civility, could also probe this period for some of the most bizarre and extreme examples of political correctness. It is not unreasonable to expect rebellion when rules of conduct start becoming ever more outlandish. When for some in the 1960s anything other than a military regulation haircut signaled a communist, when playing music too loud and too fast was a giveaway of subversive activities, it was not a surprise that members of the counterculture would want to wear their hair down to their waist and march in protest with a copy of Mao's little red book and the Vietcong flag. Similarly, if the media and cultural pundits insist on treating men like a violent crime about to happen, as they did young urban men in the mid-1990s, even to the chagrin of a feminist like Susan Faludi, there should be little surprise if male action heroes remain bitter and angry, or if their audiences begin gravitating toward foul-mouth, beer-swilling, amoral, and misogynist wrestlers.

Every side, every viewpoint in the masculinity crisis debates, finishes the argument with a call for finding a way for men and women to live side by side in a world where specialized, gender-specific roles are disappearing. Talking to the men and women of this study revealed individuals of at least two generations who appeared to be longing for this unity.

NOTES

1. Carol J. Clover, *Men, Women, and Chain Saws: Gender in the Modern Horror Film* (Princeton, NJ: Princeton University Press, 1992), 115.

2. Alan M. Klein, *Little Big Men: Bodybuilding Subculture and Gender Construction* (Albany: State University of New York Press, 1993).

3. J. Hoberman, "A Test for the Individual Viewer: *Bonnie and Clyde's* Violent Reception," in *Why We Watch: The Attractions of Violent Entertainment,* ed. Jeffrey H. Goldstein (Oxford: Oxford University Press, 1995), 116–143. Wolfe's characterization of violent entertainment is quoted by Hoberman's piece.

4. John Fiske and Robert Dawson, "Watching Homeless Men Watch *Die Hard,*" in *The Audience and Its Landscape,* eds. James Hay, Lawrence Grossberg, and Ellen Wartella (Boulder, CO: Westview Press, 1996), 297–316.

5. Neal King, *Heroes in Hard Times: Cop Action Movies in the U.S.* (Philadelphia: Temple University Press, 1999).

6. David Denby, "Movies: The Last Angry Men," *New York,* January 16, 1984.

7. Dolf Zillmann, "The Psychology of the Appeal of Portrayals of Violence," in *Why We Watch: The Attractions of Violent Entertainment,* ed. Jeffrey H. Goldstein (Oxford: Oxford University Press, 1995), 179–211.

8. Lionel Tiger, *The Decline of Males* (New York: St. Martin's Griffin, 1999), 256.

9. Patricia Leigh Brown, "Heavy Lifting Required: The Return of Manly Men," *New York Times,* October 28, 2001.

10. *Hitman Hart: Wrestling with Shadows* (12/20/98).

Bibliography

Adorno, Theodor, and Max Horkheimer. "The Culture Industry: Enlightenment as Mass Deception." Pp. 31–41 in *The Cultural Studies Reader*, edited by Simon During. New York: Routledge, 1999.

Andrews, Nigel. *True Myths: The Life and Times of Arnold Schwarzenegger*. Secaucus, NJ: Birch Lane Press, 1996.

Altman, Rick. *The American Film Musical*. Bloomington: Indiana University Press, 1987.

Ang, Ien. *Watching Dallas*. New York: Methuen, 1985.

———. *Desperately Seeking the Audience*. London: Routledge, 1991.

Barker, Martin. "The Newsom Report: A Case Study in 'Common Sense.'" Pp. 27–46 in *Ill Effects: The Media/Violence Debate*, edited by Martin Barker and Julian Petley. New York: Routledge, 2001.

Barker, Martin, and Julian Petley. "Introduction: From bad research to good—a guide for the perplexed." Pp. 1–26 in *Ill Effects: The Media/Violence Debate*, edited by Martin Barker and Julian Petley. New York: Routledge, 2001.

Berlyne, D. E. *Conflict, Arousal, and Curiosity*. New York: McGraw-Hill, 1960.

Blumler, Jay G., and Elihu Katz. *The Uses of Mass Communications*. Beverly Hills, CA: Sage, 1974.

Bobo, Jacqueline. *Black Women as Cultural Readers*. New York: Columbia University Press, 1995.

Bordo, Susan. *Twilight Zones: The Hidden Life of Cultural Images from Plato to OJ*. Berkeley: University of California Press, 1997.

Bouzereau, Laurent. *Ultraviolent Movies: From Sam Peckinpah to Quentin Tarantino*. Sacramento, CA: Citadel Press, 2000.

Braudy, Leo. "Genre: 'The Conventions of Connection.'" Pp. 435–452 in *Film Theory and Criticism*, edited by Gerald Mast, Marshall Cohen, and Leo Braudy. Oxford: Oxford University Press, 1992.

Briggs, Charles L. *Learning How to Ask: A Sociolinguistic Appraisal of the Role of the Interview in Social Science Research*. New York: Cambridge University Press, 1990.

———. *Violence on Television: Programme Content and Viewer Perceptions*. London: British Broadcasting Corporation, 1972.

Brown, Patricia Leigh. "Heavy Lifting Required: The Return of Manly Men." *New York Times*, October 28, 2001.

Bryant, Jennings, and Dolf Zillmann. *Responding to the Screen: Reception and Reaction Processes*. Mahwah, NJ: Lawrence Erlbaum, 1991.

Buckingham, David. *Children Talking Television: The Making of Television Literacy*. London: Falmer, 1993.

———. *Moving Images: Understanding Children's Emotional Responses to Television*. Manchester: Manchester University Press, 1996.

Campbell, Joseph. *The Hero with a Thousand Faces*. Princeton, NJ: Princeton University Press, 1972.

Caroll, Noel. "The Paradox of Suspense." Pp. 71–92 in *Suspense: Conceptualizations, Theoretical Analyses, and Empirical Explorations*, edited by Peter Vorderer, Hans J. Wulf, and Mike Friedrichsen. Mahwah, NJ: Lawrence Erlbaum, 1996.

Cawelti, John G. *Adventure, Mystery and Romance: Formula Stories as Art and Popular Culture*. Chicago: University of Chicago Press, 1976.

———. "Chinatown and Generic Transformation in Recent Films." Pp. 498–511 in *Film Theory and Criticism*, edited by Gerald Mast, Marshall Cohen, and Leo Braudy. New York: Oxford University Press, 1992.

Chan, Jackie, and Jeff Yang. *I Am Jackie Chan: My Life in Action*. New York: Ballantine Books, 1998.

Clover, Carol J. *Men, Women, and Chain Saws: Gender in the Modern Horror Film*. Princeton, NJ: Princeton University Press, 1992.

Crowther, Bosley. "Review of the film *The Dirty Dozen*." *New York Times*, June 16, 1967.

Cussler, Clive, and Craig Dirgo. *Clive Cussler and Dirk Pitt Revealed*. New York: Pocket Books, 1998.

Davis, Elizabeth G. *The First Sex*. New York: Dent, 1973.

Davison, W. Phillips. "The Third Person Effect in Communication." *Public Opinion Quarterly*, 47 (1983): 1–15.

Denby, David. "Movies: The Last Angry Men." *New York*, January 16, 1984.

Desser, David. "The Martial Arts Film in the 1990s." Pp.77–110 in *Film Genre 2000: New Critical Essays*, edited by Winston Wheeler Dixon. Albany: State University of New York Press, 2000.

During, Simon, ed. *The Cultural Studies Reader*. London: Routledge, 1999.

Ebert, Roger. *Roger Ebert's Home Movie Companion*. Kansas City, MO: Andrews McMeel Publishing, 1992.

Elias, Norbert. *The Civilizing Process: Vol. 1. The History of Manners*. New York: Pantheon, 1978.

———. *The Civilizing Process: Vol. 2. Power and Civility*. New York: Pantheon, 1982.

Elias, Norbert, and Eric Dunning. *Quest for Excitement: Sport and Leisure in the Civilizing Process*. Oxford: Basil Blackwell, 1986.

Faludi, Susan. "The Masculine Mystique." *Esquire*, 88–96, December 1996.

———. *Stiffed: The Betrayal of the American Man*. New York: William Morrow, 1999.

Fisher, Helen. *The First Sex: The Natural Talent of Women and How They Are Changing the World*. New York: Random House, 1999.

Fiske, John. *Television Culture*. London: Routledge, 1987.

———. "British Cultural Studies and Television." Pp. 214–245 in *Channels of Discourse, Reassembled*, edited by Robert C. Allen. Chapel Hill: University of North Carolina Press, 1992.

Fiske, John, and Robert Dawson. "Watching Homeless Men Watch *Die Hard*." Pp. 297–316 in *The Audience and Its Landscape*, edited by James Hay, Lawrence Grossberg, and Ellen Wartella. Boulder, CO: Westview Press, 1996.

Fowles, Jib. *Television Viewers vs. Media Snobs: What TV Does for People*. New York: Stein and Day, 1982.

———. *The Case for Television Violence*. Thousand Oaks, CA: Sage, 1999.

Frayling, Christopher. *Clint Eastwood*. London: Virgin Publishing, 1992.

Freeman, Arnold. *Boy Life and Labour*. London: P. S. King and Son, 1914.

Friedan, Betty. *The Feminine Mystique*. New York: Norton, 1963.

Fussell, Samuel Wilson. *Muscle: Confessions of an Unlikely Bodybuilder*. New York: Avon Books, 1992.

Gabler, Neal. "Inside Every Superhero Lurks a Nerd." *New York Times*, May 12, 2002.

Gallagher, Mark. "I Married Rambo: Spectacle and Melodrama in the Hollywood Action Film." Pp. 199–226 in *Mythologies of Violence in Postmodern Media*, edited by Christopher Sharrett. Detroit: Wayne State University Press, 1999.

Gauntlet, David. *Moving Experiences: Understanding Television's Influences and Effects*. London: John Libbey, 1995.

———. "The Worrying Influence of 'Media Effects' Studies." Pp. 47–62 in *Ill Effects: The Media/Violence Debate*, edited by Martin Barker and Julian Petley. New York: Routledge, 2001.

Gillespie, Marie. *Television, Ethnicity, and Cultural Change*. New York: Routledge, 1995.

Gitlin, Todd. "Sixteen Notes on Television and the Movement." Pp. 335–336 in *Literature in Revolution*, edited by George Abbot White and Charles Newman. New York: Holt, Rinehart, Winston, 1972.

———. *The Whole World Is Watching*. Berkeley: University of California Press, 1982.

Gramsci, Antonio. *Selections from the Prison Notebooks*. Edited by Quintin Noare and Geoffrey Nowell-Smith. London: Lawrence and Wishart, 1971.

Gray, Ann. *Video Playtime: The Gendering of a Leisure Technology*. London: Routledge, 1992.

Goldstein, Jeffrey H. "Why We Watch." Pp. 212–226 in *Why We Watch: The Attractions of Violent Entertainment*, edited by Jeffrey H. Goldstein. Oxford: Oxford University Press, 1998.

Grings, William Washburn, and Michael E. Dawson. *Emotions and Bodily Responses: A Psychophysiological Approach*. New York: Academic Press, 1978.

Guttmann, Allen. "The Appeal of Violent Sports." Pp. 7–26 in *Why We Watch: The Attractions of Violent Entertainment*, edited by Jeffrey H. Goldstein. Oxford: Oxford University Press, 1998.

Hall, Stuart. "Encoding, Decoding." Pp. 117–127 in *Culture, Media, Language*, edited by Stuart Hall, Dorothy Hobson, Andrew Lowe, and Paul Willis. London: Unwin, 1980.

Hartley, John. "Encouraging Signs: Television and the Power of Dirt, Speech, and Scandalous Categories." *Australian Journal of Cultural Studies* 1, no. 2 (1983): 62–82.

Haskell, Molly. *Form Reverence to Rape*. New York: Holt, Rinehart and Winston, 1974.

Hebdige, Dick. *Subculture: The Meaning of Style*. London: Methuen, 1979.

Hoberman, J. "A Test for the Individual Viewer: Bonnie and Clyde's Violent Reception." Pp. 116–143 in *Why We Watch: The Attractions of Violent Entertainment*, edited by Jeffrey H. Goldstein. Oxford: Oxford University Press, 1998.

Hobson, Dorothy. *Crossroads: The Drama of a Soap Opera*. London: Methuen, 1982.

———. "Soap Operas at Work." Pp. 150–176 in *Remote Control*, edited by Ellen Seiter, Hans Borchers, Gabriele Kreutzner, and Eva-Maria Warth. London: Routledge, 1991.

Hoff-Sommers, Christina. *Who Stole Feminism?: How Women Have Betrayed Men*. New York: Simon and Schuster, 1995.

Hill, Annette. *Shocking Entertainment: Viewer Response to Violent Movies*. Luton: University of Luton Press, 1997.

———. "Looks Like It Hurts: Women's Responses to Shocking Entertainment." Pp. 135–149 in *Ill Effects: The Media/Violence Debate*, edited by Martin Barker and Julian Petley. New York: Routledge, 2001.

Heywood, Leslie. *Bodymakers: A Cultural Anatomy of Women's Body Building*. New Brunswick, NJ: Rutgers University Press, 1998.

Jeffords, Susan. *Hard Bodies: Hollywood Masculinity in the Reagan Era*. New Brunswick, NJ: Rutgers University Press, 1993.

Jenkins, Henry. *Textual Poachers: Television Fans and Participatory Culture*. New York: Routledge, 1992.

Jose, Paul E., and William F. Brewer. "Development of Story Liking: Character Identification, Suspense, and Outcome Resolution." *Developmental Psychology* 20, no. 5 (1984): 911–924.

Julius, Marshall. *Action!: The Action Movie A–Z*. Bloomington: Indiana University Press, 1996.

Kael, Pauline. *Deeper into Movies*. New York: Warner Books, 1980.

Kemper, Theodore D. *Social Structure and Testosterone: Explorations of the Socio-Bio-Social Chain*. New Brunswick, NJ: Rutgers University Press, 1990.

Kent, Nicolas. *Naked Hollywood: Money and Power in the Movies Today*. New York: St. Martin's Press, 1991.

Kermode, Mark. "I Was a Teenage Horror Fan: Or, How I Learned to Stop Worrying and Love Linda Blair." Pp. 126–134 in *Ill Effects: The Media/Violence Debate*, edited by Martin Barker and Julian Petley. New York: Routledge, 2001.

King, Neal. *Heroes in Hard Times: Cop Action Movies in the U.S.* Philadelphia: Temple University Press, 1999.

King, Stephen. *Danse Macabre.* New York: Berkley Books, 1980.

Klein, Alan M. *Little Big Men: Bodybuilding Subculture and Gender Construction.* Albany: State University of New York Press, 1993.

Kubey, Robert, and Mihaly Csikszentmihalyi. *Television and the Quality of Life: How Viewing Shapes Everyday Experience.* Hillsdale, NJ: Lawrence Erlbaum, 1990.

Leigh, Wendy. *Arnold: An Unauthorized Biography.* Milwaukee, WI: Congdon and Weed, 1991.

Levy, Emanuel. *John Wayne: Prophet of the American Way of Life.* Metuchen, NJ: Scarecrow Press, 1988.

Lindloff, Thomas R. *Qualitative Communication Research Methods.* Thousand Oaks, CA: Sage, 1995.

Link, David. "Facts about Fiction: In Defense of TV Violence." *Reason* 25, no. 10 (March 1994): 22–26.

Linz, Daniel, Edward Donnerstein, and Steven M. Adams. "Physiological Desensitization and Judgments about Female Victims of Violence." *Human Communication* 15 (1989): 505–522.

Livingstone, Sonia M. "Audience Reception: The Role of the Viewer in Retelling Romantic Drama." Pp. 285–306 in *Mass Media and Society*, edited by James Curran and Michael Gurevitch. New York: Edward Arnold, 1991.

Luke, Carmen. *Constructing the Child Viewer: A History of the American Discourse on Television and Children.* New York: Praeger, 1990.

Lycett, Andrew. *Ian Fleming: The Man Behind James Bond.* Atlanta: Turner Publishing, 1995.

Lydston, G. Frank. *The Diseases of Society.* Philadelphia: J. B. Lippincott, 1904.

Marchetti, Gina. "Action-Adventure as Ideology." Pp. 182–198 in *Cultural Politics in Contemporary America*, edited by Ian Angus and Sut Jhally. London: Routledge, 1989.

McKinley, E. Graham. *Beverly Hills, 90210: Television, Gender and Identity.* Philadelphia: University of Pennsylvania Press, 1997.

McLeod, Douglas M., Benjamin H. Detenber, and William P. Eveland. "Behind the Third Person Effect: Differentiating Perceptual Processes for Self and Other." *Journal of Communication* 51, no. 4 (2001): 678–695.

McRobbie, Angela. "Just like a 'Jackie' story." Pp. 110–124 in *Feminism for Girls*, edited by Angela McRobbie and Trisha McCabe. London: Routledge, 1984.

———. *Feminism and Youth Culture: From "Jackie" to "Just Seventeen."* London: Macmillan, 1991.

Medved, Michael. "Hollywood's Three Biggest Lies about Media and Society." www.indpendent.org/events/transcript.asp?eventID=69 (accessed May 28, 2009).

Mellen, Joan. *Big Bad Wolves: Masculinity in the American Film.* New York: Pantheon, 1977.

Moores, Sean. "Dishes and Domestic Cultures: Satellite TV as Household Technology." Paper presented to the Fourth International Television Studies Conference, London, 1990.

Morley, David, and Charlotte Brunsdon. *The Nationwide Television Studies*. London: Routledge, 1978.

Morrell, David. *First Blood*. New York: Warner Books, 1972.

Murdock, Graham. "Reservoirs of Dogma: An Archeology of Popular Anxieties." Pp. 150–169 in *Ill Effects: The Media/Violence Debate*, edited by Martin Barker and Julian Petley. New York: Routledge, 2001.

———. "Visualizing Violence: Television and the Discourse of Disorder." Pp. 171–190 in *Mass Communication Research: On Problems and Policies*, edited by Cees J. Hamelink and Olga Linne. Norwood, NJ: Ablex Publishing, 1994.

Murray, Will. "The Executioner phenomenon." Pp. 135–144 in *Murder Off the Rack: Critical Studies of Ten Paperback Masters*, edited by Jon L. Breen and Martin Harry Greenberg. Metuchen, NJ: Scarecrow Press, 1989.

Nathanson, Paul, and Katherine K. Young. *Spreading Misandry: The Teaching of Contempt for Men in Popular Culture*. Montreal: McGill-Queen's University Press, 2002.

Newcomb, Horace, and Robert S. Alley. *The Producer's Medium: Conversations with Creators of American TV*. Oxford: Oxford University Press, 1983.

Newcomb, Horace and Paul M. Hirsch. "Television as a Cultural Forum." Pp. 561–573 in *Television: The Critical View*, edited by Horace Newcomb. New York: Oxford University Press, 2000.

Palahniuk, Chuck. *Fight Club*. New York: Henry Holt, 1999.

Palmer, Patricia. *The Lively Audience: A Study of Children around the TV Set*. Sydney: Allen and Unwin, 1986.

Perloff, Richard M. "Perceptions and Conceptions of Political Media Impact: The Third-Person Effect and Beyond." Pp. 177–197 in *The Psychology of Political Communication*, edited by Ann N. Crigler. Ann Arbor: University of Michigan Press, 1996.

Pope, Harrison G., Katherine A. Phillips, and Roberto Olivardia. *The Adonis Complex: The Secret Crisis of Male Body Obsession*. New York: Free Press, 2000.

Press, Andrea Lee. *Women Watching Television*. Philadelphia: University of Pennsylvania Press, 1991.

Radway, Janice. *Reading the Romance: Women, Patriarchy, and Popular Literature*. Chapel Hill: University of North Carolina Press, 1991.

Remoff, Heather T. *Sexual Choice: A Woman's Decision: Why and How Women Choose the Men They Do as Sexual Partners*. New York: Dutton, 1984.

Rosengren, Karl Erik, Lawrence A. Wenner, and Philip Palmgreen. *Media Gratifications Research: Current Perspectives*. Thousand Oaks, CA: Sage, 1985.

Sanello, Frank. *Stallone: A Rocky Life*. Edinburgh: Mainstream Publishing, 1998.

Sarris, Andrew. "Review of *The Dirty Dozen*." *Village Voice*, June 29, 1967.

Schickel, Richard. *Clint Eastwood*. New York: Alfred A. Knopf, 1996.

Schlesinger, Philip, R. Emerson Dobash, Russell P. Dobash, and C. Kay Weaver. *Women Viewing Violence*. London: British Film Institute Publishing, 1992.

Schrader, Paul. "Notes on Film Noir." Pp. 229–242 in *Film Genre Reader*, edited by Barry Keith Grant. Austin: University of Texas Press, 1986.

Schwarz, Bill. "Night Battles: Hooligan and Citizen." Pp. 101–128 in *Modern Times: Reflections on a Century of English Modernity*, edited by Mica Nava and Alan O'Shea. London: Routledge, 1996.

Seiter, Ellen, Hans Borchers, Gabriele Kreutzner, and Eva-Maria Warth. "Don't Treat Us Like We're So Stupid and Naïve: Towards an Ethnography of Soap Opera Viewers." Pp. 223–247 in *Remote Control*, edited by Ellen Seiter, Hans Borchers, Gabriele Kreutzner, and Eva-Maria Warth. London: Routledge, 1991.

Shapiro, Marc. *James Cameron*. Los Angeles: Renaissance Books, 2000.

Siegel, Don. *A Siegel Film: An Autobiography*. New York: Faber and Faber, 1993.

Stanko, Elizabeth Anne. *Intimate Intrusions: Women's Experience of Male Violence*. London: Routledge, 1985.

Tasker, Yvonne. *Spectacular Bodies: Gender, Genre and the Action Cinema*. New York: Routledge, 1993.

Tiger, Lionel. *Men in Groups*. New York: Marion Boyars Publishers, 1984.

———. *The Decline of Males*. New York: St. Martin's Griffin, 1999.

Turner, Graeme. *British Cultural Studies: An Introduction*. London: Routledge, 1996.

Vidmar, Neil, and Milton Rokeach. "Archie Bunker's Bigotry: A Study in Selective Perception and Exposure." *Journal of Communication* 24 (1974): 36–47.

Walker, Cynthia W. "A Dialogic Approach to Creativity in Mass Communication." Unpublished doctoral dissertation, Rutgers, the State University of New Jersey, New Brunswick, NJ, 2001.

Warshow, Robert. "Movie Chronicle: The Westerner." Pp. 453–466 in *Film Theory and Criticism*, edited by Gerald Mast, Marshall Cohen, and Leo Braudy. New York: Oxford University Press, 1992.

Barbara J. Wilson, Joanne Cantor, L. Gordon, and Dolf Zillmann. "Affective Response of Nonretarded and Retarded Children to the Emotions of a Protagonist." *Child Study Journal* 16, no. 2 (1986): 77–93.

Wuss, Peter. *Analysis of Film and Psychology: Cinematic Structures in the Perceptional Process*. Berlin: Edition Sima, 1983.

———. "Narrative Tensions in Antonioni." Pp. 51–70 in *Suspense: Conceptualizations, Theoretical Analyses, and Empirical Explorations*, edited by Peter Vorderer, Hans J. Wulff, and Mike Friedrichsen. Mahwah, NJ: Lawrence Erlbaum, 1996.

Yacowar, Maurice. "The White Man's Mythic Invincibility." *Jump Cut* 34 (1989): 2–4.

Zillmann, Dolf. "The psychology of suspense in dramatic exposition." Pp. 199–232 in *Suspense: Conceptualizations, Theoretical Analyses, and Empirical Explorations*, edited by Peter Vorderer, Hans J. Wulff, and Mike Friedrichsen. Mahwah, NJ: Lawrence Erlbaum, 1996.

———. "The Psychology of the Appeal of Portrayals of Violence." Pp. 179–211 in *Why We Watch: The Attractions of Violent Entertainment*, edited by Jeffrey H. Goldstein. Oxford: Oxford University Press, 1998.

Zillmann, Dolf, and Joanne Cantor. "Affective Responses to the Emotions of a Protagonist." *Journal of Experimental Social Psychology* 13 (1977): 155–165.

Zuckerman, Marvin. *Sensation Seeking: Beyond the Optimal Level of Arousal*. Hillsdale, NJ: Lawrence Erlbaum, 1979.

Index

About the Author

Barna William Donovan is a graduate of the film school of the University of Miami and he earned his doctorate from Rutgers University. He is a tenured professor and Chair of the Communication Department of Saint Peter's—The Jesuit College of New Jersey. Along with his publications in academic journals, he is the author of the book *The Asian Influence on Hollywood Action Films.*